CW01072202

Coding

4 Books in 1:

Machine Learning for Beginners

Python for Beginners

Linux for Beginners

Kali Linux

Jason Knox

Table of Contents

Machine Learning for Beginners

Python for Beginners

Linux for Beginners

Kali Linux

Machine Learning for Beginners

A Beginners' Guide to Start Out Your Journey With Data Science, Artificial Intelligence, Machine Learning and its Algorithms, Deep Learning and Neural Networks From Scratch

Jason Knox

Introduction

Machines have been a central part of human life for centuries, if not eons. The complexity of machines has varied, but in all cases machines have extended the human mind and helped to automate tedious tasks, helping to free up human beings to do other things.

Of course this hasn't always been welcomed. In the 18th century, riots ensued when machines automated the jobs of textile workers. A group known as the Luddites destroyed many machines in factories out of fear that they would lose their ability to gain employment, being outcompeted by the machines. Ironically, 50 years later there were ten to thirty times more jobs in those industries. The new job creation opened up because of the increased productivity unleashed by the machines. Sadly, even though the lessons of that experience are clear, modern day Luddites continually worry about robots and artificial intelligence destroying all the jobs around them.

Of course there will be challenges ahead, there always are. Workers will have to obtain more extensive training than they did in decades past, as they begin to work with more sophisticated machines that use statistical algorithms to learn and perform better.

Machine learning is one of the most exciting and vibrant areas of research in science and engineering today. In this book we are going to introduce you to the world of machine learning, beginning with a discussion of how machines and computers have evolved along with humans over our long history.

We will also talk at length about data science, which is a field of growing importance. Data science is now becoming one of the hottest career paths around, and it's used in multiple ways from Wall Street, to the Pentagon, and in private firms like Amazon and Facebook (no surprise there). The main focus of this book, however, will be on machine learning.

Next we will explore the differences between artificial intelligence, machine learning and deep learning, all three of which may interplay with each other while being independent fields and concepts in their own right.

After this we will discuss the steps that are followed in machine learning, including collecting data, data wrangling, analysis, training and testing algorithms, and deployment. From here we'll go over the main types of machine learning, and then talk about algorithms.

Jason

Chapter 1: What is Machine Learning – and the evolution of machines

In this chapter we will introduce you to the concept of machine learning and learn how it fits in the broader realm of computer science and artificial intelligence.

A Quick History of Computer Science

In the early days of computer science, a computer had to be given specific, step-by-step instructions in order to perform a given task. At first, these instructions were entered in the computer using punch cards that a computer system could read. Computers use a binary language where 1 means yes and 0 means no. It's possible to build up complete streams of logic and store and represent anything using only binary. That includes anything from the stock market, to your basic information like name, age, and social security number, to the pixels that make up an image.

A step-by-step procedure of the kind that computers use to accomplish a given task is known as an *algorithm*. So in the early days of computation, algorithms were written in binary language.

Early programming methods were extremely cumbersome, but computers proved very useful early on. They were used to crack secret codes in the Second World War, and to calculate the trajectories of projectile weapons like artillery. Computers are far better at performing such tedious tasks than humans, who are clever, but extremely slow thinkers. After the war, computers found broad application and entered the business world for the first time.

The use of computers would have remained extremely limited had programmers been forced to continually create algorithms using binary. While binary is great for computers, it's hard for human beings to think in terms of binary. Even people who are studying engineering and computer science have to work their minds to think in binary terms, and so in order to make things easier people began developing higher level languages.

There are two levels of higher level languages that were used in the early decades of computer science after the war ended. The first level is called assembly language. This is a lower level language that is still using a thought process, if you can call it that, which a computer would use. It's difficult to understand and many people find it quite challenging to develop large algorithms using assembly language. The kinds of steps that are involved may include telling the computer to move a piece of data from one memory location to another, or having it go through the individual steps to multiply two numbers together. Assembly language is barely a step above binary.

However, programmers also began developing high level languages. These are languages that use logical structures and flows, along with instructions that are more suitable for the human mind. Even so, programming using a high level language is still an extremely complex task, and it's extremely useful. This is why people with computer science degrees command high salaries.

You are probably familiar with some of the many high level languages that exist today. In the 1950s, FORTRAN was the king of high level languages, and it's still used in many scientific applications, such as simulating the detonation of nuclear weapons. While it's partly used in applications like that because of legacy reasons, it's also used because it's an extremely good language for doing calculations.

As the 20th century wore on, other computer languages were invented and became more popular. These included Pascal, Ada, C, and C++. The language C++ was an extension of c which introduced the concept of *object-oriented programming*. Rather than simply designing algorithms, object-oriented languages let programmers build objects inside their programs, and the objects can be acted on or experience "events", which takes the idea of an algorithm as a step-by-step of instructions to a higher plane.

Later, the invention of the internet and smart phones resulted in a wide proliferation of new languages that were specifically developed for use in certain contexts. For example, an extension of C used to program iPhones was invented called objective-c. Later that was replaced by Swift. On the internet and on Android phones we've seen the rise of Javascript and Java, among many others too numerous to mention.

The Evolution of Machines

Human beings are problem solvers, and machines are an extension of our natural thought processes. Whenever there is a seemingly impossible task, humans "put their minds together" in order to plan and figure out a way to accomplish the task. This is something that humans have always done. Eons ago, people might have had to figure out how to cross a river. Then in 1969, humans put their minds together to land two men on the moon.

The first human tools were just extensions of our hands and limbs, and substitutes for the big canine teeth and claws that we lacked. These tools included cutters, scrapers, and spear tips all made out of stone. Although their purposes are relatively straightforward, they were quite revolutionary. These were the first steps taken to extend the human mind by using machines, or tools if you want to call them that. This was indeed a giant leap, the designer of a tool has to envision it in their mind, and then carve something out of a rock that had never existed before. By using knives and spears, humans became powerful hunters with the ability to cut and tear at their prey that was far superior to anything a lion or bear could muster with their natural defenses.

As the eons passed, tool making slowly grew in sophistication. At first, the progress was extremely slow. People began making baskets and other tools to carry and store things they needed like food or olive oil. They also made plows, which made it easier to plant crops. For centuries things basically stayed the same, as if people were slightly beyond the stone age but kind of trapped in it. But as civilization became more sophisticated, so did the tools it was using.

The wheel was invented in the old world, which allowed people to transport goods and people far more effectively. The Romans build roads, and then created aqueducts to bring water from far away places. Pretty soon people were making windmills, and using the power of water to make the first machines in the sense that we understand the word.

Early machines went beyond using a simple tool, which requires direct human application of labor. The first machines used simple levers and pulleys, which are devices that distribute and magnify applied forces in order to do work. Levers, pulleys, wedges and screws were all invented in ancient Greece, and of course we still use them today.

Watermills harnessed the power of water to operate various simple machines. The importance of these developments goes beyond the direct applications and labor saving properties they had, and brings the idea of removing the human from the work to the forefront. Ever since the first watermills were used to do hammering or other work, machines have become more sophisticated and capable in the desired effect, which is to free up the human from labor completely. This process was accelerated dramatically in the late 18th century by the invention of the steam engine. From that point forward, it was possible to build more and more sophisticated machines that saved human labor. Despite the fears of the Luddites that we alluded to earlier, this process has expanded the economies of the world to such an extent that every machine advance doubles, triples, and quadruples the number of jobs available. As things get more sophisticated, people find new and more interesting things to do. As obvious as the historical data is on this point, people still fear technological and machine development as much today as the Luddites did, and they still speak about a coming world where everyone is unemployed.

The Evolution of Artificial Intelligence

If you can substitute a machine for horses carrying a wagon or for a man hammering something, while the leap in thought is larger, the next question that can be considered is whether or not the mind can be replaced as well. The early computers that broke the Nazi codes in World War II certainly raised that possibility, and it had been broached in fiction multiple times decades and even centuries earlier. Fiction writers imagined artificial beings that could think on their own. The concept of a thinking machine seems like the ultimate end game that would result from the long stream of machines that were gradually replacing tasks done by humans. But was that really possible?

By the 1960s serious computer scientists had begun developing artificial intelligence as a field. Rather than remaining in the realm of speculation and science fiction, it now became a rigorous branch of computer science that was developing rapidly.

Despite decades of research and rapid progress, the way the human brain works remains somewhat clouded in mystery. Understanding consciousness and how we learn things continues to push the boundary of science. Despite this, amazing progress has been made in AI over the past fifty years, even if the original promise of the HAL 9000 computer still seems years away.

So what is artificial intelligence, fundamentally speaking?

Artificial intelligence can be described as the development of computer systems that perform tasks normally done by humans. A simple example of artificial intelligence would be a visual perception system. Of course this isn't "simple" in the dense that a computer system that does visual perception is simple from a technology perspective or in the amount of challenge involved, but a small child has extremely well developed abilities of visual perception, just as animals do. And it's something that pretty much happens automatically.

Other computer systems that can be considered to be artificially intelligent include an automated translation service like Google Translate, a speech recognition system like Siri, and any decision making system that does what human cognition would do on some level. Chess playing computer systems have long been seen as one of the Holy Grails of artificial intelligence, and when they got as good or better than many human chess champions, this was considered an important milestone because chess is considered a pretty high level human function.

Another more sophisticated systems that use artificial intelligence include self-driving cars.

Of course from science fiction we know that the ultimate in artificial intelligence would be the construction of a robot that looked like and behaved like a human. The development of this seems to be closing rapidly as I write this book. The belief is that these devices would be working for people, but it does raise a lot of concerns and ethical issues.

At the core, what do humans do as they go through life? They learn from their experiences. As you learn, you get better at doing things, in other words your behavior adjusts to incorporate the data that you have incorporated. You might say that your behaviors are algorithms, and the algorithms changed.

This is also the core of artificial intelligence. That is the idea behind artificial intelligence is to have machines that can learn from experience, and adjust their algorithms appropriately.

Computer systems that are artificially intelligent are able to recognize patterns in data, and so they can be trained by feeding them large amounts of data.

Machine Learning

Earlier in the book when we discussed the evolution of computer systems, we noted that each step in an algorithm had to be programmed by a human programmer, and in those days this was done using punch cards to represent 1's and 0's that the computer would use to carry out the tasks. When you program in that fashion it's tedious, and the computer acts as a passive receptacle, merely carrying out the steps that you feed it to carry out various tasks, and produce pre-determined answers that are dependent on coded rules. But what if there was another way to use computers?

This is where *machine learning* comes in. The concept behind machine learning is simple (to describe). You develop a computer system that is able to learn from data it's exposed to, improve it's performance, and make decisions without being explicitly programmed to do so. It learns from data by recognizing patterns in the data and it does this automatically without needing human intervention. Patterns in data can be detected using statistical modeling. The more data it's exposed to, the better it gets at its job. This is the concept of "self-learning".

The algorithms that we've described earlier that were programmed directly a human programmer, determining every single step along the way, illustrated a very different approach to computing . Traditional computer programming involves giving the computer direct commands developed by a human or groups of humans.

Since computer systems that use machine learning improve their performance with experience (in the form of being exposed to large amounts of data), they do have some aspects of human-like intelligence at least in a gross sense. Underneath the hood, however, patterns are detected using statistical models.

In short, machine learning brings together statistical modeling together with algorithms. The algorithms will have a large number of parameters or knobs that need to be set. But rather than setting them beforehand, they are left free-floating. Then the algorithm is exposed to large test data sets, and the patterns in the data are used together with the statistical modeling to set the value of these parameters. This is how the machine "learns". We call feeding test data to the model in order for it to learn "training".

The algorithmic models look for relationships and patterns in the data in order to make predictions about the outputs. The data itself will configure the structure of the model rather than having a computer programmer do it. The system has to be exposed to a large amount of data, otherwise its not going to be able to accurately determine the underlying relationships in the data and use that to make future predictions. Remember that in the real world, there are always outliers that can throw off any predetermined outcome. In order for the system to learn well enough so that it's not making too many mistakes, it has to be exposed to enough data so that it can also incorporate the outliers and unexpected results. Of course the model is not going to be 100% accurate all the time, even a well trained model is going to have misses.

We can think of an example of how machine learning could be applied in the real world. Imagine developing a machine learning model that could be used to approve an application for a loan. The model would be fed data on large numbers of people who had applied for this type of loan in the past. The data could include demographic, educational, employment, and income information as well as the past payment and credit history of the applicants. The system would then use the data to try and determine what patterns in the data existed that would then be used in order to predict the outcome, that is whether or not a given applicant would pay off or default on a loan.

Obviously, although on the surface we expect that this would be an easy problem to solve, in reality it's nuanced. The system needs to be fed more data in order to avoid making erroneous predictions. When it comes to debt, this is an interesting problem, because a human is able to meet with an applicant and would be able to make a judgment on whether or not someone unqualified on paper should actually get a loan based on other factors. Those are factors a computer system is unlikely to be able to tease apart, at least in a traditional sense.

Let's suppose that we made a system based on traditional programming methods. That type of system would approve or reject a loan based on hard-coded options that are put in place by a human programmer, for example the programmer would set a minimum credit score, income level, and so on. But a machine learning model would not have any of those parameters set, but instead would learn from the previous data. It's not going to be perfect, but this would help it tease out cases that added some variance to the data with people who using strict rules would not be approved for the loans. But maybe like the human banker, a machine learning system, given enough data would at least in some cases decide to approve a loan for someone who would not be eligible on paper.

Remember that there is no human intervention once the algorithm is set up and the machine is then fed the data. It may detect many patterns in the data that we are not even remotely aware of. But more exposure to data and further testing and training can help the model become better.

Training and Test Data

There are two phases of development using machine learning that are used before it's ready to be actually applied in the real world. In the first phase, the algorithmic model is developed by feeding it *training data.* During this phase, the system will seek out patterns in the data and use them to start refining itself as it learns, by tuning the knobs or parameters in the model. This entire process is conducted without direct human involvement, the only human involvement will be feeding the data to the model and getting it started.

Once the system has been exposed to all the training data, test data, that is additional data the system has not seen before, are fed to the system so that it's predictions can be tested against known outputs. It may be that more refinement is needed, or it may be that the system is ready to be applied. Remember that either way, humans do not intervene by modifying the model themselves. They may check results, and they may feed data to the model, but they don't actually set parameters or modify it. If the model is demonstrating that it's not quite up to par, then you would feed more training data to the model.

In today's world, there are many machine learning models that are operating in many of the systems you use, it could be on websites, in mobile apps or messaging, or in programs like Microsoft Word.

For example, YouTube is using a machine learning model to curate videos for you. Most people probably feel that it does a fairly good job, but that it's not quite accurate. The same thing may hold true with a dictation system, that is learning your voice when you attempt to dictate documents, or word predictive models that are used on some email systems or in messaging. The reason they don't work perfectly is because they have a small subset of data, and you being an individual are going to be throwing random events to the system all the time. So you can see why a credit checking system would probably work better than YouTube telling you what videos to watch or your email suggesting what you should say in response to an incoming message.

Machine learning also has some fun applications. Big video game companies are using machine learning algorithms to have their games learn from the experience just as the player is doing so, and this can make the games more challenging as the player advances to new levels.

Machine Learning vs. Artificial Intelligence and Deep Learning

Machine learning is actually a subset of Artificial intelligence. You probably have an intuitive understanding of what artificial intelligence is. You can think of a robot from a science fiction movie as your reference point. That is, artificial intelligence is a system that has cognitive abilities that would at the very least try to mimic the human mind, and possibly exceed it, at least in certain tasks. These cognitive skills can include problem solving abilities, and the ability to learn from examples. An artificially intelligent system would have some ability to perceive its environment, and then take actions to increase its probability of success. An example of this would be a self-driving car, image processing, or a facial recognition system.

So you can see fro this that machine learning is actually a *subset* of artificial intelligence. Humans obviously learn from experience, and that is one of the goals of AI, which is accomplished by machine learning.

The overall goal of artificial intelligence has traditionally been to get computers to perform tasks that they are not very good at now, but that humans can do really well. In the early days of artificial intelligence, it was thought that you could use a set of rules to create an artificially intelligent system. That is a model that is kind of based in the thinking patterns used with the old style programming methods, that is just passing the computer a set of logical statements. Starting from this point, computer scientists thought that you could add more and more logical rules that would make the system smarter. This approach turned out to be completely faulty, and this was an early setback for AI from which it has strongly recovered. We are now starting to see the fruits of artificial intelligence all around us, even if it doesn't quite meet the visions of independently minded robots and androids in Star Wars and Star Trek.

There are three broad types of artificial intelligence. The first is general artificial intelligence or general AI, which would classify a machine that would be able to complete any task that a human could perform. You could put the androids here.

Narrow AI is where you have a machine that would perform a specific task better than a human can. This type of AI would be used to say create robots that would load and unload boxes in a warehouse. They never get tired or ask for breaks and work at a predictable pace. These types of robots already exist.

Another example from narrow AI are self-driving automobiles. That may be a work in process, but you see that the task for the AI system is narrow in scope – operating a motor vehicle. Notice how machine learning applies here as well, a self-driving system could learn from experience on the road, incorporating more and more situations into it's data set. Also, you can see how at least in theory the machine would be able to do the task better than a person. Whether that is really true or not remains to be seen, but development in the area has been stunningly rapid.

Finally we have strong AI, where machines can perform a task better than a person can. We already have computers doing this without AI, since they can tally up numbers, multiply and divide them, and calculate averages and standard deviations on data sets on an instant, when it would take a human hours. However image processing applications and chess playing programs are a good example.

Strong AI utilizes neural networks. A neural network is a set of interconnected nodes (aka functions). The interconnections are reminiscent of a nervous system, where individual nerve cells act as the nodes and they are interconnected with other nerve cells. A simple arrangement is to have input directly connected to the nodes which are connected to the output. This is generally the idea behind machine learning.

Shallow Neural Network

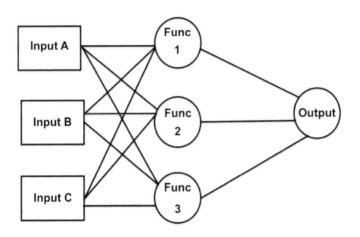

Deep learning uses a more complicated neural network that has hidden layers of nodes in between the input and output.

Deep Neural Net - Multiple Layers

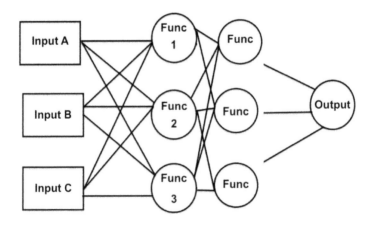

Therefore, machine learning is a subset of AI, and deep learning is a subset of machine learning. The models in deep learning are more complicated than the models in machine learning, but the basic concepts are the same.

What Sectors and Industries Use Machine Learning

Machine learning is used throughout the world of business and government. The applications are wide ranging and varied, after all this is meant to be a generalized method that can be used to apply computing power. We've already touched on a couple of specific examples, now let's get some idea of how machine learning can be used in different sectors and segments of society.

Government

As you might imagine, the government has a significant interest in machine learning. The interest of government spans all levels, from local governments through the Federal government. And of course internationally, many of the world's centralized governments are utilizing machine learning for a wide variety of purposes, some good and some bad.

The military is utilizing machine learning for all of its operations. This will help the military develop more efficient machines that can operate without significant or any human input. Depending on the application, this can be seen as a positive or as something that might raise ethical concerns.

As we've seen, Southwest Airlines and other companies like UPS have used machine learning to identify issues impacting wasted time, fuel, and money. The U.S. military might not seem that similar to Southwest Airlines and UPS at first glance, however remember that in addition to fighting wars the military is a logistics and transportation powerhouse. The military needs to keep troops supplied in remote locations, and it needs to be able to move heavy equipment from one point to another with absolute efficiency, as well as transporting large numbers of people by air, sea, or over land. Machine learning is being used to improve logistics and transportation in the military in order to cut fuel costs, reduce idle time, and make the movement of people and supplies more efficient.

Target recognition is an important application of machine learning for the military. Machine learning can help soldiers identify and track possible targets. This can help improve the accuracy and efficiency of targeting operations in real time, while reducing the risk of creating civilian casualties. In the training phase, the model can learn by being presented with data of past enemy behaviors and movements.

One area where machine learning is proving to be valuable is in cyber security. Algorithms that have been trained using machine learning can help detect fraudulent attempts to access a network, deal with cyber attacks, and even launch counter strikes. Since this is a branch of artificial intelligence, machine learning systems involved in cyber security can act autonomously. The applications of machine learning to cybersecurity span all levels of government, inside and outside the military.

The internal revenue service is another federal department that has increased the role of machine learning in its operations in recent years. In particular, the IRS is interested in using machine learning to help detect fraud and identity theft. It can also study past data from fraud cases in order to detect patterns that emerge from this data, that can then be used to predict where fraud is occurring in the future.

The Centers for Disease Control is beginning to use machine learning for a wide variety of purposes. For example, one proposal is to use machine learning to study epidemics. This could help healthcare workers identify epidemics faster, and then act when necessary in response. As it is now, data is often de-centralized and not processed until after the fact, when patterns of cases showing up at various hospitals could be used to detect when an epidemic is in formation and predict it's future course.

Local governments are using machine learning as well, to help deliver services more efficiently and prevent fraud and theft. While it's controversial, police departments can use machine learning to scan faces in a crowd and pick out criminals they may be searching for, or they can use it to scan license plates and track movements. Some local governments are using machine learning so that they can allocate resources more efficiently. This can be done for any task that local government does, such as roadwork, spraying and maintaining sewers, distributing police patrols in different areas, and restaurant inspections. Machine learning can also be used to model criminal activity. By having the algorithm learn from past patterns of criminal activity, once trained it could estimate where crimes will occur in the future, what types of crime, and the level of police resources that should be directed toward each area.

Another area which local, state, and federal governments are interested in is using machine learning to predict the behavior of people that have been arrested. As you might imagine, this is quite controversial and may run into constitutional issues in the United States. The way it would work is it could estimate, based on the data points associated with a given individual, the likelihood that they would show up for a trial if they were released. The system can allow people to be released on their own recognizance, set bail, or even recommend that a suspect be held without bail. The system can also analyze the data points associated with the subject and make estimates on the chance of reoffending if they are convicted.

As you can see, the government is using machine learning in many other contexts, and throughout many different departments. These applications are not without controversy, but because of their power governments are going to try and implement them. So expect to be hearing a lot about this going forward.

Financial Services

It won't surprise you to learn that banks, mortgage companies, and financial service companies of all types are using machine learning to enhance their operations and make them more efficient – from their perspective. The applications of machine learning to financial services are seemingly endless, but the first area where they are used extensively is with fraud detection. This can be used to determine when it appears someone is setting up a false account, is using an account for fraudulent activity, or is using identity theft to obtain financial services. A simple example that may touch some of our readers is use of a debit card in a manner that is consistent with the patterns seen when cards are stolen. If you have experienced this, having your card shut off even though you have it but are just running errands and paying with your debit card, then you can see first hand the pitfalls that come along when machine learning gets it wrong.

Another area that machine learning has taken over when it comes to financial services is credit checks and loan approval. The days of having to speak to a loan officer are rapidly disappearing, and in some cases are already gone. This is actually one of the most straightforward applications of machine learning, the algorithm is easily trained on the reams of data that have been collected on the past from the financial behaviors of tens of millions of people. This can teach the algorithm quite well and have it predict who among today's applicants is likely to default on their loan. Of course as we mentioned earlier, these types of processes are never going to be perfect and so mistakes are bound to happen.

Transportation and Shipment

We've already noted that Southwest and other airlines have been able to use machine learning to allocate their resources more effectively and to avoid wasting fuel and time unnecessarily. The same techniques used by the airlines can be used in any application involving mass transit, or with hauling and shipping.

For example, machine learning can help a trucking company use it's resources in the most efficient way possible to cut fuel costs and reduce idle time among drivers. Machine learning makes shipping more effective, by being able to determine how to sort goods for shipping and what goods should be loaded on what ships, working autonomously and more efficiently than a human. We also face the possibility that at some point there will be self-driving trucks, railroads, and self-propelled/directed ships that travel back and forth to their destinations without human interference. Of course there are many legal and ethical issues that come along with these applications, and so it's not clear how much the potential applications will see actual use on a large scale.

Mining, Oil and Gas

Machine learning has immediate application to the oil and gas industry, and also to mining. One area where it can be used is in the search for new deposits or energy sources. This can make companies far more efficient when they seek out areas for experimental drilling. Using machine learning, they can quickly filter out areas that are likely to be less promising. A large part of the mining, oil, and gas industries is transportation and storage. Once again, the ability of machine learning to help make transportation and logistics more efficient is able to help these industries a great deal. Machine learning can also be used for more efficient distribution and maximizing the efficiency of storage. These applications are not without risk, it's possible that a human geologists would spot an area for experimental drilling that a system based on machine learning would miss, in fact that is likely to happen sometimes. However, overall the application will be more efficient and effective.

Retail and Online Marketing

Everyone is talking about it these days – you are probably seeing ads online that seem to read your mind. The technology that lies behind these systems is based on machine learning. If you are looking for a new pair of shoes, you are going to see advertisements for shoes all over the place. It's not clear that this always works, the algorithms are not able to pick out intent when someone is looking at something online. If they aren't already, these systems are likely to be tied with your behavior in physical or "brick and mortar" stores, not just with online activity. This is one area where privacy advocates are not pleased, it remains to be seen where this will go. However, since its producing powerful results for marketers and generating a lot of advertising revenue, it's going to be pretty difficult to end the practice.

Healthcare

One interesting area where machine learning is starting to have an impact is in healthcare. While medicine often requires a lot of problem solving skills and interpretation from medical professionals, a lot of it is rule based, with treatments that can be easily picked out by machine learning systems. You can imagine how a system could be trained using databases containing the characteristics of large numbers of people who have high blood pressure, and studying the drugs that were chosen by physicians. A machine learning system can easily replicate this behavior and maybe even do a better job, as it would be able to look at the characteristics of a person and tease out the patterns seen in the large databases of patients to look for patterns that associate one treatment over another with success, or conversely with side effects. One can envision a system of prescribing for illnesses, when the prescriptions are essentially routine, as being done in a completely automated fashion. This could also be done for prescriptions of antibiotics for sinus infections or sore throats, or even to prescribe oral medications to diabetics. This would free up doctors for other activities that are a better use of their talents, and improve the overall efficiency of the healthcare system.

Machine learning can also be used as an assistant for a doctor in more complex cases. An algorithm can spot something that a doctor might miss, leading to more accurate diagnoses and treatment.

Interestingly, machine learning and AI are being used to create surgical robots, that can either assist a physician or even replace them. Obviously, this is a more advanced application of the technology. It may be used in the future to help bring medicine to rural areas where doctors and hospitals are becoming scarce.

Machine learning can also be used to help with staffing, scheduling appointments, and distribution of patients in a large healthcare facility. As you can probably guess by now, machine learning is very good for developing systems that solve and manage logistical problems like this. Given the high level of inefficiency in the healthcare system, this could potentially save large amounts of money over time.

Chapter 2: Introduction to Data Science

Data science is an emerging interdisciplinary field that spans computer science, mathematics, and statistics. It's closely tied to machine learning since large amounts of data are involved and utilized in data science and in machine learning. In this chapter we will give an overview of what data science is about and how it extracts knowledge from data.

What is Data Science?

Data science is a field that attempts to extract knowledge from large data sets. In short, machine learning is a tool that is used in data science as part of the effort to reach this goal. In particular, companies are interested in detecting the hidden patterns that exist in the large data sets that they have collected. While it's possible for a computer to spot these patterns, humans are ill suited for doing so. We are good at looking at small chunks of data at a time, especially when it's highly structured. But in the modern world, the amounts of data collected by governments and large corporations are absolutely enormous. And although people know ahead of time that there are probably lots of patterns within the data, they don't know what those patterns are or how they can be used in a predictive fashion.

The job of the data scientist is to use machine learning algorithms to analyze the data and come up with results. Ultimately a human must interpret and direct, choosing which algorithms to use and which to actually employ after training. Once they are employed however, machine learning systems run autonomously without any human input.

You may have also hear the phrase "data mining", this phrase can be taken to mean the activity taken by data scientists. Data mining seeks to discover patterns that exist in large data sets. Returning to our example from the last chapter, we can imagine some characteristic in common that people who default on loans might have. It could be something unexpected that would only emerge after the examination of large amounts of data, such as a tattoo on their left ankle.

In addition to doing "data mining" the field of data science can be paired with "big data", another jargon word thrown around to describe this field. Big data refers to dealing with extremely large data sets that are normally too cumbersome to deal with. Since the turn of the 21st century, the increase in the amount of data has been astronomical. More and more, people are living their lives through the computer, whether it's browsing the internet or using their smart phone. This leaves a large trail of financial data, entertainment data, shopping data, and more. This can require sophisticated systems that use machine learning or it might just require large amounts of computer power, storage, and processing, or some combination thereof. Data science, big data, and data mining have come at a time when the storage capacity of computers has become virtually unlimited and low cost. Large facilities maintain banks of computer storage at a capacity never seen before.

Is Data Science Really a Thing?

There is some argument as to whether "data science" is really a distinct field of study. Some consider it a buzzword that is being used in place of statistics, and that the modern "data scientist" is just a statistician using the tools of machine learning and big data in order to extract information out of large data sets.

Buzzword or not, data science is taken to sit at the intersections of computer science, math and statistics, and the field of business. Data scientists know how to extract meaning from large data sets, and it's true that statisticians also know how to do that. But a true data scientist will be versed in computer science as well, that isn't necessarily the case with a statistician. Moreover, a data scientist is expected to have business knowledge, and many statisticians do not. Data scientists will work with raw databases that contain large amounts of data within which they hope to find patterns.

However, the power of data science lies in its wide applicability. It can be used in medicine, business, or by the military just to name a few examples. What makes data science unique and powerful, and takes it beyond traditional fields like statistics or computer science, is that it lies at the intersection of multiple fields, and so a "polymath" is needed to be an effective data scientist.

The role of machine learning in data science

Machine learning is a tool that is useful for data scientists. By utilizing machine learning, the data scientist can increase their productivity by allowing the machine learning systems to do a lot of pattern recognition without the need of direct human intervention, which would be impossible given the large nature of todays data sets in any case. The data scientist can then focus on what humans do best, in that they interpret the patterns that machine learning has found in the data.

The Tasks of Data Science

Data science will use statistical modeling and machine learning among its tools, but what are the goals or outcomes that data science hopes to deliver? There are many ways that data science can be used. We can't possibly list them all, but in this section we will discuss some of the major ways that data science is applied in practice.

Predictive Analysis

The first major way that data science is used is in *forecasting* and *predictive analysis*. This can be any type of forecasting, data science could be used to forecast a company's expected performance in the coming year, for example.

Forecasting is similar to basic prediction modeling, which is a large part of machine learning. So what data science is looking for is the ability to predict a particular outcome based on the inputs provided.

One area where predictive analysis is being utilized quite effectively is in retail. Companies have collected enormous amounts of data on people. Every time that you go to the grocery store and use a "shopper's card" to save a few dollars, the company is tracking every purchase you make. They use this data, in conjunction with the data they have collected from millions of other people, in order to predict what you're going to buy next and also to determine what advertising you'll be susceptible to.

This brings us to a related application where data science is being used with increasing regularity. This is for the purpose of product recommendations. You will see this on Netflix, Amazon, or YouTube. By analyzing your previous habits and the habits of those who are like you, data science is able to estimate movies, books, or videos that you are likely to be interested in. Sometimes this works pretty well but sometimes it doesn't.

Prescriptive Analytics

Data science and machine learning is finding many uses in a field known as prescriptive analytics. In this case, the machine learning is used in order to accomplish some specific tasks. Researchers in this area are aiming high, looking to replace or augment humans in tasks that they actually do pretty well. One area where this might be familiar is a self-driving car. Data collected from autos being driven by human beings can be used to train the machine learning systems.

This has also been used for sometimes with air travel, with "autopilot" being used when flying the plane is pretty routine, so the pilots sit back and supervise, letting the computer direct the plane unless an emergency arises.

Pattern Recognition

If you have the new iPhone X, then you're familiar with another type of data science, which is recognition. Data science powers the ability of the phone to use your face to unlock it. This is also done on the older models where the thumbprint, rather than the face is used for the same purpose. This kind of technology could also be used in many other ways, like picking out the face of a criminal in a crowd.

In the last chapter, we mentioned an idea of using a machine learning algorithm to approve people for a loan or not. In fact using machine learning algorithms for scoring of customers or ranking has long been one of the most frequently applied areas of data science. FICO or credit scores are a good example of this.

Classification and Anomaly Detection

Simple classification schemes are a part of data science. Do you have a Gmail account? If you do, then you know there is a Promotion tab, a Social tab, and a Primary tab. It also includes a spam folder. The system uses machine learning in order to route incoming messages to the correct location. Unfortunately this doesn't work perfectly, and Google has chosen for us what "social" and "promotion" mean, as a part of their attempt to shield us from what they think are unwanted marketing emails. That is another example of something that works most of the time but you're going to find out that it is certainly not close to 100%.

Anomaly detection is another area where data science is used. Unusual data patterns can often represent cases of fraud, but once again they don't always do so. If a book on Amazon had been up for three months, and was only getting a few downloads a month and suddenly it got 40 reviews over the course of one or two days, the system would note that this was anomalous behavior. I don't know how Amazon works internally, but it's possible they would check into it, and remove the reviews if they turned out to be fake. Such behavior can be used to alert a human to intervene in the situation.

The brains of animals and humans are wired in part to recognize patterns in the external world. But when it comes to big data, our brains are too slow and only able to analyze small bits of information at a time. When presented with large data sets, they are simply too complex for humans to take in or recognize the patterns that are hidden in the data. For example, in order to determine what characteristics people have that might lead them to purchase a pet cat and then go bankrupt, you would have to examine a large number of characteristics of tens of millions of people. It's pretty obvious that a human being lacks that capability at a fundamental level. You might be able to recognize a pattern studying 4-5 characteristics of a group of 10 or 20 people.

Computers, on the other hand, are lighting fast and able to find patterns among large collections of data that humans couldn't possibly pick out. Since they are able to check multiple scenarios quickly and iteratively, a computer system is going to be able to spot things that people simply can't detect. Since people can't or at least can't readily detect these patterns, we often say that they are 'hidden' in the data.

There are many ways that pattern recognition can be used in machine learning. For example, criminal behavior often follows distinct patterns. Auto thefts are going to occur in some specific areas of a city far more often than they occur in other areas. They may occur more often during particular times of year. Sure, a person might be able to sit down with a few data points and determine this with some measure of accuracy, but a computer would be far more accurate. Using machine learning, it could examine tens of thousands of cases of auto theft over a dozen years, and in the process it would probably find patterns that a human being simply would not be able to detect.

A grocery store could also use data science in novel ways. By issuing shopper's cards, the store not only can determine what individuals may purchase, but now they also know where their customers live. They can determine how often people from different neighborhoods shop in the store, and possibly find patterns as to time of day people shop, what days they shop, and how much they spend each time they visit the store. This would help the grocery store laser target their advertising. Their machine learning tools might also detect unusual patterns the store's owners or managers haven't thought of, for example detecting that a lot of the customers come from a distant location. This could propel them to open a new store close to the location where these people lived, so that they could increase efficiency of distribution and make shopping more convenient for their customers.

Examples of Data Science in Use

Data science has been used by industry to make big changes and safe money in their operations. In one famous example, Southwest Airlines claims it determined how much time its planes were spending idling on the tarmac before takeoff, and it was able to use this information to save hundreds of millions of dollars by reducing fuel waste. Other airlines are using data science in order to do better planning of their routes, and improving their logistics.

Data science has also been used by companies like Netflix to help them recommend movies for you to watch, based on your past habits. You can see from this example how machine learning and data science are deeply intertwined. Of course data science is a field for a human, and so machine learning is one tool that they rely on.

Data Science as a Career

There is no question that data science is a hot career path right now, and it will continue to be one for the foreseeable future. Most universities don't have a specific data science program, that is something that you can create on your own. In order to do that you could major in either computer science or mathematics and statistics. But either way, you will want to take course in the other field as well as in business. Remember in our discussion above we noted that a statistician would have to learn a lot of computer science as well as get some business education before they could actually be considered a data scientist. You don't necessarily have to get a PhD in order to make a career out of it, but in competitive science related fields an advanced education is definitely going to give you an edge. In computer science, you should focus on AI and machine learning in order to pursue a career in data science.

If you are interested in a career that uses machine learning, data science is but one path. You always have the option of going straight through computer science with a specialty in machine learning. It's a certainty that you will be very employable if you choose this path.

Chapter 3: Supervised Machine Learning

In the earlier chapters we have just glossed over the concept of machine learning. It turns out that there are four major types of machine learning that need to be considered. In this chapter we are going to find out what they are, and how they are used in order to achieve the goal of machine learning. There are four main types of machine learning that are used. These include supervised learning, unsupervised learning, semi-supervised learning, and reinforcement learning. Understanding the differences between these is an important part of understanding machine learning.

Supervised Learning

With supervised learning, the goal is to determine a functional relationship or mapping between outputs Y and inputs X. You can think of this as a mapping relationship that would be similar to mathematics. That is Y is some function of the inputs X:

$$Y = f(X)$$

So the inputs act as an independent variable, while the outputs Y are a dependent variable. In this case, the input and output variables are known beforehand for the training data. As a loose analogy, think of the square of a number. In that case, you would know the input 2 would produce the result 4, and the input 3 would produce the result 9, and so on. When the input and output variables of a data set are known, they are called *labeled*. Of course in machine learning the relationship between the input and output variables isn't known beforehand, even though the associations between the inputs and outputs is known, and the problem is much more complex that squaring a number. The system is fed both the inputs and outputs together during the training process.

In the real world, in many, if not most cases, the relationship between an input and an output variable is not a direct functional relationship, but is instead a probabilistic one. For this reason, a data scientist must have an advanced understanding of probability and statistics in order to be effective.

The job of the algorithm during training is to find the patterns behind the relationship between X and Y.

Eventually, the system would be able to predict the outputs Y for new inputs X for which the results were not known in advance.

The algorithm uses an iterative method in order to seek out the patterns that will allow it to correctly predict the outputs. This process of feeding the model labeled data is analogous to teaching the model. It's similar to a teacher in an algebra class teaching the students the concept of a squared number, and the teacher knows what the answers are.

Data used for supervised learning is grouped in a row and column format, just like a spreadsheet. Each column is given a label called an *attribute*. The various characteristics of a data point or object are also known as *features*. A single data point would consist of one row from the data set. So a single data point can have multiple attributes. Data can be numerical or *categorical*, which simply means it's any kind of data that is not numeric. Categorical data takes the form of characters.

Here is an example dataset organized in this fashion. Suppose we have a group of people and we want to predict whether or not they will have diabetes in five years. The challenge in this case might be to determine if one ethnicity or another has a higher risk of developing diabetes, given similar input conditions.

Blood Sugar	Height (in.)	Weight (lbs)	Age (yrs)	Race or Ethnicity
120	67	200	52	White
126	65	190	54	African American
130	70	195	53	Hispanic
128	72	204	50	Hispanic
110	69	201	50	White
130	68	200	56	White
127	70	205	48	Native American

In this case, a data point would be an entire row, so picking the highlighted row in the middle, (128, 72, 204, 50, Hispanic) would be one data point. The data (128, 72, 204, 50) are numeric data, and "Hispanic" is categorical data in this example. In the case of supervised learning, we would know beforehand which of these cases developed diabetes and did not, and could train the algorithm to learn to pick them out by repeatedly feeding it the data until it attains an accuracy that we desire.

As another example, we could use the characteristics of homes for sale in the Orange County, California area to develop a model that could take that data as input and then predict the selling price. During the training phase, if we are using supervised learning we'll use data from homes that already sold with an iterative process in order to teach the model the relationship. The training will be repeated as many times as necessary in order to get the model trained well enough that it's at an acceptable level of accuracy. In this case our data set might look like this:

SQFT	Bedrooms	Bathrooms	Age	Location
1400	3	2	25	Irvine
1250	3	1.5	30	Orange
1500	3	2	10	Whittier
1100	2	1	40	Santa Ana

In this case, using row 2, *Orange* is the categorical data, and the rest is numeric data.

During the training process, using an iterative process, the algorithm gradually creates a model that can accurately predict the outcome given new, never seen before data inputs based on the patterns that it has found in the data. The data used for training purposes are actually paired data, with the desired output. So the machine is given the output as part of the training process. Using our diabetes example, taking one row of data, the system would be fed the inputs (130, 68, 200, 56, white) along with the known result (Has Diabetes). Or using the homes dataset, we could have the pair (1500, 3, 2, 10, Whittier) paired with a known result ($450,000). Often data is input to models using comma separated value file formats.

A set of data points that are input for machine learning of the form (A,B,C, ...) is called a *vector.*

The goal of training is to have the algorithm refine it's model so well that it's able to predict the outcome accurately enough (often termed "reasonable") when it's presented with never before seen data.

Supervised learning follows a path of well defined steps. This begins with human input, by selecting the types of training examples that are going to be used in the training process. Once that has been decided, real world data with known outputs is collected from databases. Vectors are then created using attributes or features that are desired to play the role of inputs and they are assembled into rows as illustrated above. Although it might seem like the more features you have the better, it's actually preferable to have a relatively small number of features that are used in the training. This will make it easier for the system to accurately determine the patterns and relationships that exist in the data. It will then be more able to accurately predict future results.

Once the data has been gathered, the algorithm is tested on the training set. The algorithm will adjust its own parameters as it determines the patterns in the data. Then the accuracy of the algorithm is evaluated. If necessary, the process is iterated in order to keep refining the algorithm, using more test data.

Selecting an Algorithm

When the model is in the design phases, the data scientist will choose an algorithm that will form the basis of the model. In this case, the algorithm is a type of model used to determine functional relationships. We will be investigating this in more detail later, but for now we will note that these types of algorithms include linear regression, decision trees, nearest neighbor analysis, or non-linear regression, to name a few. Don't worry if you don't understand what these terms mean, we will discuss that in detail later. They are general techniques that can be applied to data sets in order to determine functional relationships.

The amount of data that will be required to train an algorithm is going to depend on the complexity of the algorithm. A simple algorithm will require less data than a complex algorithm. One of the most important things to understand in this context are how output errors are characterized in machine learning systems.

Bias Errors

A *bias error* is simply the difference between the average prediction a given model will give for a specific input as compared to the real or correct value. The average prediction given by a set of models will actually be a range of predictions, because when fed different data sets the models will learn differently, and therefore be parameterized in different ways. Bias is simply the difference between the average and the true value.

A model can be trained on any number of data sets, and from the perspective of a human managing this process, it may not be possible to say whether one model is any better than another. However, using a particular data set is going to bias the model.

Variance Errors

Here we again imagine using a process to build multiple machine learning models, each one trained on its own data set. A variance error is the error between the prediction of the model and the actual result when one data point is considered. In the earlier section, we gave an example of a set of data points that could be used to predict whether a specific individual would become diabetic given height, weight, age, blood sugar, and ethnicity. So you'd put in a specific case, and note the error between the models and the actual prediction.

A model that is flexible is one that is going to have a larger variance error. Total prediction error is the sum of bias error and variance error.

High variance is also a consequence of data sets that contain a large number of inputs. The more inputs the higher the variance error. That is, we can see that it might be relatively easy for a machine learning system to determine the probability that a given person will get diabetes within five years given their height, weight, age, and fasting blood sugar or A1C value. But if you keep adding more information to each data point, such as height, weight, age, fasting blood sugar, ethnicity, occupation, years of education, prior military service, born by cesarean section etc., it becomes more difficult for the model to learn, and hence their error rate will be higher.

Noisy Data

Another error that can arise with machine learning is the case of measurement or human error when the input data is concerned. Measurement error is common, and of course we all know that human error when it comes to data input can be common as well. It's straightforward to recognize that bad input data is going to train the algorithm badly, and so it's going to have erroneous predictions.

Classification vs. Regression

Generally speaking, supervised learning can be divided into one of two different types, *classification* or *regression*. Classification is a simple learning process that can be binary or more complex. The prototypical example of classification is determining whether or not an email is spam, or whether it's a genuine message. Although this seems like a simple question, I am sure that most readers have had one or more experiences with spam detection systems that misclassifies either valid emails or lets spam through the filter.

Classification systems can go well beyond simple binary classification. Examples of this include speech recognition and handwriting analysis. There are several types of algorithms that can be used in machine learning for classification purposes. We will review these in more detail later, but list them here for reference:

- Neural Networks
- Decision Trees
- Support Vector Machines
- Nearest Neighbor

- Naïve Bayes Classifier
- Boosted Trees
- Random Forest

Regression models use linear regression in order to predict output values. These types of models use a set of parameters to determine or estimate the relationship between one or more input variables and an output variable. The simplest possible model used for regression is:

$$Y = c + b*x$$

Here, x is the input or independent variable. The regression coefficient is b, and c is a constant. In order to train a model it would be fed data and the values of b & c would be adjusted in order to come up with accurate predictions.

Variations on Supervised Learning

In a minute, we are going to discuss a different way to use training for machine learning, called unsupervised learning. The basic concept behind unsupervised learning is that the data fed to the algorithm for training is unlabeled. That means that the expected output values are not provided to the algorithm for training purposes.

It's possible to have a hybrid model between the two. This is called semi-supervised learning. When this training method is used, a subset of the data will be labeled, that is it will include the desired output values. The training data will also include a subset which is unlabeled. In most cases, the subset of data that is labeled is smaller than the unlabeled set.

Active learning is an interesting and powerful variation of this. When using active learning, the machine can request output data as part of the learning process. Some of the data sets used in training for these purposes could be labeled, but most would be unlabeled.

Chapter 4: Unsupervised Learning

In supervised learning, the training session involves the programmer or data scientists feeding the machine or algorithm data sets that not only include sample data, but also include the outputs. This is called labeling. Now we are going to consider a method of learning that uses unlabeled data. That is the system is trained on data sets that don't include the outputs. This type of method is more independent from the perspective of the machine, or we might say its more autonomous. In this case, we are leaving it up to the machine itself to determine what patterns exist in the data and it can learn for itself what the outputs should be. In this case the algorithm may be able to learn from mistakes. This is a more sophisticated type of machine learning that is reminiscent of the way that humans learn in most cases.

Different situations will call for different approaches. That means that sometimes supervised learning will be more appropriate to use, while at other times unsupervised learning will be the better choice.

There are three general types of machine learning that fit under the category of unsupervised learning. The three that we will discuss include:

- Clustering
- Neural networks
- Markov algorithms

Let's begin by considering clustering.

Clustering

Clustering is a relatively easy form of machine learning to understand. The basic principle behind clustering is that you can take any set of data and group it or classify it in different ways. Let's take the diabetes example once again. If we are interested in what people are most likely to get diabetes over a specified time period, we could group the data by: age ranges, gender, ethnicity, last measured fasting blood sugar, body weight, BMI.

Using unsupervised learning, there is an open ended approach to pattern recognition, so while we focused on only one classification in the previous examples, in this case we might want to have our algorithms examine all of these cases to determine which classifications were the best predictor of a future case of diabetes.

So when clustering is used, each data point is placed into a defining group. This is done because it's believed that members of a certain group are going to have some characteristics in common. For example, dog owners are going to have different characteristics in common as compared to cat owners, and people who own dogs and cats may have unique characteristics of their own.

This concept has a wide array of applications, one of which is the creation of a 'lookalike' audience in Facebook advertising. The principle behind this system is nothing more than clustering – Facebook will analyze the features of people who have purchased a particular type of product in the past, and then use that to create a new listing of people who have yet to purchase the product but based on probability estimates, are likely to purchase the product in the future because their features match up with previous buyers.

When using clustering, the data scientist can determine the numbers of groups or clusters that are used for the learning. These go by the fancy name of cluster centroids.

There are several different types of clustering that can be used, but we will only be able to review two of them here. These are relatively simple to understand, and they form the basis of other clustering techniques. So once you understand the basics then you'll find it easy to pick up different algorithms.

K-Means Clustering

The first type of clustering we are going to examine is *k-means clustering.* The idea behind this approach is to determine the center, or mean of the clusters. The data scientist can start this process off by choosing the number of clusters, and it's been suggested that manually examining the data is appropriate in this case. So you can eyeball the data to estimate how many clusters (that is groups or categories) should be used for the data. We could do that with our database data, and maybe we would use ethnicity and gender, or ethnicity, gender, age, and BMI.

The algorithm then proceeds, first it determines or computes a "group center" or mean data point for each group. Then the distance of each member data point from the group is calculated. The goal of this process is to refine the results multiple times, and so this is followed by recalculating the group center. Then the entire process is repeated.

The iteration process should make the mean or group center more accurate as time goes on. K-means clustering is a commonly used method, and it's simple to understand and easy to use.

Mean Shift Clustering

Mean shift clustering is another averaging based approach. The idea behind this method is that there is going to be a tendency for data points to be dense and sparse in different areas. For example, people who become diabetic are going to be clustered more around ages 45-54 than they are around 18-24. The latter age group will have some diabetes cases, but they will be comparatively rare as compared to the 45-54 age group.

In order to find the dense zones of data points in a large data set, a technique known as windowing is used. Again calling on the diabetes example, we might imagine that we have a database of a million people to examine. That is certainly not something that a human observer is going to be able to look at and tease out the patterns from the data, but you can see how the human observer would be able to look at a small subset of the data and then determine the different classifications that should be used when analyzing it. The algorithm will try to find the centroid of each group or class.

Now we start by making a window. A window is a range of data points that we use to examine subsets of the data. For example, if looking at age, we could use a four year inclusive window to examine the density of data points. The algorithm could start at age 18, and the first step would be to examine the window of all data points in our set for ages 18-21.

This type of algorithm uses what is called a 'sliding window'. So we slide the window to the next age range, which in this case would be 22-25. As the algorithm is searching, it will be looking for the most dense concentrations of data that will help us heighten the predictive power of our diabetes model. For example, it's probably going to find high density areas between 45-49 and 50-53.

We can also look for clusters of data that have a lot of data points for the groups that have been defined by the data scientist. Let's say that we are using a database of people who have applied for new home loans in the southern California region. We could classify them by current address, age, ethnicity, income level, education level, and so on. The data can be sliced and diced in any way you see fit, for example you might want to classify the data by income level, then within each income level you would look at the other characteristics mentioned such as educational attainment or current address.

This is where the commonality comes in. If you recall, we mentioned the possibility or probability that data points that cluster are likely to have many features in common. As an obvious case, looking at the home loan data we'd probably find that there is a clustering of people with college educations or higher among the group that has an annual income over $150,000 a year, while a group with an annual income of $75,000 a year or less is more likely not to have a college education.

The process of clustering is an iterative process, and it's continued until the mean or centroid stops changing, or changes at a rate that is below some level that you have pre-determined to be an acceptable level of error.

It may be the case that the first time you use this procedure, it's not working perfectly for you. In that situation the procedure used is to try it again, while using different groups or clusters.

Neural Networks

We touched on the basic idea of neural networks earlier. The fundamental idea behind a neural network is to set up interconnected nodes. In some sense, this is a representation that mimics the way the brain is structured. It's interesting to think about the fact that the brain isn't just structured this way at the cellular level. In fact it's following this model all the way to the highest levels. There are many independent regions in the brain that perform specific tasks, and they are interconnected with each other. For example, one area of the brain processes visual input. Another area of the brain processes listening to speech, while another processes actually speaking. Still other areas of the brain govern the formation of memory and emotions. These are the nodes of high level neural processing in your brain. They are all connected to each other by nerve axons which form communications channels.

The idea behind neural networks was to create a computer system that could learn in a similar way that the human mind learns. In the case of a neural network, the specialized areas of the brain or individual nerve cells if looking at it on that level are replaced by independent functions, which in computer science terms can be thought of as independent black boxes. They are connected to each other through parameters that are exchanged.

Once again, the concept of pattern recognition comes to the fore. A neural network is designed to learn by seeking out patterns in the data that it receives.

In your brain, nerve cells have different numbers of connections with other nerve cells. Connections can strengthen, the more you learn something. If you forget something, the connections will be pared back. A neural network attempts to mimic this behavior, strengthening connections between particular nodes in the network.

The fundamental idea behind neural networks is the same as that used for other types of models. The nodes in the network can be considered to be a single black box, so you can view the neural network from the outside and not worry about the internal details. Like other models, the neural network will have a set of tunable parameters. The way to tune the parameters is to continually feed data into the black box – that is we train the neural network.

Then, as it gets trained on more data, the parameters get more finely tuned, and more likely to give the correct answers when fed new, never before seen data. Does this sound familiar? The same basic concepts are here, but with a different implementation.

We use unsupervised learning with neural networks, and so they are not going to be fed the correct output answers. Instead they will get unlabeled data. The basic structure of a neural network is shown below. On the left, we have a representation of our input data which is fed to the network. In the middle, the hidden layers or black box is shown (we are peeking inside, so it's a dashed box instead of black). Then on the right side is the output.

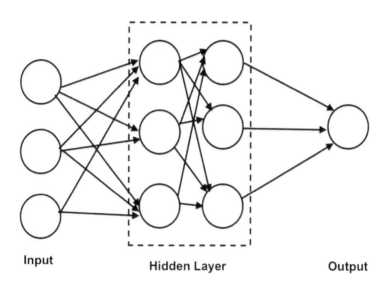

Input   Hidden Layer   Output

There is no specific number of hidden layers. In the image above, we show two, but you can start with only one hidden layer and add more layers as necessary to refine the algorithm so that it comes up with more accurate answers.

The number of nodes in the hidden layers can be varied. Here we have shown three nodes per hidden layer. A general rule of thumb is that you should not try to "overfit" the data. Overfitting occurs when there are twice as many nodes as there are in the input data. Here, we have three nodes for the input data, and so the overfitting condition would be six nodes per hidden layer. Often, the number of nodes chosen is about the average between input and output data. For simplicity, we've only shown one output node, but obviously there can be more. Using the average, in this examples the best case scenario would be 2 nodes in each hidden layer, but it's an approximate relationship and so three is fine.

When using neural networks, in the same manner that you do with all types of machine learning you will set a desired error level that is acceptable to you. When the system gets to that error level, training stops because the neural network is performing as well as you need it to perform. You can also have training last for a fixed number of iterations. With each iteration, the model will improve itself, and then continue until it reaches the number of iterations that you have specified.

The inputs and outputs of a neural network are similar to what we've already seen. For example, we could set up a neural network to classify borrowers as high risk, medium risk, or low risk. The inputs to the system could include age, gender, occupation, income level, credit score and any other parameters that we felt were relevant.

Each node of the neural network is some function, so its basically one of the functions that we've seen before. In the beginning, the "brain" is considered stupid, so you might start out with one layer, and a bias is assigned to each node in the hidden layer. The bias assigned to each node is random.

Each input node has a weight that is assigned to it. So if credit score is more important than occupation, then the weight of the credit score node could be assigned some value like 0.7 and the weight of the occupation could be assigned a value of 0.45, say. These are then fed into the different nodes. In the beginning, the system starts by using guessing, until the *activation function* takes over.

The data is then run through the activation function for each node. The activation function creates a nonlinear estimate of the output, and then this compared to the correct answer to get error estimates. This gives you how far off the guessing that was generated by the assigned bias of each node was in getting to the correct answer. This information is then fed back into each node. Then the bias of each node is adjusted. The weights of the inputs can be adjust as well, so if you find that the model used above underestimated the weight of the credit score in determining the loan, the weight could be increase, so say we adjust the weight of credit score to 0.72 and the weight of occupation is adjusted downward to 0.42.

In neural networks, the learning rate is the amount that the biases and weights of the system are adjusted with each iteration. Momentum is a measurement used in neural networks to determine how much past results affect the weights and biases. When the neural network has gone through the entire dataset, that is an iteration, and these are repeated either a fixed number of times or until the level of error is acceptable.

With each iteration, the neural network is strengthened. This is analogous to the strengthening of your neural connections when you learn something new and practice it or study it hard. The more the neural network is exposed to the data, the more the biases and weights will be adjusted and the performance of the neural network will continue to improve.

Neural networks have many applications. They are particularly effective at recognizing objects in images. They are also used to detect anomaly's in data, for predictive analysis, risk management, fraud detection, and sales forecasting. Like the brain, which is "general" in its intelligence, neural networks are very useful when applied to any problem involving pattern recognition.

Markov Algorithm

In this section we will cover the third type of unsupervised learning that we are going to discuss in the book. This is called the Markov algorithm. This type of algorithm can be used when you want to take a data set and translate it into a different type of data set. The data in the Markov algorithm are sets of strings. It searches for patterns in the sets of strings that should be replaced. The rules that are used for the operation of the Markov algorithm have been described as "grammar like". The translation method used is a simple substitution formula. An easy application of this would be in the transcription of DNA and RNA. You may recall that the DNA uses four nitrogen bases that form the basis of the code. These are adenine, thymine, guanine, and cytosine. These bond together into pairs. Adenine always bonds to thymine and guanine always bonds to cytosine. So one translation algorithm that could be used is substituting adenine for thymine, and thymine for adenine. Then guanine can be substituted for cytosine. Using these simple rules, the Markov algorithm could go through a data set representing a DNA sequence and make a new, translated data set that would encode the opposite strand. Alternatively, another Markov algorithm could be used to generate the RNA strand from a given DNA code, in this case it would substitute Uracil for thymine.

Chapter 5: Reinforcement Learning

We saw that in the case of supervised learning, the answers to each input in the data set were provided during the training phase. Reinforcement learning withholds the answers, but uses the concept of reinforcement to guide the correct behavior. The model has a reinforcement agent that decides on its own what to do. The agent's task is to find the best path to get a reward that acts as reinforcement. So far we have described a cartoon model, but this is a pretty accurate description as far as the basic concept – think of giving a reward as a feedback mechanism to improve the output. Typically reinforcement learning is used when there are multiple solutions to a problem, so this is an alternative to supervised learning which has one correct answer for a given input. The programmer is more involved in this case. When the algorithm produces a given output, then the programmer can decide to reward the model or not in the correct fashion to guide it to the answer.

Another difference between reinforcement learning and supervised learning is that reinforcement learning uses sequential inputs. This works in the following way. The model is presented with the first input. Then the second input to the model depends on the first output. This process is continued on through the data. In the next iteration The second output would then be a dependency for the third input, and so on.

Types of Reinforcement Learning

You know that when training animals or teaching small children, you can use different methods of reinforcement in order to shape the behaviors that you want. Let's consider a horse as an example, and look at some of the different methods of horse training that can be used.

In the old days, horse training methods tended to be harsh. In other words, they relied on a negative reinforcement type of system, that is also known as punishment. The trainer might carry whips and ropes with them, and when the horse did something that the trainer didn't like, they might use the whip to strike at the horse on its lower legs or on its rear end. This type of training relies on creating fear in the horse, which we might consider to be the agent in our analogy. The desire here is to get the horse to produce the output we want by behaving in a specific fashion and carrying out certain work duties, such as being tame for riding or pulling a wagon.

You can also use a positive reinforcement mechanism. When using positive reinforcement, the trainer would keep some treats with them. When the horse did something the trainer wanted the horse to do, then the trainer would give the horse a treat.

A similar method is used with dogs. You can praise the dog verbally, give him a pet, and then feed him with a treat when he does something that you want him to do.

There is even a third alternative, which is to use a combination of positive and negative reinforcement. In the case of animal training this would involve using force or punishment when the animal did something wrong, and then responding with a treat with praise when the animal does something desirable.

So the formal definitions of positive and negative reinforcement in reinforcement learning when it comes to machines are actually similar. Let's take the case of negative reinforcement first. In negative reinforcement, a reward is given when a negative behavior is avoided. This will strengthen the behavior of the agent toward the correct end goal. However, this type of reinforcement is believed to only bring the system up to a standard of minimum behavior. By analogy, you can go back to our discussion of horse training. If you only used negative reinforcement, the animal would avoid doing things that the trainer didn't want, but would stop there. The animal would not be performing the desired tasks that the trainer ultimately seeks.

In order to maximize performance, reinforcement learning should include positive reinforcement. When the agent exhibits desired behavior the agent is rewarded. This strengthens the behavior, and this is likely to result in an improvement of performance that gets stronger with time.

Don't get too carried away with our discussion of horse and dog training, that was only a loose analogy. It is to get you in the frame of mind of being able to see how different reinforcement mechanisms can shape the behavior of a system. In that case the system would be the horse. People aren't used to thinking of children or animals as "systems", but hardcore computer scientists might be doing so.

Humans also learn in part through this interaction model. One common way that reinforcement learning is explained is to imagine a child approaching a fire. Suppose that it's winter and it's cold outside because there has been a major snowstorm. A child may approach the fireplace in order to get warmth. As the child approaches, the child feels better. They can get very close to the fire, and they still feel good, warming their body up after having been outside in the snow. The child may have an urge to put their hands out facing the fire in order to warm up their extremities. This will feel good to the child, and so it acts as a positive reinforcement mechanism. Then if the child reaches out further to actually touch the fire, they will feel the burn and extreme heat, and pull their hand away and start crying. This is negative reinforcement, which teaches the child not to actually touch the fire. We see that in the same situation the child has learned two things through positive and negative reinforcement. The first is that fire provides warmth, as long as you stay a little bit distant. The second lesson is don't touch the fire.

In summary, the agent learns the correct behavior by performing the correct actions and seeing the results. This type of machine learning is particularly effective for making artificially intelligent versions of games. So for example, we can make a chess game, or a computer version of Go that uses artificial intelligence. In both cases, the agent and reward model would be used. Consider a chess game, the agent is the computerized chess player. They learn by playing games, and making the right moves that bring rewards. From this experience the agent learns what the right moves are and gains experience. In the beginning the agent is dumb, it may know the basic rules of the game but its not going to know what the best moves are in different situations that will lead to victory when playing chess games against talented opponents.

The State Model of Reinforcement Rearning

Reinforcement learning begins with the system in a certain state, or configuration. If you are unfamiliar with this concept, think of a lamp. The lamp has two states – on and off. The lamp begins in the state OFF, and there is one action an agent could take with respect to the lamp, which is to flip the switch to turn the lamp to the ON state.

You can think of more and more complicated examples. A calculator (more likely an app on your phone than a physical calculator these days) begins with a state zero. That is there is a number zero displayed on the screen. As the agent, you can take actions on the calculator to change its state.

An agent in machine learning will be operating in some kind of environment. This kind of model is often used in video games, and so the environment will be the scene that the game is played in. In the case of chess, the environment will be the chessboard.

The agent can take an action based on the state provided by the environment. In a chess game, the human player may open with a specific chess move. The agent will analyze the situation, and then it will decide to make a certain move in response. A reward may result from the action.

Reinforcement learning is a loop based system. After the agent has made it's first move, the new situation forms the basis for the input to the next state. You can view a chess game as iterating through a series of different states. As each player makes their move, the state of the game changes.

In reinforcement learning, the goal of the procedure of reward for good behavior is to maximize the reward in a cumulative fashion. Think of it as saving money in the bank. You are rewarded the most by saving money at regular intervals, and the amount of money adds up, sometimes to prodigious sums of cash as more and more money is saved and the process of compound interest grows the sum.

Short Term Rewards

The concept of short term and long term rewards is considered with reinforcement learning. The idea behind this is the following. You might have your eye on the ultimate prize, which is the long-term reward. However, you are also less likely to receive the long-term reward as you are to succeed in attaining nearby, short term rewards. In reinforcement learning, this is described by a parameter called the discount rate, which is sometimes described by a number gamma that ranges from 0 to 1. Since you don't know if you are going to be able to get the long term reward, you are better off getting the short term reward first.

When gamma is small, the discount is large. When gamma is large, the discount is small. Thus gamma and the discount have an inverse relationship. A large gamma is associated with an agent that seeks out the long-term reward. An alternative way to state this is that a small discount is associated with an agent that seeks out the long-term reward.

But if gamma is small, the agent prefers to get the short term reward. At least the agent knows that they will get something. As we said above, this is also the case when the discount is large.

Have you played the Pac-man game? In this game, you control the main character, and you can try to get through to the next level or focus at first on eating up as many coins as you can to earn points. The game is setup so that you're going to have an inclination to do this. Might as well build up some points before running into an enemy character and getting killed. Pac-man can be thought of as having a large discount for the games main player.

When are Rewards Given

Let's think in terms of a video game to understand this concept. If the rewards are given at each stage of the game, it's called temporal difference learning. So you can get a reward during game play. The alternative is Monte Carlo, where rewards are cumulative and handed out at the end.

Temporal difference learning is also known as Q-Learning. The key here is that you get the reward when you get the reward. It doesn't matter what the state of the system is, so you're not waiting to reach the next level.

Episodes

Reinforcement learning can be divided into episodes. Each episode has states, actions, and rewards. New states are created based on the outputs from the states before them. Tasks are instances of reinforcement learning programs. When you have episodes, tasks are episodic.

An episode in a game can be the first iteration of play. If you are good at the game, you can get through the entire first level without being killed. The end of the level would be the end of the first episode. However, you don't have to make it to the end to end the episode, getting killed also ends it. You can then replay the episode if you haven't run out of lives.

Continuous Tasks

A game can take a different approach, and rather than having levels it can be continuous. An endless runner or flappy bird type game could be continuous. At every instant, the agent is interacting with the environment and can be rewarded or punished for exhibiting the correct behavior.

Q Tables

A q-table is a collection of states and actions in pairs, arranged in a table. The Q-table is updated when each episode is completed. Depending on performance, the q-value, which is initially set to zero, is updated. The agent can use the q-value in order to determine its next action, based on the reference in the q-table.

Chapter 6: Algorithms for Supervised Learning

There are many different algorithms to choose from when considering machine learning. In order to get a firmer grasp on how this all works behind the scenes, let's take a look at some of the most important algorithms that are used. These include linear regression, logistic regression, decision trees, random forests, and naïve Bayes. We have already discussed clustering, Markov, and some of the other approaches used in unsupervised learning.

Linear Regression

Linear regression is a relatively simple mathematic technique that is used to determine the functional relationship between two variables. It's simple enough that it's often taught in algebra courses. Linear regression begins with an input variable that is considered the independent variable. The output from the model is the dependent variable. Using ordinary functional notation, this is expressed as

$y = f(x)$

Since linear regression has become closely associated with data science, independent and dependent variable labels are not used as frequently anymore. You can also refer to x as the predictor, and y as the response (output is also acceptable). When there is only one input or predictor, the model is said to be simple, and so if you hear the phrase simple linear regression, this means that it's linear regression with one input variable. A model that had six input variables would not be simple. Instead, that would be called multiple linear regression.

Linear regression can be used on any mathematical relationship of the form y = f(x), but researchers are interested in using the technique when it's known that there is a relationship but it's not known what the form of that relationship is. In this case, we say there is a statistical relationship. When two variables have a statistical relationship, it is not absolute or deterministic in nature. When there is a statistical relationship, if you plot a graph of x and y on a plot, you are going to see individual data points scattered about the chart. Often a line is seen drawn through the data.

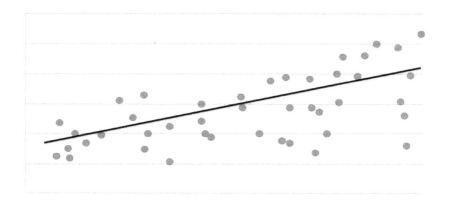

The line that is drawn through the data is actually calculated using linear regression. That is why the term 'linear' is used, it's a linear representation of the relationship between the input and output variables. This type of model is not going to give an accurate prediction of what the output would be every single time. What you can say is that it uses a line which fits the empirical or measured data that will give you the trend between the input and output variables. Suppose for example, that the above chart gave the heart attack rate for men who were aged 50 at different body mass index. The horizontal axis would be the body mass index and the vertical line on the chart would be the heart attack rate. What we have here is a line that fits the data, so we can give you a statistical answer of what the heart attack rate is for a given BMI. However, any one individual is not necessarily going to fit the statistical data.

Since linear regression gives you a straight line representation of the relationship between the input and output variables, it's the same equation of a line that you remember from school. It's in the form:

y = mx + b

When used in machine learning, the job of the system is to learn on a large data set to determine the values of m and b as accurately as possible. The more data and more iterations that are used, the closer m and b will become to the idealized values.

The error of this model can be calculated by comparing predicted results to actual results. If we call w the measured value and y the predicted value, the error is given by a simple formula:

e = w − y

In practice, what's done is you calculate e for a large range of data points, and then you square the differences, and sum them up. So now we have a measure of the total error. In order to make the model as accurate as possible, we want to minimize this quantity. This is called the 'least squares method' because we are trying to get the least or smallest value of the sum of the squared errors.

This is a simple calculation, and the values calculated are used to find m and b in the formula that gives you the straight line. So this is a very simple type of machine learning, but don't be fooled by its simplicity. It has enormous value in research and has great predictive power.

Researchers are going to note certain things about the relationship between the input and output variables. For example, what is the trend? If the line is sloped upwards, that means that the output increases when the input increases. On the other hand, if the line is sloped downward, the output decreases when the input increases. Simply knowing this relationship can be very important for many applications. For example, there is a relationship between the HDL cholesterol level and your heart attack risk that follows that type of pattern. HDL cholesterol would be the input variable, and heart attack rate is the output variable. If you were to get a large set of data from a health study and build a linear regression model from it, you would find that when HDL cholesterol level increases, the heart attack rate decreases. So any linear fit that you got between the two variables would have a downward slope.

Not all graphs are as scattered as the one shown in the picture, in fact in most cases where linear regression is used you're likely to see the data points clustered closely about the line used to fit the data. If the model didn't have strong predictive power it wouldn't see used so much. Once the machine has learned on a set of training data, it will be able to predict output values for new inputs that it hasn't seen before.

There is much more you can learn about linear regression, there are entire courses taught about this one topic alone. You can do yourself a favor by becoming extremely well acquainted with it. One nice thing about this model is that it's simple enough that you can really understand the model. This can be done by using it by hand with small data sets to see how it works. You can do the calculations by hand and then get some larger data sets and setup a linear regression model in a spreadsheet, or write a small computer program to implement it.

Although we didn't discuss it here, you can use linear regression with multiple input variables, but it's more complicated. That is something that you are probably going to want to take straight to the computer.

Logistic Regression

Logistic regression is another method used to determine a statistical relationship between input and output variables. In this case the first situation we are going to look at is when the output variable is binary, that is it can only have one of two states. This can be yes or no, male or female, 0 or 1, etc. When this is the case, data scientists say that the variable is 'dichotomous'. There can be one or multiple input variables for a logistic regression model.

Logistic regression is used any time there is a yes or no answer to the question you seek. It could be used to detect spam email, since whether or not you put an email in the spam folder is a yes or no question. Linear regression can be used to solve such problems as well, but with linear regression you would have to pick a threshold to determine whether some input variable produced a "yes" or a "no".

There are certain mathematical functions that can be used to take input data and generate a yes or a no answer. These functions will smoothly but rapidly approach one value or the other. The power of these functions is they can help the modeler set a threshold to determine whether or not something is a "yes" or a "no".

Consider the case of a spam email. A spam email might have certain characteristics, like a claim that you are about to receive money. Or it may ask you for personal information, or appear to come from a certain source when an analysis of the computer system it came from shows that this is deception. It may use certain language, like claiming you have received a free gift. Each characteristic that has been identified as being associated with a spam email can be given a score or weight. Then when the email has been thoroughly examined, the weights can be put together in order to develop a composite or total spam score. There will be a threshold set by the system to classify whether or not something is spam. If the email passed the threshold, then it will be identified as spam. If not, then the email is going to be routed to your main inbox. The threshold used to make the determination is known as the decision boundary.

Of course the system is going to make mistakes. Many emails that fall below the decision boundary will actually be emails that the user wants to receive. However, since machine learning systems are always able to learn, the user can move a given email from the spam folder, and this will teach the system that next time an email comes from that sender, it's not spam.

Simple logistic regression begins with a model that is similar to that used for linear regression. The output will be 0 or 1, and it will use a linear relationship of the form $y = mx + b$. So at the core of this algorithm, we find that there is a linear regression model that is used to fit the data.

However, another component of logistic regression is a mathematical function known as the sigmoid function. This can be used to threshold data. A sigmoid function of t is positive if t >= 0, and it smoothly and rapidly approaches 1. If t < 0, the function rapidly decays to zero. An example is shown below.

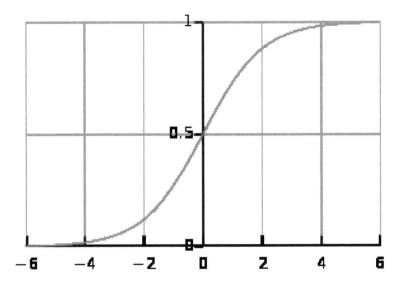

The output of the logistic regression model is framed in terms of probabilities. Using the spam model, the characteristics might be analyzed and the model might come up with an estimate such as there is a 75% chance a given email is spam. The sigmoid function is actually going to give you the probabilities that an output variable is 1 or 0. The mathematical details are beyond the scope of this book, but for those who are interested this is a good start.

Of course not every question is binary. But what is the core characteristic of a binary output? My answer to this question is that it's discrete. Something is either 1 or 0, there is no in between. Of course in reality this questioned can be nuanced depending on the application. In the case of email spam, we are only offering the probability that the email is spam, and then in the final output it's binary.

There can be discrete outcomes with more than two choices. You can have three, four, or any number that you like. The beauty of the logistic regression model is that you can expand it and extend it as far as you need to in order to build your model. This is called multinomial logistic regression. In this case there is no ordering but there are discrete possibilities.

For example, we could use it for a study of voting results. There are discrete possibilities (Democrat, Republican, Green, Libertarian, Did Not Vote ...). You can also envision building a model that tried to predict what type of diet people followed based on various input variables. For example, you could have (vegan, keto, carnivore, Mediterranean). Your training data would be a set of people that actually are following one of the diets, and the task for machine learning would be to seek out patterns in the data that could be used to predict what diet a person is likely to choose given the input characteristics. This makes sense to use for a logistic regression model because the relationship is going to be statistical and not absolute. Therefore there would be thresholds for each possibility.

It's also possible to use ordered data sets. This case is known as ordinal logistic regression.

Decision Trees

A decision tree can be used for categorical or numerical data. You can think of moving through the decision tree by asking a question at each branch or node. These are called decision nodes, and they are made up of two or more branches. A leaf node is called a classification or decision. The best predictor is the root of the tree, or the root node. At each node, some question is answered in yes or no fashion, and the algorithm proceeds through the tree until it arrives and an answer. These trees are actually usually presented "upside down" with the root node at the top of the tree.

A machine learning model can learn a decision tree by splitting the data into different subsets based on different attributes. This is done using a process called recursion, where a function calls itself based on revised inputs, that come from the outputs of the function. Target variables are set based on values of attributes. The recursion continues until it has reached a point when everything at a given level has the same value of the target attribute.

For example, we could classify students in a school, by whether or not they are going to attend college. There may be many factors that will determine whether or not they can attend college or not. For example, we could consider their GPA. Is the GPA above 3.0 or not? We could also consider the score on the SAT exam. The idea here would be to use a minimal set of criteria, you are not looking to see if the student will enter Harvard Law school. Each criteria is framed in terms of a yes or no questions. So the root of the tree could be "Is this student a senior graduating this year?". If the answer is no, then the process would stop. If the answer was yes, then it would proceed to a new node where another yes or no question was asked. The next node might ask "Did the student take the SAT or ACT". Once again, a no answer would stop the process. A yes answer would then continue forward, asking the next question, which could determine whether or not the student attained the minimum score in order to enter any college.

One area where decision trees can be used effectively is with simple medical diagnoses. For example, we could determine whether or not a patient has a bacterial sinus infection or not. The decision tree would ask multiple questions that were arrived at by training the machine learning algorithm. The training would enable the algorithm to find patterns in the data that could be used to determine whether or not a specific patient was likely to have a viral, or bacterial infection.

It could start by asking whether or not the patient had a fever over 100 degrees. If the answer was no, then the patient probably has a cold virus. If it is yes, it's possible the patient has a bacterial infection, but they may have a more serious viral infection that only involves telling the patient to go home and rest. Therefore more questions are necessary on the tree. For example, the next question might be how long the fever has lasted. Using the same procedure, the machine would continue asking questions that would be related to rules doctor use to estimate whether or not an infection is bacterial or viral in nature.

Decision trees can be numerical but are typically oriented to classification problems similar to those we have illustrated here. The rules that are generated with decision trees are actually simple and easy to understand. They can be read and understood by a human observer, even if large data sets were used to generate them.

Since the primary use of decision trees is simple classification, they are not computationally intensive. As you can see from the examples given, a simple check of a question and answer using the attributes of a data point is all that is necessary.

However, decision trees are best used with simple classification problems. If there is a large number of classifications, errors can result. Decision trees are known to overfit training data.

Random Forest

A random forest is a variation on a decision tree that attempts to overcome its weaknesses. In many applications, a decision tree will be more than adequate for the tasks that you are facing. However, if the task appears to be complex enough to bring out the weaknesses of the decision tree, a random forest will be more appropriate. The random forest will create multiple decision trees during training. One advantage of a random forest is that it won't have the overfitting problem that decision trees can have.

So a random forest consists of multiple decision trees. The decision trees are random. One way that they are made random is to build a given tree on a random sample from the training data. That means that each tree in the random forest will have used a unique data set for it's training. During the construction of the tree, splitting at nodes is done in a random fashion.

This is done by randomly selecting which attributes to use at each node.

Nearest Neighbor

The k-Nearest Neighbor model can be used in either regression or classification problems. Although it's used in both, it's normally used more frequently in classification problems. To apply the algorithm, different classifications are assigned to the objects of study. A "vote" is tallied among the neighbors that are nearby.

In a nearest neighbor model, a data point can be classified by comparing with the values of nearest neighbors. This is done on a plurality basis, so for a given attribute the nearest neighbors don't have to be a strict majority.

A k-nearest neighbor algorithm works as follows. You begin by selecting a value for k. Don't worry about that yet, you will see in a moment how that will work. Then you have the system go through all of the data points. You need to find the distance between each point.

Then the data is sorted in this fashion. That is we arrange the distances from smallest to largest. If the distance is small, then two data points are alike, and if the distance is large the two data points are not alike. This is where k comes in, it is going to determine our criteria for determining whether or not two data points are similar or not.

You use k to pick out the top k rows of the data. Since our data is organized by distance, it picks out the k-nearest neighbors. Remember the top row of the data is the smallest distance between data points.

Now we have our "vote". This is done by determining the most frequent classification that occurs in the top k rows. That is the *predicted* class.

Chapter 7: Tips for Your Work in Machine Learning

Machine learning is a very exciting field of study. In this book we've learned a lot about how machine learning is done, including how to teach the algorithm and all the various types of algorithms that are available. We've also learned a great deal about supervised and unsupervised learning, and some of the many applications of machine learning, from saving airline companies with fuel costs, using predictive behaviors to determine what advertisements people see online, to using machine learning for extremely complex tasks like driving a car. These developments are interesting and definitely exciting.

One of the challenges of machine learning will be selecting the right algorithm for the right problem. You're also going to need to know how to determine what data sets to use for training, and whether or not you should use supervised or unsupervised learning. These are some of the many challenges that a newbie will face when trying to enter into this field. It's important to learn all of the nuance associated with these questions and others, so that you will know how to go forward with machine learning and be successful.

Understand the Difference Between Prediction and Classification

One of the simplest and yet most important distinctions that you are going to have to learn to make without error is understanding the difference between prediction and classification. Some models are quite frankly better for classification, some are only suitable for prediction, while still other algorithms may be suitable for both depending on the circumstances. You are going to need to be clear about this. The first step in this direction is to make sure that you can look at any given problem and immediately identify it as one or the other. Then, depending on how you have classified the problem – as classification or as prediction – you can then go from there to choose the algorithm that is going to be the best one for the given situation.

Choosing the wrong algorithms could not only lead you in the wrong direction and waste time, but companies that are hiring data scientists aren't going to be interested in people that make that kind of mistakes. While people are often excited about trying to get going with the advanced material, learning the algorithms in detail and coding them up, if you don't have a solid foundation in place from the very beginning then you are unlikely to have any kind of success. People are not going to be interested in working with someone that doesn't have a firm grasp on the fundamentals.

A good exercise is to review famous cases online, and see what algorithms were chosen for them. This way you can learn from the experts who have already been working in the field. You will want to compare different types of problems. For example, image detection, facial recognition, logistics, approving someone for a loan, or showing someone an online advertisement. Each of these problems is quite different in nature and scope. Even more to the point, they are going to require different approaches when data science is applied.

It is a good exercise to write down a list of twenty common problems that are tackled using machine learning. Then for each problem, determine whether or not it is a classification problem, or a prediction problem. Be careful with nuance here. If we are talking about determining whether or not someone should get a loan using a machine learning model, whether or not it's a predictive or a classification model can depend on what we are asking. We might simply have a cutoff that uses multiple factors like credit score, annual income, previous bankruptcies, etc. During the training phase the algorithm will pick out the patterns in order to determine what criteria are actually used. It may also determine a cutoff score of its own choosing, based on what it learned about people below the cutoff score from the training data. But you can see that this is a classification problem. People are either classified as being creditworthy or not.

Framed another way, the problem at hand may be to determine whether or not a person will default on a loan. In that case, the same general problem, possibly using the same data sets, would be a predictive problem instead.

Try looking at many different problems in this way so that you can determine how good you are at determining the correct way to view a problem. This is the first step in being successful.

Knowing Which Type of Learning to Use

The learning portion of the process of developing a model is one of the most important. You need to understand why you would choose supervised over unsupervised learning, or vice versa. Remember that it's not whether or not one is ultimately better than the other or not, the question is whether or not one is best suited for the problem at hand or not. One case is obvious, and that is if you have the answers to the questions, that is you have the output data for the inputs in your data set. Remember that supervised learning is a case where the system is given the outputs. But don't stop there. Depending on the nature of the problem at hand, you may or may not actually want to go ahead and give the answers to the system. In some circumstances, even though you have them, it might be better to use unsupervised learning instead.

Also remember that you can use a combination method. That is you can supply the model with the answers for a subset of the training data, and then use unsupervised learning for the rest of the data. This is one area that you should consider for further study after finishing this book. Learning which is the best approach is an important skill, and if you lack judgment in this area you are unlikely to go very far with machine learning.

One way to test yourself is to follow the suggestions given in the previous section. That is, look at what people did in previous examples. You can start by looking at simple, artificial cases, but you should become familiar with how this has been done in the real world. Rather than just looking up the answers, challenge yourself. Begin by simply looking at the problem is framed. Then you work out for yourself what the right way to proceed should be when it comes to the learning. After you have done this, and only after, you can then go ahead and find out what people decided to do in the real world.

Data Selection

Many people get overly excited about the algorithms and the process of machine learning itself. Equally important however, is the data that you select to use in your training. If you choose the wrong data that can mean that your model delivers bad or irrelevant results. Your career as a data scientist will be short lived indeed, if that is the case.

You'll also want to focus on using data sets that are the right size for the right problem.

One way to get a handle on this is the same approach that you would use in any other situation. Look and see how other people have handled this problem, in particular for real world cases. Read any literature you can on case studies to help educate yourself on these issues. Being able to choose the right test data is as important as deciding whether or not you should use supervised or unsupervised learning, and what algorithm you should use in a particular case.

It's important to learn from the experiences of others, seeing what types of data are best suited to different algorithms. Sometimes, you might let the data choose the algorithm for you. At others it's going to be the other way around.

Sometimes you're just going to have to let the results speak for themselves. When you run your tests with a given data set, if you are not getting the results you are expecting, you might have to re-examine your choice of the data. It could be that you are using the wrong algorithm but you might also be in a situation where the data set just isn't right. Maybe the data set isn't large enough, or it might not have the right attributes. You will have to evaluate each case independently.

At other times, you might actually be using too much data. This can be in an absolute sense, for example perhaps you are feeding it too many rows. On the other hand the problem might lie with the attributes. It's more than possible to try and feed an algorithm too many attributes. There is a sweet spot in every single case. An algorithm has a need for a proper number of attributes in order to find patterns in the data. If it can't find the patterns, it might be because there aren't enough attributes.

We can return to our diabetes question for an example. If you wanted to find out whether or not one gender was more likely to become diabetic by age 55 than another, you could feed the machine data with two attributes, A1C store and gender. But that might not be enough information for the model to find any patterns or determine any relationships. So having it learn by looking at other attributes that are factors in the development of diabetes will help it recognize the patterns it needs to recognize. These could include body mass index, age, family history of diabetes, and other factors.

On the other hand, if we feed it too many features, then the algorithm might not do so well in its pursuit of finding meaningful patterns that are hidden in the data. Maybe the birth place of each person is also included in the data set. Is that really relevant to the question at hand? It is probably only of tangential interest unless you're specifically studying whether or not people born in certain locations are more likely to develop diabetes. But for determining whether or not one gender is more likely to get diabetes than the other by a specific age, that data point probably has no relevance whatsoever. Including it is going to reduce the efficiency of your model.

A good way to attack this problem from the front end is to do an analysis of every attribute and feature in the data. Simply take a look at each attribute, and ask yourself whether or not it's important for the question that you are asking in this particular test. If the answer is no, then jettison it. You can always add it back later, but you will save yourself a great deal of headaches by taking a proactive approach to your setup.

Tools to Use

It turns out that you don't have to be the world's best programming expert in order to succeed with data science, although I advise getting a formal education. The good news, however, is there are some relatively simple tools that you can use in order to become well acquainted with this field. In order to do data science you don't have to become an expert on building large scale software projects using object oriented programming. In fact when you get down to brass tacks, while the contributions of computer science to the field are important – and I urge you to get a solid background in it – understanding the algorithms in a way that might come better from statistics and probability is going to be more important.

One of the most popular tools used for machine learning is Python. The first thing to note about Python is that it's a lite tool. Second, you can use it on any system. Python is fast and great to use for calculation, and it's also something that can be used to "model" more complicated software that might be written using a more sophisticated programming language later.

There are many books available on Python, find the one that is the most suitable for your tastes and experience. I recommend taking it step by step. Nobody should try rushing through the process of learning any technical field, and that includes data science and machine learning. Going step by step means that you should find a solid book and work through the examples, but you should choose books that are going to challenge you to work on your own projects that gradually increase in complexity.

There are also many well regarded free resources that can be used to teach yourself how to do coding with Python. You can find many videos on YouTube, or consider taking a low priced course on Udemy. You might check out the Kahn Academy which remains free and offers a huge library of videos that will help you become a master of nearly any subject.

Another tool that is widely used in studies of machine learning is R. This is a package made for mathematicians. The purpose of R is to provide a ready made suite of tools that can be used for statistical analysis. R can perform virtually any task that we have described in this book, and it's particularly suited for linear regression and least-squares problems. I do not believe that R charges for you to download and try the program. You might look for some books on R to learn it thoroughly if you decide that you want to use it.

The reality is that you should not select one tool or another. You should learn both Python and R. In the competitive world of data science, you are going to be better off if you have become a master of both tools. After you have learned them, then you can switch between one or the other as required by your work. You can have your preference, and that is fine. But remember that people that you work for may have their own preferences that might be different.

You should also not assume that you are going to be able to work using Python and R all the time. This is why I strongly recommend that people get a diverse background in multiple programming languages. Different situations may call upon the use of different programming languages, and you may be required to know more sophisticated programming languages as a part of your job requirements. The best way to deal with this is to prepare ahead of time, but to have a realistic picture. When I was in school, there was a much smaller set of programming languages. Today they have proliferated, but the utility of so many different languages is very questionable indeed. What you should do is make sure you are comfortable in the top 3-5 programming languages. You don't have to be an absolute expert in each one, but if someone were to hire you for a job using one of the languages you should be able to tell them you know the language, and you know it well enough that it's not going to slow you down on your job.

Again, one of the best ways to take care of this is to get a degree or at least a minor in computer science. Doing so, you'll probably be exposed to at least three different programming languages, but that will depend on the university that you attend.

Another reason that I recommend computer science is that it's not really about the programming languages. Success in science or engineering actually comes from your ability to solve problems, and this is what computer science actually teaches. Computer science isn't about 'coding' or specific computer languages, it's about teaching you how to think as a computer scientist– that is training your brain. For many people it's a very challenging curriculum. One thing that I will guarantee is that someone who goes through it is going to be able to outcompete someone who simply learns 'coding' on the internet. So learning coding using resources on the internet is a good way to get started, but you should not cut any corners on the way to a career in data science if that is your objective.

In addition to learning R and Python, you should definitely be learning statistics and probability at an advanced level. That doesn't mean you have to actually get a PhD to do it. But you should take as many courses on these subjects as possible, since they form the core of data science.

Practice

In the beginning, start simple. Like I suggested, starting with a good book that has a lot of examples that you can work through is important. You should practice coding your own models using Python or R, and then you should seek out sample data which is available online. There is nothing like practice, remember they say practice makes perfect. There was a book that came out a few years ago called Outliers, one of the assertions of the book was that great people become great at what they do by devoting 10,000 hours of time to their chosen pursuit. If you play golf for 10,000 hours, you're more likely to be able to compete with Tiger Woods than if you just went on your own natural talents. Unfortunately, many people see the value of playing golf for hours on end but they don't apply the same logic to technical and professional topics. You might consider bucking the trend, and devote enough time and energy to data science and machine learning as you would if you were a member of a professional sports team. You can practice and study enough to become an expert in the field. When you do that, you are going to be someone who is highly sought after, and you are going to be better at your job and be able to deliver the kinds of results that people are expecting. One of the challenging things about data science is that while it's in high demand, and there are lots of jobs all around, if you don't deliver you aren't going to survive.

Utilize Mixed Learning Models

An important tip that has served me well is to try mixed learning models when I don't seem to be getting the results I expect from one type or another. If you are not seeing results from supervised learning, then consider using a subset of your data for unsupervised learning, and vice versa. There are many options to consider, remember that there are many hybrid variations of partial-supervised learning. The best ones to use will depend on the circumstances.

This is a great way to breathe new life into a project that seems to be going nowhere. If something is stuck, it can help you revitalize things and get it launched off the ground. Don't be afraid to try multiple approaches. One of the worst things that can happen to any engineer or scientist is to get caught up with just one or two beloved approaches that they are afraid to give up. Or, maybe they are afraid to try something new.

Have Realistic Expectations

It's important to have realistic expectations. Not every case of machine learning is going to be the next big breakthrough. In fact, in some applications machine learning might produce disappointing results. If that is the case for one of your projects, don't be afraid to cut it loose. This may mean changing algorithms, refining the test data, or even abandoning the project all together. Sadly, there has been a great deal of hype surrounding machine learning. And as excited as I am about it, it's hard to say that maybe sometimes the hype is a little much. That doesn't mean I'm abandoning the field. All it means is that you need to keep things in some perspective.

Chapter 8: The Future of Machine Learning

Machine learning has been one of the most exciting developments to come out of computer science and artificial intelligence in a very long time. Of course machine learning began its long road to its present form many decades ago. But it's only recently that we've seen machine learning getting widespread application to the extent that it's actually changing the way that society is operating. Understanding these changes is going to be one of the most important things going forward for the data science community and society at large. I try to stay optimistic, there are some reasons for concern but I have to keep believing that Machine learning is going to provide many tools which are going to help improve peoples lives. Every tool development machine learning doesn't have to be the most dramatic and breakthrough development of that man has ever seen. We can probably go through history and I would have to say that people like Nicholas Tesla or Thomas Edison we're probably a lot more impactful on society then a lot of the new technologies that we are seeing today. I would say that's the truth for any given individual technology.

However when you take a look at the sum total of the changes that we are seen from machine learning, society is going to be transformed a great deal in the coming decades.

One of the things that we are definitely going to see is there going to be a great deal of jobs that are eliminated. We have already seen the development of robots that can stack and manager warehouse just as well as any human worker. They haven't yet been deployed in a real situation, but the fact is it's only a matter of time before that happens. Second, we've already seen the developments of robots that can do many menial labor jobs. The most famous of these is a robot which is able to cook hamburgers in a fast food restaurant. This may be unfortunate for those pushing for a $15 an hour wage for that type of work because right now the robot is too expensive to be practical. But if you keep pushing it at some point the robot becomes a cost-effective investment. Regardless of what happens, regarding the wages, the downward pressure on costs that usually happens with technology almost ensures that robots that do menial labor are going to be taking a lot of jobs over the next 5 to 10 years.

Remember that this is nothing new however. I hate to bring it up yet again, but people in the 18th Century had great fears of losing their jobs to the new machines that were then making their way throughout society. The concerns of those people turned out totally misguided. In fact they were dead wrong. Of course that doesn't mean that we should mock anyone who has concerns about these lost jobs now, nor does it mean that we should dismiss them. We can't assume that because jobs were created in much larger numbers in the past due to technological changes that this is always going to happen. However if I have to been on it, I would definitely suggest that that's probably the case. One thing that people are really good at is finding new things to do. Look around you and observe all the things that we do now that were even existing as a mere thought 50 or hundred years ago. As an example consider the video game industry. Today it generates billions of dollars and it employs tens of thousands of people. Every time that human labor is liberated new uses for it are quickly found.

It's hard to say where the future machine learning lies, but one thing it's going to do is allow people to have a more personalized existence. We've already seen great strides towards this over the past decade or so. Now everything is personally curated from music to videos. This process is in their early stages of development. It's only going to accelerate in the coming decades.

Another thing were likely see is the application of machine learning to more and more areas throughout life. The growth of data science and machine learning has been explosive in the past 10 to 15 years. That trend is likely to continue.

When I was in college one of my computer science professors what at the time seemed like a completely ridiculous proposal. He said that in the future you could eliminate the need for programmer. He did envision this system of black boxes where you built up a layer that reduced the complexity and moved away from having to talk directly to the computer, replacing it with something extremely simple that practically anybody could understand. So people will be able to program just by moving around objects on the screen and connecting them with lines. This dream is already being realized. One example is a product named build box. This is a simple example that you should check it out online to understand the power behind it. It's a tool that allows people to develop video games without using any programming whatsoever. The selling point of this product is that it eliminates the programmer. All you do is drag and drop objects on the screen like you are using PowerPoint or keynote. It's really something else. And while is used primarily to develop mobile games, the general principles behind it can be used for any type of programming.

One very important factor which I will call the Ace in the hole is quantum computing. It's unclear at this point whether quantum computing is something that will become practical or remain in the realm of theoretical investigation. If practical and functional quantum computers are ever built it will be a game changer on the scale of the Industrial Revolution. How quantum computing is merged with machine learning could be one of the most interesting intellectual challenges in the coming century. There is no question that if quantum computing becomes a practicality life is going to be very different afterwards. The changes that we're experiencing right now are going to seem incredibly trivial.

Conclusion

Machine learning is becoming more and more important as time goes by. This is an exciting time to enter computer science and data science and learn how to use these tools in order to complete amazing tasks. Although machine learning seems brand new, the concept of machines and learning goes back to the dawn of time. Human beings have always been tool makers and tool users, and todays machine learning systems and artificial intelligence are merely the latest 'iteration' in the long history of humans extending their minds through the use of tools.

And that is an important concept. Unfortunately, these days there is a lot of fear mongering regarding artificial intelligence. The old Luddite fantasy, which held that jobs would be stolen by machines and people would have no way to earn a living, finds open ears when it is discussed today. People seem to be vulnerable to the same old fantasies even if the empirical evidence says otherwise. The Luddites were wrong, the machines actually created 10 – 100 more jobs than they eliminated. Machines free up people to engage in more productive activities, and when productivity is increased jobs, activities and opportunities increase as well.

The same holds true today, as it always has. Each new generation brings up the old Luddite ideas, only to see them die yet again. This happened in the early 1980s when the invention of spreadsheets and accounting programs on personal computers led people to a state of fear where they imagined accountants and office workers would no longer be necessary. Then they did the same thing with word processors, imagining that secretarial work would be eliminated. Neither happened.

Now here we are again. After languishing for decades, artificial intelligence is finally coming to life. Robotics are enhancing the capability of manufacturing companies to produce more output with less cost and labor. Despite the fact that as I am writing this the economy is at full employment, politicians and people in the media are once again making the Luddite charge. This time artificial intelligence and machine learning are coming for your jobs. The short-sighted people who promote these fears miss the point entirely, they fail to see that the changes the world is currently going through are going to do what they always have and that is raise productivity and free people to do other things.

Hopefully they won't stop this exciting engine. I suspect they won't be able to. Governments and corporations are already in love with machine learning. The reason is simple. Machine learning works. After decades of oversold promises, computers are now in a position where they can learn, and once trained, they work autonomously. Machine learning makes corporations run more efficiently and helps government identify fraud, prevent cyberattacks and do a million other things. Since intelligence is general, the applications of machine learning and AI are general.

AI holds out a special fear for people who hold the Luddite perspective. It's one thing to say that a machine is going to destroy your job, but people also have unrealistic fears of machine learning systems. They seem to think that AI and robots are going to take over the world as if they are living in some kind of science fiction fantasy. There is no doubt that as the years go by machine learning is going to continue to improve and be able to take on more tasks, but what those tasks are used for is entirely in human control.

These tools can be used for nefarious purposes. In the Republic of China, machine learning tools like facial recognition are being used to control and harass people. Tools that in the United States and Europe are used to determine someone's credit worthiness for a loan are being used in China to give people a 'social score'. According to news reports, the social score can be used to keep people from traveling or being able to leave the country.

So there is no question that in the wrong hands, the tools of machine learning can be used with bad intent. But that has nothing to do with the tools themselves and this kind of situation applies to any technology that human begins have ever invented. We can't control what everyone does in other countries, but we can control how the tools are used here. Each of us has a responsibility in doing this. If the government misuses these tools, then they need to be called out for doing so and you should vote for politicians who will manage AI in an ethical fashion. With private companies that task is easier, simply avoid any private company that uses them in an unethical fashion.

At this point I'd like to personally thank every reader for taking the time to read the book and making it all the way to the end. I hope that the book has been educational, and that you've learned a great deal about machine learning and how it works. If you are new to machine learning, my hope is that you've come away with some of the mystery behind it stripped away. It's not as complicated as it might seem when you are first exposed to the ideas, or just hearing about them in the media.

If you read this book just to become more informed on the topic, I hope that this book has satisfied your curiosity. If you are really interested in machine learning and would like to become educated in it and possibly pursue it as a career, the best place to start is to learn how to code. In order to get a job in this competitive field you are probably going to need some kind of academic degree and this is one of the few areas in college where you can go to school and directly learn the skills you are going to need on the job. But you can get started by learning python, which is a simple programming language that runs on any system. You can get online and search for machine learning algorithms built in python that can use small data sets to start giving you practice in this field.

If you decide to go further, my advice is to either major in statistics or computer science, or ideally double-major in computer science and mathematics. Studying computer science alone is probably inadequate because you need to have an advanced grasp of probability and statistics in order to actually pursue a career in data science.

I would also recommend taking a few business courses. You will want to learn about things like logistics where data science is often applied to generate solutions for large corporations. It works well and I can guaranteed that one thing you will be able to count on is you will be able to get a job doing this if you get the right education.

How far you go is up to you, the more the education the higher level at which you are going to start and these types of fields can be very competitive. A masters degree would be great and for those who want it a PhD will put them in the best position. If you have followed my advice with a double major, you can pick one or the other for a masters degree, it's not necessary to continue trying to get more academic credentials in both.

Working with machine learning is a different type of activity than traditional computer programming. Of course traditional computer programming is still around and alive and well, so let's not kill it off yet.

Thanks again for reading, and please visit Amazon and leave a review for this book!

Python for Beginners

A Step by Step Crash Course to Learn Smarter the Fundamental Elements of Python Programming, Machine Learning, Data Science and Tools, Tips and Tricks of This Coding Language

Jason Knox

Introduction

Congratulations on purchasing *Python for beginners: A Step by Step Crash Course to Learn Smarter the Fundamental Elements of Python Programming, Machine Learning, Data Science and Tools, Tips, and Tricks of This Coding Language*, and thank you for doing so.

This book is made for all those interested in learning from scratch how to start coding and programming on Python. If you already have some knowledge of this language or another one, you will find very interesting and important information here that we are sure you didn't know.

In the following chapters of this book you will be able to get started into the world of programming, starting with an introductory chapter, where you are going to learn about the Python differences, advantages, uses, some information about Machine learning and Data science, and even how to install it according to your operating system. After the introductory chapter, are all of the fundamental elements of Python like data types, operators, control statements, loops, functions, modules, OOP (Object-oriented programming), file management, and some other extra information.

It is really important to start programming and putting into practice everything here explained, since, if this is not done, commands, syntax and many other things will be forgotten.

Good luck, and welcome to the future.

There are plenty of books on this subject on the market, thanks again for choosing this one! Every effort was made to ensure it is full of as much useful information as possible, please enjoy it!

Chapter 1: Introductory Chapter

What Is Python?

Python is a very versatile interpreted language developed by Guido Van Rossum. It is a high-level programming language with a user-friendly approach, it is an object-oriented programming language, with dynamic typing and easy to interpret syntax, all these features make this language ideal for scripting, as well as we can use it to make applications in a variety of areas.

Programming is a fascinating, creative, and rewarding activity. That is why, in this book, we are going to explain to you from the simplest point of view how we can program in this language, assuming that we all need and want to know how to do programming. You need to know Python's vocabulary and grammar, as well as how to correctly interpret the words of this language, and how to build well-formed phrases. Once you know correctly how to work in this language, it will be much easier to work in other programs such as

JavaScript or C++, where you will be able to realize that each language has its own grammar and vocabulary, but, after all, the solution to each of the problems is going to be the same regardless of the programming code you are using.

Learning Python for beginners is basically like learning to write and to interpret that writing, this language has a very reduced vocabulary, conformed by words that have a particular meaning for Python, the particular meaning that has each word is what is known in language as "keywords", as an example of these words in Python we have the following:

And, as, assert, break, class, continue, def, del, elif, else, except, finally, for, from, global, if, import, in is, lambda, nonlocal, not, or, pass, raise, return, try, while, with, yield, among others, are some of the "keywords" that you will use in this programming language.

Python has the advantage of being a free code and easy access, with a quite large library, in addition to a very large community of programmers, making it much easier to use, it also offers a better error checking than programming in C. This a language of very high level, among its many other features Python will allow you to separate the program into modules that later you will be able to reuse, in addition, it has a collection of standard modules that you can use as a base for your programs.

Python is also an interpreted language; this term tells you that you will not have the need to compile or link particularly. You will be able to use this interpreter interactively. This programming code will allow you to write compact and readable programs, besides Python programs are considerably shorter than those made in C++, for example, and this is particularly due to the syntax used.

Which Are the Advantages of Using Python?

As the main advantage, we can mention that this language has a method that simplifies programming a lot more, and this method is based on proposing a pattern to follow, which is why it is considered a great language for scripting. It is a script code; this means that you don't have to declare constants and variables before using them. Also, as it is an interpreted language, when you run the program, all the lines of the program are not read, only those that are being executed at that moment, so it can be said that it goes line by line, which makes it more manageable. It has a high speed in development; it can be used on multiple platforms; it is an open-source language; therefore, communities and users can create their own versions or create add-ons that may or may not be added to the following versions of Python.

Another advantage is that it is an elegant and flexible language, where the language itself has the ability to give you a large number of tools, and the flexibility allows you not to worry so much about the details. It is versatile, which will allow you to develop websites, create graphical user interfaces, software and games, system prototypes, client applications, distributed systems, scientific tasks such as simulations or prototypes. Another of its great advantages is that it is easy to develop, simple and fast, and its library does most of the work. Moreover, it supports large database storage and is ideal for combining several components, which is why it is also known as a glue language, and this way, we can use Python with C, with Java, etc.

Differences Between Python and Other Programming Languages

Python runs programs on the operating system, and generally, if you want to run some JavaScript on the operating system you have to use **NodeJS**, you can take it as a Python interpreter, because thanks to this program you will be able to run JavaScript programs just like you would run Python ones.

There is no better language than another, what differentiates them are the tools used by each one, and the applications that each one can generate. The main objective is to be able to solve a problem in the best and most optimal way.

In the case of Python and JavaScript, both are interpreted languages, so you will see in practice a file, and you will write your code in this file, you save it so that the computer can execute it, but for this to happen you will need an extra program that interprets these codes and allows the computer to read it, and this is what an interpreter does, if we install it in Linux you will be able to interpret the code in Linux, if we install it in Windows you will be able to interpret the code there and in the same way in Mac. Both languages would then be multiplatform.

Both languages have Open Source syntax; this means that you can see how the codes of the standard libraries are written, so you will be able to see more easily how each of these programs is developed.

Now let's talk about the differences between both languages. JavaScript (JS) was a language that was born to add interactivity to the browser. In JS, the functionality that brings the language itself is very minimal, since it lacks a large amount of codes it is complemented with another tool called **npm**, this way you will be able to download codes from the internet to complement this functionality because JS does not include all of the tools. It is at a disadvantage compared to Python because you are going to find a wide variety of codes that you will have to choose which one you are going to use. In Python, you will find certain types of applications in which it is unique. In JS, the most popular default type of application are web applications, web-based applications, both in the server and browser environment.

Python, unlike JS, was born as a general-purpose programming language, that is to say, it was not born for the purpose of the browser as JS, but was born to create any type of application that runs on the computer, whether desktop applications, web, server applications, and that is already a great advantage in itself over JS.

It has a huge amount of libraries already included by default, while JS is very different because it has quite minimal information. You can also extend the functionality of Python by installing **pip** for Python, which would be more or less the equivalent of **npm** for JS if you like.

In Python, you will find packages with specific functionality while in JS, it is easier to find several packages that do basically the same thing.

As for Python and the programming language C, in the case of Python, it differs mainly because this is an interpreted language, and C is a compiled language, although it is true that Python is a slower language than C, it is also easier to learn and use.

C is a language used for real-time systems, operating system kernels, for low-level hardware programming, such as microwaves, digital clocks, sensors. While python has many more commercial applications and a variety of environments, including websites, desktops, programming small computers like Raspberry Pi, and many others.

Introduction to Data Science

Data is defined as facts and statistics stored for reference or analysis. It is a technique for analyzing data and having a series of analytical reports with different visualizations. Data Science refers to a series of applications that we use to analyze the data of either a company or a particular investigation. This discipline is composed of activities related to data mining, analytical processing, and reports.

It is the extraction of knowledge from a variety of structured and unstructured volumes through the use of data mining techniques and predictive analysis. What is basically wanted is to combine several tools to obtain an expected result. All this is achieved with Machine learning, data mining, etc.

A data is a symbol or set of symbols, whether alphabetical, numerical, or graphical, used to represent or describe a numerical value, a fact, an object, or an idea. While information is the set of data organized in a suitable way to be objective of treatment, and knowledge is the meaning extracted from that information.

Today, data and information are often represented by binary codes. A digital system such as TV, telephone, and so on, stores, transfers, and processes the information in binary code.

Our universe moves around data, scientific data, such as astronomy data, for example, genomics, while, in social sciences, historical data, digital books. In companies and commerce, we have corporate sales data, for example, market transactions, censuses, airline traffic. In the area of entertainment, we can have data from images, movies, mp3 files, games. In medicine, we can have data from patients, scanners, and results.

Now, in summary, Data Science is an interdisciplinary field that applies mathematical, statistical and computational techniques that are implemented in different areas, for example, in the area of biology, sociology, medicine, etc..

When we merge computation with statistics, we will obtain what is known as Machine Learning, but when we merge computation, statistics, and research in a particular area and with the data we have at our disposal is what we will know as Data Science.

In this sense, a Data Science will have as its main objective to model, analyze, understand, visualize, and extract all the possible knowledge from the data we have available.

The procedure is handled in several states or steps until we get to obtain the final results. The first one is when we have to focus on the understanding and approach of the problem we are going to evaluate. This information we have will be fed back with the understanding of the data that are associated with the problem we are evaluating. This whole process is done iteratively.

Then comes the stage of preparing the data we handle, thus creating our database, and then making the models.

Finally, we arrive at the final step where we evaluate the results obtained, and we see if the model is generated correctly with the chosen technique, if indeed the model is adequate we will proceed with the implementation of the model. If the opposite happens and the generated model is not the one we are looking for, the process returns to the initial state, and we would start the iterative process again.

Fundamentally, if you want to join the world of Data Science, you must have knowledge mainly in modeling, visualizations, database, and programming. In the analytics part, you handle information about statistics, artificial intelligence, machine learning, primitive models, natural language processing. On the other hand, you must have the knowledge of database management, data recovery, in addition, you must manage large volumes of data which is what we also know as Big Data, acquire knowledge in the area of computer science, such as programming, privacy, security, distributed system, and last but not least design art, where data, interpretation, and models must be visualized correctly.

Data Science needs the use of a programming language and fundamentally needs an excellent computational efficiency to be able to handle this large amount of data. Therefore, if the language we use makes all the programming slow, it will not work; we need to have a good and large library, which, as we know, we have in Python. In Big Data and Data Science is strictly necessary to have libraries specially designed to manage large volumes of data and get a high calculation speed in complex data structures. Next, we will mention some of the libraries that are available for Python; Apache Spark (large scale data processing, available for Python, Java), Apache Mesos (computational resource management, available in Python, Java, C and C++), Open MPI (high performance parallel computing, available in Python, C, C++, R, Fortran, MATLAB), Tensor Flow (for machine deep learning models, available in Python, C and C++).

Machine Learning

In the case of Machine Learning, we are talking about an area whose objective is to develop algorithms that allow computers to learn.

In order to better understand the concept of Machine Learning (ML), let's start with a brief summary of some of the applications that are made with ML, since these algorithms are used daily, for example, when we use emails we are using ML, in fact, was one of the algorithms with which it began in this branch of artificial intelligence, and began to apply massively.

When we classify a mail in the inbox, by new or unwanted mail, this classification is done by learning the algorithm, taking into account parameters already established. What happens with this algorithm is that it learns from the user, when he selects an email and classifies it as unwanted, for example, the algorithm learns from this information provided by you, and when we receive an email from this user again, it will go directly to the spam or junk mail tray.

This is one of the ML applications that had the most impact at its time and gives us an idea of the years the scientists and programmers have been studying, analyzing, and developing AI.

Another application of ML is the facial recognition of photos; this is one of the algorithms used and constantly perfected by the company Facebook. Its principle is essentially the same as the previous case when we download a photo on the platform the application will perform a scan of it and compare it with the data it already has stored, so it can relate the names of each of the people who are in the photo.

Following another example of ML; we have the recommendations of the Netflix movies, in this application, a series of algorithms are conjugated that, together, make the recommendations of the movies and series of the Netflix platform.

The algorithm learns not only from the films seen but also from the ones we no longer see and the ones we include in our list of visualizations. All this information serves as a database for the algorithm to learn which the most-watched films are.

What Is Machine Learning?

ML, or automatic learning, is a scientific discipline in the field of artificial intelligence, which consists of using algorithms so that they can learn automatically based on a set of data, without having to write a specific code for the problem.

How Is ML Classified?

- **Supervised Learning Algorithms:** this type of learning occurs when an algorithm learns from data from examples and associated target responses, which may consist of numerical values or string labels, to later predict the correct response when presented with new examples. Examples include voice recognition, spam detection, and handwriting recognition, among others.

- **Unsupervised learning algorithms:** refers to when the algorithm learns from simple examples without any associated response, letting the algorithm determine the data patterns itself. For example, detect morphology in sentences, classify information, etc.

- **Reinforced Learning Algorithm**: in this type of learning, the algorithm decides how to act to perform its task. In the absence of training data, the algorithm learns from experience, collects examples of training through try and error while attempting its task. For example, navigation of a vehicle in automatic decision making.

- **Learning by Natural Language Procedure**: this learning formulates effective mechanisms for communication between people and machines by means of natural languages. For example, spelling and grammar correction, analysis of opinions and feelings, language comprehension, or automatic translation.

- **Deep Learning:** uses the principles of the basic ML algorithms together, attempting to model high-level abstractions in data using computer architecture. It is a complex definition, but with this algorithm, almost anything can be done, the algorithm carries out the Machine Learning process, using an artificial neural network composed mainly of a hierarchical number.

What Are Some of the Current Applications of ML?

Machine Learning is a system based on the processing and analysis of data that is translated to discovery and can be applied to any field as long as you have an extensive amount of data. Some of the most developed uses are:

- Economic predictions and fluctuations in the stock market, such as the stock exchange.
- DNA sequence classification.
- Mapping and 3D modeling.
- Medical diagnostics.
- Fraud detection.
- Internet search engines, for example, shortcuts to predict the searches we have already done.
- Voice recognition systems, which we get on our phones with Siri or Alexa, so that they recognize the voice of users.

Artificial Intelligence (AI)

Artificial intelligence is a recent science and currently embraces a wide variety of subfields, ranging from general-purpose areas such as learning and perception to more specific ones such as chess, the demonstration of mathematical theorems, poetry writing, and the diagnosis of diseases.

Defining artificial intelligence is not easy, as there is no general consensus on its definition. For this reason, we will give you several concepts that exist today.

We could enclose in a few words the definition of Artificial Intelligence as the "art of developing machines capable of performing functions that when performed by people require intelligence" (Kurzweil, 1990)

"Computational intelligence is the study of the design of intelligent agents." (Poole et al., 1998)

"It is the automation of activities that we link with human thought processes, activities such as decision making, problem-solving, learning, ..." (Bellman 1978)

Finally, we could add that artificial intelligence is the study of intelligent agents that perceive perceptions of the environment and carry out actions based on them. An agent is either a human being, a robot, or a program that perceives data or information from the environment and also has a way to interact with it. The intelligent agent is an entity that acts in the best possible way in the time it has, according to the information it has to achieve an objective that provides the highest performance expected.

Warren McCulloch and Walter Pitts (1943), have been recognized as the first authors of the first work of artificial intelligence. They started from three sources: knowledge about basic philosophy and functioning of neurons in the brain, the formal analysis of Russell's and Whiteheady's propositional logic, and Turing's theory of computation. (Proposal made by Alan Turing in 1950, which was designed to provide an operational and satisfactory definition of intelligence.), they proposed a model constituted by artificial neurons, in which each one of them was characterized by being "activated", or "deactivated", and the "activation", was given as a response to the stimulation produced by a sufficient quantity of neighboring neurons. They showed, for example, that any computing function could be calculated through any network of neurons interconnected, and that all the logical connectors (and, or, not...) could be implemented using simple network structures

Artificial intelligence became an industry from 1980 until the present. In 1981, when the Japanese announced the "Fifth Generation" project, a ten-year plan to build intelligent computers. As a response, the United States created the Microelectronics and Computer Technology Corporation (MCC), a consortium in charge of maintaining national competitiveness in these areas.

Fundamentals of Artificial Intelligence

We will mention some of the disciplines that have contributed with ideas, points of view and techniques to the development of artificial intelligence, some of them are philosophy and psychology, being Aristotle the first in formulating a precise set of laws that governed the rational part of intelligence, mathematics. Philosophers delimited the most important ideas of artificial intelligence, but to move from there to formal science it is necessary to have a mathematical formulation in three fundamental areas: logic, computing and probability; computing, cybernetics, linguistics, economics, with decision theory, game theory, operational research, among others, neuroscience and biology, these are some of the disciplines that are used in artificial intelligence.

Why Is Artificial Intelligence Used?

Artificial intelligence is booming; some think it is a new revolution that could change the life of our planet. Turing thought that if a machine behaves in all aspects as intelligent, then it must be intelligent. So, if a high number of humans cannot differentiate a machine from a person in a conversation, it is because it behaves intelligently, this is what is known as the Turing Test. And the first program to pass it was Eliza that imitated the behavior of a psychoanalyst in an internet chat.

The AI has been given as an objective for the study and analysis of human behavior. In this way, AI applications are mainly located in the simulation of man's intellectual activities. By imitating through machines that are mostly electronic, as many mental activities as possible, and perhaps be able to improve human capabilities in these aspects.

His field is very extensive, and we can illustrate it to you with these three points of view:

- Those who argue that it is possible to make "really thinking devices," a viewpoint called strong AI.

- Others who think that it is possible to simulate mental states (without being mental states) of our brain by means of computers, a point of view called weak AI.
- The "dualists", who give separately the dimension of body and spirit, and in this way, there would be "truth judgments" to which computers would never have access.

AI has become an important science since the subjects it covers to attract a great deal of discipline.

An AI program manipulates symbolic information in the form of concepts, objects or rules. In classical computing, it is only numerical data, whereas AI systems use heuristic methods ("heuristics is the art of invention"), contrary to classical algorithmic methods.

The use of heuristics makes it possible to deal with problems without an algorithmic solution such as perception, conception or decision making, and problems whose algorithmic solution is a problem, such as, for example, the game of chess.

Artificial Intelligence and Programming Languages

AI can be programmed in almost any programming language, although it is true that there are languages that were expressly created to handle AI, so they are much more powerful in this area, but there are also other languages with which we can work easily.

One of the first programs that handle AI is LISP, it is the second-highest level program used in the world, it was created many years ago around 1958, and it is still very useful. LISP that means List Processing, because the chained lists have an important role in this language. This language allows manipulating the source code as a data structure, leaving programmers the possibility to create new syntaxes of programs with a specific domain.

The next language is PROLOG, created approximately in 1970, is based on problem-solving by means of predicted calculations obtained through database queries and mathematical tests. PROLOG, instead of searching for an algorithm to look for the solution, rather it says how the solution to a problem should be and traces that solution through searches applied to the logic of the predicates.

As a third language we have OPS5, it is not well known, but it is very fundamental in the world of AI, it is a language that is based on rules, OPS5 rules are preconditions that have to be given before any action can be done.

The Haskell language, being a purely functional programming language, of general purpose, the dose of intelligence provided by an antispam system, makes Haskell a wonderful language.

Java is one of the most important languages, an example that embraces the fusion between Java and artificial intelligence is the system called WEKA, which is a software platform for automatic learning and data mining written by Java.

And last but not least, thanks to the simplicity of Python, it is considered one of the best programming languages for artificial intelligence. Unlike languages such as Java, C++ or Ruby, Python proves to be more effective and allows the user to save time. An example of AI is a well-known PyBrain, a powerful library with flexible algorithms for automatic learning. It specifically contains algorithms for neural networks.

Python and Artificial Intelligence

As we mentioned earlier, this programming language is one of the best used to apply it to AI and neurons, we can work better with it because it has a larger community that supports it and also proves to be superior to Java, has a number of libraries that offer their open-source AI resources and is a dynamic language with a shorter learning time compared to other languages.

What Are the Features and Advantages of Python with AI?

As it is an interpreted language, it does not need to be compiled and we can use it directly and apply the program, so we consider it a complete language.

Python can occupy matrixes, arithmetic, objects and variables as you will learn in the following chapters, it also has automatic memory management which accepts a wide variety of programming paradigms, it is also available for all operating systems.

Python has libraries such as NumPy, PyBrain and SciPy, which are used for scientific, advanced computing and machine learning. In addition, it can use IDE for code checking and is very useful for developers working with different algorithms.

Together with NumPy, Scikit-learn, IPython Notebook and matplotlib, are the basis for us to start an artificial intelligence project. Matplotlib is a 2D tracing library and can be used by up to six users of the graphical interface of python scripts toolkits and web application servers.

We also have among the python libraries for AI the following:
- AIMA: used to manage AI algorithms.
- pyDatalog: it is a logical programming engine that uses python.
- SimpleAI: an easy to use, well-documented library.
- EasyAI: provides game transposition and resolution tables.
- SciKitLearn: a very good tool to be used as

machine languages, analyzes data using python and also with open source.

- PyMI: can be used with Linux and Mac OS X.
- MDP-Toolkit: it is a Python data processing framework and contains a collection of learning algorithms.
- PyBrain: it is an automatic learning library, by modules that has a great variety of environments to test.

Characteristics of Artificial Intelligence

AI is an area that could be considered new in the field of technology, despite having many years of study and research. It includes several fields of development, such as robotics, understanding and translation of languages, recognition and learning of machine words, which are responsible for reproducing human behavior.

Within the AI are neural networks, which are programs capable of simulating some of the learning functions of the human being, a neural network has the ability to acquire experience automatically and systematically analyzing data in order to determine the rules of behavior. And based on these predictions can give information on new cases.

The AI and robotics, in this case, we are talking about devices composed of sensors that receive input data and order the robot to perform a certain action. When we talk about AI and robotics, it is enough to think about chatbots, each time we recur to AI to meet the needs of customers by computers. This is what we know as "Natural Language Generation," a sub-discipline of AI that converts text data and allows computers to communicate ideas with impressive accuracy.

In Which Areas Is AI Applied?

In management and control, intelligent analysis and target setting, as well as in planning, design and development of simplified robotics and computer vision. In education, engineering, design, control and analysis. Medicine, biology, chemistry.

In design, specification, teaching, verification and software maintenance. Weapons systems. Finance, data processing.

Artificial Intelligence applied to voice recognition; as

an example, we have the already recognized SIRI; also, we have Cortana, Alexa, Google Assistant and others.

The virtual agents are programs capable of interacting with humans; as an example, we have the chatbots, some of the companies that provide these agents are Amazon, Apple, Google, Microsoft, Satisfi.

Machine Learning (ML) platforms, being this a sub-discipline of computer science and a field of artificial intelligence, develop techniques that allow computers to learn. Providing algorithms, programming interface, development and training tools, big data. It is a platform that day by day is gaining popularity in the artificial intelligence industry. Some of the companies that sell ML are Amazon, Google, Microsoft, SAS, Skytree.

Why Python? Why It Is Highly Recommended in the Above Topics?

Python is a programming language that meets the necessary characteristics for Data Science, it is a language with a good philosophy, with well-defined standards, with simple, explicit languages. In addition, the fact that, as we mentioned in several opportunities, this language has a library of free codes for mathematics, statistics, machine learning and science topics in general.

Python has approximately six main libraries and many others, but we are going to explain specifically which are the most important, we are going to find Python libraries for visualizations as they are: Matplotlib, Seaborn, Bokeh. Data visualization allows us to better understand the data we are processing or analyzing, and these libraries are very good for handling this type of information. Matplotlib is Python's graphical library, generating excellent quality graphics, whether time series, histograms, power spectra, bar charts, error charts and others. Seaborn, specializes particularly in the visualization of statistical data, offering a high-level interface, to create visually attractive statistical graphs with informative quality; and Bokeh, visualizes data iteratively, in a web browser, we can also create interesting, interactive graphs.

When it comes to libraries for numerical calculations and data analysis, we have NumPy, which provides a universal data structure that enables not only data analysis but also data exchange between different algorithms, SciPy provides efficient numerical routines, performs numerical interaction, optimization, interpolation, Fourier transforms, linear algebra. Pandas is useful for data scientists, widely used for finance, statistics and social sciences.

Python is also capable of executing codes from other general use languages such as C, FORTRAN and Java, in addition to being a complex alternative to scientific languages of specific use, as they are: Cython, that executes code C; F2py allows to execute codes in Fortran, Jython/Jep, integrates with Java, Numpy/SciPy is a good alternative for MATLAB, among others. So, we could say that Python, in one way or another, can embrace everything.

How to Start Installing Python and Its Interpreter?

We have already talked about the advantages, features and even the various applications that this versatile programming language has.
But now we are going to learn in an easy way, how we

can do the installation of Python. And for that, it is necessary to understand some key programming concepts. When programming in Python, it is necessary to have a "text editor" or an "integrated development environment" (IDE), where the code that will be executed later will be written in order to be able to see the program's functionality.

There is a great variety of text editors and IDE development environments, with which we are going to be able to program in this language. Some of them are Windows Notepad, Linux Gedit, Mac TextEdit, Sublime Text 3 for Windows, Linux or Mac. Now, when we talk about created developments, (IDE), to program specifically in Python, we have PyDev and PyCharm, Jupiter, Atom, Visual Studio, Spyder, IDLE.

There are many of which we can choose, however, as this is a beginner's book, let's start with the basics and is using Python's IDLE, and so be able to program.

An integrated development environment for Python is what the word IDLE means; it's just an elementary graphical development environment that allows you to edit and run programs in Python.

In Windows and Mac, IDLE will be distributed together with the Python interpreter, meaning that when we install Python in both operating systems, IDLE will also be installed.

Whereas, in Linux, IDLE will be distributed as an application that can be installed from the repositories of each distribution.

It is fundamental for every beginner in this area to focus on the knowledge of the language rather than on the editor or development environment. And that is because the editor and the environment are going to be able to be changed at the moment that the user wants.

Now, to begin the installation for Windows and Mac users, we must, first of all, go to the Web site; www.python.org:

Once you have entered this page, you will be able to confirm that you are on the official Python site. After that, in the page you will see a menu, place the cursor on the tab that says "Download", and additionally you will get a submenu, where you will be able to see the operating system you are using, which in this case would be Windows or Mac. If you are a user whose operating system is Mac, select the tab of the download submenu and you can see all available versions to date of this programming language.

In order to know which version is the one we should choose at the time of downloading Python, you have several recommendations, when you select the tab of the download menu, you will observe on the right side that appears "Download for Windows", one of the advantages that this Web system has, is that it is able to identify the operating system in which you are entering its page, so by default you are going to be recommended the version that you should download for the operating system you are working. Easy, isn't it? In case your operating system is Windows, it will recommend you to download the latest version of Python for Windows, and likewise for other operating systems, whether Linux, Mac, etc..

Once you have the knowledge of which version you are going to download for Windows in this case, select the option that says Python followed by the version number until the last verification at the time of writing the book, the latest version of Python was 3.8.0. It should be noted that every time this language changes version, generally only some new features are added, which you will be able to use in your programming code.

Once you click on the Python version you selected, you will see how it automatically downloads to your operating system. Once the download is finished, you will look for the file in your computer, which is usually in the download folder of your desktop, being this file the Python installer.

In the case of Windows, you click on the right button and you will run the program, the Python programming language installer interface will open immediately, and in this step, it is advisable to select the box that says "add Python 3.8.0 to PATH". This recommendation is due to the fact that PATH is an environment variable of the operating systems, where the paths in which the interpreter must look for the programs to execute will be specified.

When following the recommendations, you select this box, what happens is that you will be able to use text editors and commands to be able to program and execute our code in Python.

Finally, the system asks how you want to install the programming language and you can choose the customized version, where the user decides what he wants to install and how he wants to do it, or you can choose the recommended option by default, which only consists of the path where Python will be installed and will also tell you that it includes IDLE, which as explained above refers to the integrated development environment.

Then when you select "install now", the installation on your operating system begins. Once the installation is complete, you verify that the program actually ran.

A quick way to search Python is to place the word IDLE in the Windows search engine and we will see immediately the IDLE that, when opening, you will be able to see that the programming language is already downloaded and installed.

If the operating system is Linux, you will have to open a command terminal. In most cases, when working with Linux as an operating system, it is very common that you already have Python programming language by default. However, it is important to verify that this is indeed the case, and it is done in the following way:

You write on the command line:

sudo apt install Python 3

When you press the "Enter" key, in case your Linux operating system has a security key, it will ask you for it at that moment. Once placed the key and pressing the key "Enter" again the system will try to install Python, and in case you already have it installed by default, what will happen is that if it is an older version, it will be updated, instead, if you have already installed the latest version, it will remind you that you already have Python and that you already have the most recent version.

This way, you can be sure that you have Python in your Linux operating system. Afterward, it is recommended to verify if IDLE is installed and to do so you have to write the following on the command line:

sudo apt-get Install Idle

By pressing the "Enter" key on the system, it will install the IDLE, in case the operating system does not have it, or update it in case it has one, but an older version, in the same way as in the previous case. So finally, you already have Python installed and also the development environment (IDLE) with which you are going to program in the Python programming language.

To be able to open IDLE in Linux, you place IDLE on a command terminal and the environment that is going to be used for the language will appear on the screen.

When you have the programming language in the operating system that you are using, either Windows, Mac or Linux, which were the three cases explained, you start with the settings to customize your Python language if you want, according to the liking of each user. For example, if you select the options tab in IDLE, it will open an interface where you will be able to modify the sizes of the letters, the color, the background of IDLE, to mention some of the things you can do.

Using Python with Shell and IDLE

Once you have Python in your operating system, the next step is to compile and run a program with Python.

A program is a series of instructions that have been previously coded and that will allow you to perform a series of specific tasks on your computer. These coded instructions are what are known as source code; these codes are what the user or programmer sets in his computer.

The source code is written in the Python programming language and this language will later be converted into an executable file and for this to happen, in other words, for the source code to be converted into an executable file, the help of a compiler will be necessary that will later be executed in a "central processing unit" (CPU) and all this will happen with the help of an interpreter.

In summary, we have that a compiler is going to convert our source code into an executable file since it is a translator that transforms a program or source code into a machine language so that it can be executed; this translation process is what is known as compiling.

There is a difference between a compiler and an interpreter since the first one translates a program described by the programming language into the machine code of the system, while the interpreters only perform the translation, be it instruction by instruction, and also do not store the result of this translation.

Therefore, we have a source code that is going to be executable in two ways by either a compiler or an interpreter who will execute it immediately.

When we open the IDLE in our system, in the same way that we did it before, we are going to observe the screen that we find when we open our IDLE, which is called Shell, or we can also call it as the interpreter of our Python language.

Every time we open our interpreter or Shell, we will always find a kind of header, which will always be the same, where it has Python information, such as the version in which it is working, date and time, for example. This type of format helps us appreciate that we are working with the Shell interpreter.

By means of this example, we will be able to visualize how our Shell interpreter is doing the translation from Python language to machine language instruction by instruction.

We write a line of codes in Python, starting with the very famous phrase in Python for every beginner "Hello World" and we will do it in the following way: The syntax is written as follows:

```
1    print("Hello world")
```

Already written the instruction that we want the program to execute, we only have to press the "Enter" key and automatically the interpreter will translate instruction by instruction and will not wait to receive another additional instruction but executes once we press the "Enter" key.

Additional detail of the interpreter is that it can also be used from the command prompt, which is also available on Windows, Linux and Mac.

In order to use the interpreter from the command prompt, simply type in the word Python and press the "Enter" key. This way, you start to run the Python interpreter and we know that we are effectively in the interpreter because, as in the previous case, we are going to see the same header as we saw before.

Now we can start to execute instructions written with Python:
--- print ("Hello world"), the interpreter is going to translate this line and immediately shows us the result "Hello world".

Chapter 2: Basic Concepts

In programming, a variable is a space in memory where the data used by a program will be stored and retrieved. Each one of these variables must have a name so that it can be identified and you can refer to them during the development of the program.

In the Python language, the names of the variables cannot coincide with the names of the commands assigned to this programming language; besides, the variables cannot contain blank spaces. What all this means is that a variable cannot be called "print", for example, because "print" is already a command that makes an assignment in Python. Nor could it be called "na me", because as mentioned above, it has blank spaces in the phrase.

There are two types of variables that are common in Python and they are as follows:

The variables that store numbers, in this type of variables, are subdivided into two types:

Integers, called "int".

Decimal or real numbers, which are called "float".

In addition, all variables that store text are called "strings" (str), so the content that is placed within these variables must be in quotes.

How Can We Declare a Variable?

The first thing that is done to be able to declare a variable is to assign a name to it, when doing so a memory space better known as variable is created immediately, then we place the equal sign, after the variable name so that we can indicate to the program that is going to store a data that will be in the memory space or variable and finally the data that will be saved is assigned, in this way and following with all these indications it will be possible to store this data to the variable.

One of the advantages of Python is that it can identify the type of data to be stored, which means that we do not have to tell the program that we are storing an integer, as is usually done in C, because the language itself detects it.

For example,

number_one = 2

In the case that we store a decimal or real number, what Python does, in this case, is to tell the variable that it is going to receive a real value and therefore it must meet the characteristics in order to receive it. The same happens with the values of type text or "strings"; Python can identify the type of data to be stored.

Data Types

The Python programming language has several types of data, numeric, text, where a single value can be True or False and some others. When we store data in a variable, the result obtained will depend specifically on the type of data we are working with.

Therefore, we can say, that the types of data are those which allow us to order a type of information, so that later on we can store in the variables, this data, and then, by means of the use of the variables, to carry out the operations that the programmer requires.

It is advisable to know what type of data we are using, to enhance the scope of the code or know how far we can go because if we do not know what type of operations we can do with a type of data, we would often get errors when programming.

Numbers: This type of data is the one that allows us to perform all kinds of arithmetic operation, from adding, to compare two numbers. They are absolutely necessary to make functional programs because, as you know, there are mathematics everywhere, and programming is not an exception. Among the types of data that make up the numbers, we have:

1) Integers: This type of data is used as a number, specifically as an integer, as its name says, with the help of this type of data, you can perform different types of operations, both the addition, subtraction, multiplication and all that you can imagine, of course, as long as you can make a number. To be able to declare an integer variable, the syntax is the following:

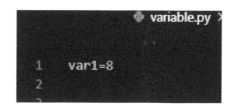

2) Float: This type of data is also a number, but in this case, it is a floating one, by which we mean that this has a greater number of decimals than integers, or is a number of higher precision. To declare a variable that is of the floating type, the syntax is the following:

3) Complexes: This type of data is used, because they have a real and an imaginary part, in real life the imaginary numbers are very used in engineering, specifically in electronics, for the calculation of factors and phases. To be able to declare a variable that contains the type of integer data, the following syntax will be needed, which will be

different from the one we have been seeing.

```
variable.py  X

1    var3=complex(1,5)
2
3
```

Strings: This type of data is extremely used since it is the one that allows sending messages because it allows us to assemble a cumulus of characters and to send it, it is for that reason that also this type of data, can be denominated string of characters.

The syntax to declare the variables that have within them the data type of character string is very simple, as you only need to write the string between single quotes or double-quotes. To get a better understanding of this concept, let's look at the following example:

```
variable.py  X

1    var4='Hello 1'
2    var5="Hello 2"
3
```

This type of variable, which has strings inside them, is used a lot to add interactivity to the program; it is used both in the input function and the output, which will be explained later.

Also, there is a fundamental operation on the strings, since there are occasions in which it is necessary to add two strings of characters, for that the (+) is used, as you can see next:

```
variable.py ×

1    string="String1 "
2    string2="String2"
3    concat=string+string2 # concat="String1 String2"
4    string3="This "+'is '+"a "+'example'
5
```

As we can see here, two strings are created, and then concatenated into concat, and the next case is that the variable string3, is the concatenation of four strings.

Boolean: This type of data is used to perform logical operations, which are widely used in programming, the same may be True or False, and from this, different programs can be made, this type of data will take importance in the following chapters, where it is necessary to use the conditions.

Lists: This type of data is very special, better said, this data structure, since they allow us to group several items inside them, the same ones are extremely useful, because they are very used inside the programming.

To be more specific, if you have some kind of previous knowledge in the programming, the lists are very similar to the arrangements in C, but if you do not have the knowledge, then a list is a way to order a certain number of items, in an orderly way. An important feature of the lists is that the items can be integers, strings, booleans, etc.. An example to declare a list, will be the following:

```
variable.py ×

1    list1=[1, "hi", True]
2    list2=[1, 2, 3, 4, 5, 6, 7, 8]
3
```

As we can see, in the last example, we created two lists; the first one has three items, the first one is an integer, the second one a string and the third one, a boolean. While the second is a list that has within it, eight items, which are integers and go from the one to the eight.

But this type of data does not end here, as you can perform different types of operations with the same, such as inserting new items at the beginning of the list, insert them at the end of the list, also remove elements from the list or even look for some specific element within the lists.

```python
variable.py ×
1    list1=[1, "hi", True]
2    list2=[1, 2, 3, 4, 5, 6, 7, 8]
3    list1.append("last") #[1, "hi", True, "last"]
4    list1.insert(0,"first")#["first",1, "hi", True, "last"]
5    list1.remove(1)#["first", "hi", True, "last"]
6    result= "find" in list1
7    print(result)
8    result= "last" in list1
9    print(result)
10
```

Being this, a complete example on working on lists, and as previously explained, two lists were created, *list1* and *list2,* then, the next command, what it does is to place a new item in the last place of the list, in this case, was placed "last", then another item was inserted in the first position of the list, as you can see, the function *insert()* has two arguments, one is the item we want to place, and the other, is the position in which you want to insert the item, the other statement that was used, was to remove an element from the list, this is done with the use of the *remove* function and specifying the specific position you want to remove, and finally, you want to verify if there are certain elements within the list, and that is achieved through the use of the *in* statement, which must return a boolean, which will be true or false.

Tuples: This is also a data structure, which works in a similar way to the lists, but in this case, the tuples, analogous to the lists, organizes a number of items, but unlike the lists, after created the items, can not be modified; therefore, they remain so until the end of the program. One of the benefits of using tuples is that you work faster with them, in addition, that these will not be modified; therefore, it is not possible to make any data error.

```
variable.py ×

1    tuple1=(1, "Hello", "try", False)
2
```

As we saw, to create a tuple, you only need to put the items in parentheses, unlike the lists that are in brackets. In an analogous way with the lists, you can do the searches on the tuples with the sentence in.

Dictionaries: As we have seen with the last two data structures, here we also find a structure; in this case, each word has a key, working like a dictionary, but to understand this a little better, it will be important to see a simple example.

```
variable.py ×
1    dicc={"zero":0, "one":1, "two":2}
2    a=dicc["one"] # a=1
3    print(a)
4    dicc["try"]="ok" #{"zero":0, "one":1, "two":2, "try":"ok"}
5    print(dicc)
6    del dicc["one"]  #{"zero":0, "two":2, "try":"ok"}
7    print(dicc)
8
```

As we could see in the previous example, the first thing we do is to declare our variable as a dictionary, and for it, we use the curly brackets; as we can see, each key has its pair, as for example "one" is the key, and the integer 1 goes with it. Then we print the value of a, on screen, then we proceed to add an item more in the dictionary and the only thing that is done is to place a value to a new key, then print the dictionary and verify that no error has been incurred; finally, we will remove an item from the dictionary, and this is done, using the instruction del and knowing which is the key you want to remove.

An important detail of the dictionaries is that they do not admit repeated keys inside their items.

Operators

Operators that can be used in Python can be classified into five categories:

1. Arithmetic Operators

These are operators that have the ability to perform mathematical or arithmetic operations that are going to be fundamental or widely used in this programming language, and these operators are in turn subdivided into:

1.1. Sum Operator: its symbol is (+), and its function is to add the values of numerical data. Its syntax is written as follows:

```
>>> 6 + 4
```

1.2 Subtract Operator: its symbol is the (-), and its function is to subtract the values of numerical data types. Its syntax can be written like this:

>>> 4 – 3

1

1.3 Multiplication Operator: Its symbol is (*), and its function are to multiply the values of numerical data types.

Its syntax can be written like this:

>>> 3 * 2

6

1.4 Division Operator: Its symbol is (/); the result offered by this operator is a real number. Its syntax is written like this:

>>> 3.5 / 2

1.75

1.5 Module Operator: its symbol is (%); its function is to return the rest of the division between the two operators. In the following example, we have that division 8 is made between 5 that is equal to 1 with 3 of rest, the reason why its module will be 3.

Its syntax is written like this:

>>> 8 % 5

3

1.6 Exponent Operator: its symbol is (**), and its function is to calculate the exponent between numerical data type values. Its syntax is written like this:

>>> 3 ** 2

9

1.7 Whole Division Operator: its symbol is (//); in this case, the result it returns is only the whole part.

Its syntax is written like this:

>>> 3,5 // 2

1.0

However, if integer operators are used, the Python language will determine that it wants the result variable to be an integer as well, this way you would have the following:

>>> 3 / 2

>>> 3 // 2

If we want to obtain decimals in this particular case, one option is to make one of our numbers real. For example:

>>> 3.0 / 2

2. Comparison Operators

The comparison operators are those that will be used to compare values and return; as a result, the True or False response as the case may be, as a result of the condition applied.

2.1 Operator Equal to: its symbol is (= =), its function is to determine if two values are exactly the same.

For example:

3 = = 3 Is True

5 = = 1 Is False

2.2 Operator Different than: its symbol is (! =); its function is to determine if two values are different and if so, the result will be True. For example:

3 ! = 4 Is True

3 ! = 3 Is False

2.3 Operator Greater than: its symbol is (>); its function is to determine if the value on the left is greater than the value on the right and if so, the result it yields is True. For example:

5 > 3 Is True

3 > 8 Is False

2.4 Operator Less than: its symbol is (<); its function is to determine if the left value is less than the right one, and if so, it gives True result. For example:

3 < 5 Is True

8 < 3 Is False

2.5 Operator Greater than or Equal to: its symbol is (> =), its function is to determine that the value on the left is greater than the value on the right, if so the result returned is True. For example:

8 > = 1 Is True

8 > = 8 Is True

3 > = 8 It's False

2.6 Operator Less than or Equal to: its symbol is (< =), its function is to evaluate that the value on its left is less than the one on the right, if so the result returned is True. For example:

8 < = 10 Is True

8 < = 8 Is True

10 < = 8 Is False

3. Logical Operators: Logical operators are the and, or, not. Their main function is to check if two or more operators are true or false, and as a result, returns a True or False. It is very common that this type of operator is used in conditionals to return a boolean by comparing several elements.

Making a parenthesis in operators, we have that the storage of true and false values in Python are of the bool type, and was named thus by the British mathematician George Boole, who created the Boolean algebra. There are only two True and False Boolean values, and it is important to capitalize them because, in lower cases, they are not Boolean but simple phrases.

The semantics or meaning of these operators is similar to their English meaning, for example, if we have the following expression:

X > 0 and x < 8, this will be true if indeed x is greater than zero and less than 8.
In the case of or, we have the following example:
N % 6 = = 0 or n % 8 = = 0

It will be true if any of the conditions is indeed true, that is, if n is a number divisible by 6 or by 8.

In the case of the logical operator not, what happens is that it denies a Boolean expression, so, if we have, for example:

not (x < y) will be true if x < y is false, that is, if x is greater than y.

4. Assignment Operators

Assignment operators basically assign a value to a variable, using the operator (=).

4.1 Operator Equal to =

This equal to the operator will assign to the variable on the left side any variable or result on the right side. The general syntax of this type of assignment is:

```
>>> a = 5
>>> a1 = a
```

So we can say that a1 equals 5

4.2 Assignment operator subtract (-)

This operator will subtract the value of the variable. The general syntax of this type is:

```
>>> a = 5
>>> a - = 10; a
-5
```
So we can say that a equals -5

4.3 Sum Assignment Operator (+)

This operator will add the value of the variable. The general syntax of this type is:

```
>>> a = 5
>>> a + = 10; A
15
```
So we can say that a equals 15

4.4 Multiplication assignment operator (*):

This operator multiplies the value to the variable. Its general syntax is:

```
>>> a = 5
>>> a * = 10; a
50
```
So we can say that a is equivalent to 50.

4.5 Division assignment operator (/):

In this case, the operator divides the value of the variable. The general syntax of this type will be:

```
>>> a = 5
```

```
>>> a / = 10; a
```
0

As far as we can tell, a is zero.

4.6 Exponent Assignment Operator (**)

For this type of operator, the exponent of the value of the variable will be calculated. Its syntax is as follows:

```
>>> a = 5
>>> a ** = 2; a
```
25

So we can say that a will be equal to 25.

4.7 Integer division assignment operator (//):

In this case the operator calculates the integer division of the value of the variable. Its general syntax is:

```
>>> a = 5
>>> a // = 10; a
```
0.5

4.8 Module assignment operator (%):

This operator returns the rest of the division of the value of the variable. Its general syntax is:

```
>>> a = 5
>>> a % = 10; a
```

5

So we can say that a is equivalent to 5.

5. Special Operators: These operators are exclusive to Python, and we will explain them to you by means of some simple examples.

Be a = 3 and b = 8

The operator is, indicates if they are the equals:

print (a is b)

The operator is not, indicates if they are not equal:

print (a is not b)

 If we have a list = (1,2,3,4,5,6,7,8,9), the operator in, indicates if the value is inside.

print (an in list)

The not in operator indicates if the value is not inside.

print (a not in list)

Interactivity and Its Importance

The interactivity of Python is what allows the user to work and have interaction with the program, since, through this, it is able to show messages on the screen, so that the user receives messages from the program, on the other hand, another function of the interactivity is the input of data by the user, thus making the program make decisions, depending on the input of the user.

Basic Functions for Interactivity

In this section, we will name the two most important functions for interactivity in Python, which are print(), standard output, on the other hand, the standard input is input(), which we will explain below.

Standard Output with print()

The print() function is used to display information by the standard output that normally corresponds to the computer screen.

In Python2, print is a reserved word, while in Python3, print() is a function, so the content will be expressed as a parameter within a function, or, said in another way, must be in parentheses.

```
interactivity.py ×

1    print("Output")
2    print("The end")
3
```

As we can see in this simple example, we make use of print and should appear in console two strings, both "Output" and "The end".

It is important to note that there are many occasions in which you have two variables that are strings, and sometimes, it is necessary to use both in the same print; therefore, we proceed to concatenate and print the two strings of characters together.

Standard Input with input()

For Python3, the default function is input(), which is responsible for obtaining some input value entered by the user, it will have to be assigned to a variable, so you get a string. An important feature of this function, is that you can also show a message on screen, thus achieving to show users what they have to enter and that the programmer can write a message so that it tells what type of data has to be entered, as for example, to tell the user that needs to enter a natural number for the calculation of the area of a rectangle, but to understand a little better this, it is important to look at the following example:

```
interactivity.py ✕

1     var1=input("Put a number:")
2
```

In this example, we see that the variable that was initialized, var1, is equal to the entry that the user enters, it should be a number, since the function specifies the user to enter a number, the same entry, is going to become a string, because the function input(), always return a string, and from there, you can make the calculations.

Escape characters: These are some types of character combinations, which behave differently within the strings, as they allow us to do things we can not do easily, such as a line break.

\\	\
\'	`
\"	"
\a	Sound
\b	ASCII regression
\f	Page advance
\n	Line break

\r	Carry Return
\t	Horizontal Tabulation
\v	Vertical Tabulation
\ooo	Octal value character
\xhh	Hexadecimal value character

Triple Quotes: They are used to place multiline character strings, this can be done with single triple quotes '''text''', or triple double quotes """text""" an example of its use is as follows:

```
interactivity.py X

1   string='''Hi
2   how are
3   you
4   '''
5   string2= """This
6   is
7   a
8   example"""
9   print(string+string2)
10
```

In this example, we created the two variables, string and string2, we used both the triple single quotes and the triple-double quotes, in which we placed several line breaks, without the need to make escape characters, in this case without the \n. Finally, we will print on the screen the concatenation of the variable string and string2.

Chapter 3: Conditionals

Many times, at the time of programming, it is considered necessary to make the decision about whether or not we should execute a specific piece of the program, and even in a given condition, it is necessary to execute several pieces of code. It is the text terminal and the standard input is the keyboard.

For this type of case, we have the sentences called "if", "else" and "elif".

Conditionals such as *if*, *else* and *elif* in Python are mostly used to execute an instruction in the case of certain conditions, in which one or more are met. We can see the conditional as the moment in which the decisions to take in our program are presented; depending on them, the program can be executed or not.

It is very important to understand correctly the use of conditionals since they will be the basis for our programs to be dynamic and perform certain tasks according to their condition. Since as you know, the programs are not as simple as you imagine, they will gradually become more complicated codes, but do not worry, practice will achieve success.

If Statement

This statement is responsible for evaluating a logical operation, which can give a result of the type "True" or "False" and then executes a certain piece of code as long as its result is true.

Now, how can we see this? Well, this statement is very useful when programming. Between these statements and loops, we can cover a large part of the codes that exist today, so it is of the highest importance to understand the *if*. Imagine the hypothetical case that you are presenting an admission exam to a university, and there is a program designed to enter the grades of all those who have presented the exam and to indicate whether it is admitted or not. If the grade is greater or equal to the expected value to enter the university, the same program will be responsible for placing the student in the database as a new entry to the university, but in the opposite case, nothing will be done and move to the next.

The syntax of the *if* is as follows:

```
1   x = 14
2   y = 21
3   if y > x:
4       print("y is bigget than x")
```

We observe that a simple evaluation of two variables "x" and "y" is made, the condition of the program will be that, if the condition is fulfilled, the program prints us the text; otherwise it does nothing.

This conditional could be interpreted as:
- If the young person is of legal age, he or she can enter the club.
- If the student passed his exams, he has passed the subject.
- If the consumer has already paid, he can withdraw his order.

Another case we can use, which is very important, is to apply this knowledge to real life, the same cases, could be the calculation of the area of a rectangle or can also be the calculation of a division. The same ones can be used, but there are cases in which the same ones can fall in errors and can be processed with an *if*; let's see the following examples to know a bit more of what we are talking about.

```
  if.py          ×

1    h=input("The height of the rectangle: ")
2    b=input("The base of the rectangle: ")
3    h=int(h)
4    b=int(b)
5    if(h>=0 and b>=0):
6        a=b*h
7        a=str(a)
8        print("The result is: "+a)
9    print("Bye")
```

The first thing we can observe in this example is that two variables were initialized, both *h* and *b*, which are *input* type, one is related to the height of the rectangle, and the other is related to the width of the base, respectively.

Immediately afterwards, what we did was to convert these variables into integers, since, at the moment of initializing them, they are a string, because this is how inputs are defined, it is important to note that when the *input* function is used, the variable that is associated to it becomes a string type; when observing this, it is necessary to make the variables integers, since it is not possible to perform mathematical operations with ASCII characters but with numbers, whether decimal, binary or hexadecimal; for that reason, the *int()* function is used, which converts the string that is as an argument, into an integer.

Already, at the moment of arriving at the condition of the *if*, we take into account two events that are related and to occur simultaneously, in order to be able to proceed to make the mathematical calculations; they are: first that *h* is greater than zero, and also, that *b* is greater than zero, Why that? Well, everything has to happen simultaneously, because if not, three things can happen:
- h<0 , which indicates that a negative area may arise.
- b<0 , which indicates that we will also have a negative area.
- b<0 and h<0, and even if we find an area greater than zero, it is not good to say that a measure of length is less than zero.

When observing this, the only valid condition is the one mentioned recently, which is that the two length measurements are greater than zero simultaneously. And at the moment that this condition is True, we proceed to enter into the if block, within which, we proceed to calculate the area of the rectangle, then convert the variable into a string, and finally print on the screen the value of the area of the rectangle.

Finally, "Bye" was printed on the screen in order to know that the program has been successfully completed.

Now, we can also make another example, which is very useful at the moment of dividing, since it is known that the division between zero is not defined; therefore, we have to force that the denominator is different from zero, as we can see next.

```
if.py        ×

1   d=int(input("Please enter a number for the denominator: "))
2   n=int(input("Please enter a number for the numerator: "))
3   if(d!=0):
4       print("Result:"+str(n/d))
5   print("OK")
6
```

The first thing we can see in this example is that we declare two variables: the first is the one we call *d*, the same is related to the denominator of the division, on the other hand, the variable *n*, is from the numerator of the division; it is clearly seen that a precondition of the program is that a number must be entered, any, logically, the denominator different from zero, but does not have any other restriction. A curious thing that we can find in the code is that it uses the function int(), and then, within it, the function input, and...Why? Well, because as you should know, the variable input, returns a string, which depends on the input the user wants, therefore, what we proceed to do is convert the string into an integer in a more compact way in code.

Then, the condition that must be met is that the denominator should be different from zero, or specifically in code, that the variable *d*, should be different from zero. In the case that this condition is fulfilled, the obtained result will be printed on the screen, but you may observe that the string "Result:" is concatenated with the string resulting from the division between *n* and *d*.

Finally, it is printed on the screen, to show that the program has finished in the correct way and there is nothing to worry about.

Else Statement

This statement could be seen as a plug-in to the *if* statement since it provides you with other code alternatives when executing a program if its evaluated expression is of the "False" type.

Then we can say that this sentence is very necessary, since it is the case in which a condition is not met and you want to perform an action because of that, because as we saw in the example above, specifically in the areas or the division, something more is needed, that can be intuited, because it is true, no error was made, but it needs something to tell the user that he entered some wrong value. This is one of the reasons why an *else* is necessary, but not only that, we can also take this to another level; Imagine that you are programming the communication of a fuel plant and in the hypothesis that the condition is that if there is no spill, a green led will turn on, but in the case that this is not true, and the *else* does not exist, then it would be a real disaster; therefore, in that case, we introduce a *else* to notify customers that a problem is occurring in the plant.

The syntax for "else" is as follows:

```
1    x = 21
2    y = 14
3    if y > x:
4        print("y is bigger than x")
5    else:
6        print("x is bigger than y")
7
```

In this case, we can observe that it is similar to the if case, but there is a case in which the condition of the *if* is going to be of the "False" type. If this case had been presented to us in the previous example, our program would have remained in the air without any response, in this one we will have the "else" that will give another way to the program in which it will be of the "True" type, and this one will be able to continue executing.

This conditional could be interpreted as an escape to a sentence *if* and we can see it as:

- If the young man is of legal age, he can enter the club. If not, it will have to move away from the entrance.

- If the student passed his exams, he has passed the subject. If not, the subject must be retaken.

- If the consumer has already paid, he can withdraw his order. If not, he must pay before consuming.

We cannot leave aside the other previous examples of the *if* because, in this case, they are also important. We will focus first, in the example of the area of the rectangle:

```python
if.py              ×

1    h=input("The height of the rectangle: ")
2    b=input("The base of the rectangle: ")
3    h=int(h)
4    b=int(b)
5    if(h>=0 and b>=0):
6        a=b*h
7        a=str(a)
8        print("The result is: "+a)
9    else:
10       print("Error")
11   print("Bye")
12
```

In this example, we can observe that, in an analogous way as it is done in the example of the *if* that was related to the area of a rectangle, two variables are initialized, *h* and *b*, these variables need that we enter the value of the height and base, then, these variables will be transformed to integers by means of the function *int()*.

Subsequently, and having the variables as integers, we proceed to enter into the conditional block and thus to calculate the required area. Firstly, we see the condition, in this case, has to be satisfied, so much that the number that relates to the base and the number that relates to the height, are positive, but simultaneously, as previously explained. If this condition is true, we proceed to calculate the area, we initialize a variable that has the value of the multiplication of the other two variables, and finally, we convert it into a string, so we can make the *print()*.

Now in the case that the condition has not been satisfied, it will be shown in the screen a string that will say "Error", in order to make it clear that an error has happened in the program.

Finally, to finish the program, a print is made, which will inform us that the program has finished and that will print a "Bye" on the screen.

On the other hand, if we get to make the example of the division, this would be very similar to what we have just done, since the *else* would also make a print of "Error" and also the condition of the *if*, will be equal to what was done in that example, because what has to be met that the denominator will be different from zero.

Elif Statement

This will be a combination of the above cases. It is used to link a variety of "else if" without having to increase their tabulations.

If you have some kind of experience programming, for example in "C", you will be waiting for the use of switch, but in Python, such a sentence does not exist, for it you get the *elif* sentence, because with it you can see several cases and study different possibilities that can occur with certain conditions. For that reason, it is important to use it, and if you are initializing from zero in the programming, you will be able to see gradually the importance of the same one.

Its syntax will be:

```
1   x = 21
2   y = 14
3   if y > x:
4       print("y is bigger than x")
5   elif x == y:
6       print("x and y are equal")
7   else:
8       print("x is bigger than y")
```

- If the youngster is of legal age, he can enter the club. If he is a celebrity, he can enter. If not, he must move away from the entrance.

- If the student passed his exams, he has passed the subject. If it is possible to take a recuperative exam, it does so. If not, the subject must be retaken.

- If the consumer has already paid, he can withdraw his order. If you are a contest winner, you may withdraw immediately. If not, you must pay before consuming.

As we did with the case of *else*, let's do the examples of the calculation of areas and divisions, to continue seeing the power that has this sentence.

```
if.py          ×

1    h=input("The height of the rectangle: ")
2    b=input("The base of the rectangle: ")
3    if(not h.isnumeric()):
4        print("Error, h not is a number")
5    elif(not b.isnumeric()):
6        print("Error, b not is a number")
7    else:
8        h=int(h)
9        b=int(b)
10       result=h*b
11       result=str(result)
12       print("The result:"+result)
13   print("Bye")
14
```

In this case, we will do the code example to calculate the area of the rectangle. For it, we will take into account more conditions.

You have tried, in the previous codes, when you were asked to enter a number. Have you entered a letter instead of a number? If you have done it, then you will realize that an error will be thrown; therefore, you will not be able to finish the program in a correct way for it; we show you this example to see how we can face these problems.

The first thing we do is to declare the variables, both *h* and *b*, for it, we use the function *input()*. Later, we enter in the conditional part, and the first thing is that we verify that what the user enters, is a number, for it we will obtain True, in the case that *h* is numerical, then we deny this condition. Why? Well, since if *h* or *b* is numerical we will enter directly to those blocks and it will print us in screen that this entered value is not numerical; for that reason, we proceed to deny it, since we will only enter to communicate that there was an error of data; in the case that the variables are not numerical, therefore, the above mentioned result will be denied and a True will be obtained to enter to the errors, this is done, so much for *b* as for *h*.

Then, if both variables are numbers, we proceed to make the calculation of the area, converting both *h*, and *b* into integers, then create a variable, which stored the value of the multiplication of both variables and then converts it into a string, so prints the result of the area of the rectangle.

Finally, it will print on the screen the string "Bye" to tell the user that the code ran satisfactorily.

But you may wonder "why, in this case, the comparison was not made if the number was negative or not?" This was not done, because the isnumeric function will only return True for natural numbers, by this we mean from zero onwards.

Then, with the other example, the one of the division, we can say that the process would be very similar, with the difference that if it would be necessary to make the comparison that the denominator has to be different from zero, but by the other conditions we can say that the code is similar.

As has been done throughout the book, this type of statement can be used in different cases, which can be from hobbies at homes to industrial protocols. A practical example can be where a robot is going to move because, depending on the conditions it has, it will move to a different place.

Chapter 4: Loops

In programming, a cycle (also called loops or control structures) are statements used to execute certain instructions in a repetitive way whenever necessary.

Its operation is very simple because it is based on variables and conditions that are previously structured; this way, we can control the number of repetitions in our code.

Loops are extremely important for different reasons and they can be used for many applications, such as programming a counter, which can then function as a stopwatch, to program a code, which repeats the same instruction several times, until the user enters the correct data.

While Loop

The while loop is the one that allows us to execute periodic sequences, which in turn allow us to do multiple sequences in a row. This will be executed as long as its internal condition is of the "True" type, and if the opposite occurs, that is, that the condition is of the "False" type, the cycle will finish and will continue with the normal execution of the program.

This type of loop is widely used, since it has different utilities, from those that are controlled by counting to those that can become infinite.

The syntax of While is the following:

```
1   x = 0
2   while x <= 14: #The loop will run as long as the
3                  #condition that variable x < 14
4       x +=1
5       print (x)
```

This example is very simple; we declare a variable with the name "x" whose value will be 0, we establish a condition where the loop will be executed as long as *x* is less than 14. If this is executed, the program proceeds with the execution and prints the result.

There is a variety of *while* loop types; in this chapter, we are going to talk about *while* loops controlled by counting and *while* infinite loop.

Loop "while" controlled by counting: This type of loop is going to have a counter, which will repeat the process as many times as we have indicated.

This type of while can be easily replaced by a for

Example:

```
loops.py  ×

1    count=int(input("Number of cycles:"))
2    if(count>0):
3        x=0
4        while(x<count):
5            print("Cycle "+str(x+1))
6            x+=1
7    else:
8        print("Error")
```

As we can see in this example, we create the variable count, which is an integer, and depending on the input of the user, it will serve to enter the number of cycles you want to use.

Then, we enter a conditional block, which specifies that if count is greater than zero, the case will be true, therefore, we create the variable x, which will be equal to zero, then we enter the cycle *while*, and the condition of the cycle will be that the cycle will be repeated until *x* becomes less than count, then print on screen the cycle in which we are and finally will increase by one unit the counter of *x*.

In the opposite case, it will print in screen the string of error, since if the number of cycles is negative there will exist an error, as it is logical.

Loop "while" infinite: In this type of loop, when a case arises in which we have a number of indeterminate instructions, we will only have that our condition is of the *while*(True) type, and this will allow the program to work properly.

```python
1    import time
2    x=1
3    while(True):
4        print(x)
5        x+=1
6        time.sleep(1)
```

In this example, we import the time module, although we have not yet explained the use of modules, we help ourselves from it.

Then we initialize the variable x, that possesses the value of one; later, we enter in an infinite cycle, as the condition is True, it always repeats itself, we print in screen the value of x, then we increase in a unit the value of x and finally, with the help of the module time, we proceed to use a delay of a second, to thus wait for a small-time, specifically a second, until the cycle repeats itself. As you can imagine, in this example, a simple chronometer was programmed.

Statements Used in the While Loop

Break statement: This statement allows us to interrupt cycles and even abandon them when they have not yet finished their execution regardless of whether the expression being evaluated while remains in the True position.

```
1   while True:
2       a= input("insert 0 to break out the loop while")
3       if(a=="0"):
4           break
5       print("you did not insert 0 so i can break up the loop")
6   print("Finish")
```

In this example, we have implemented a *while* cycle of the infinite type since the condition of this will always be True and, therefore, will be infinite.

Then we continue to declare a variable "a"; this is directly related to the *input* function that will wait for any value entered by the user; in this case, should be 0 to break the infinite cycle, and if you do not enter that number, the cycle will continue.

In line number three, we can find an *if* statement, which will give the condition that if the zero value is entered, this cycle is broken. And if not, the program will print on the screen "you did not insert 0, so I can break up the loop".

Finally, if the condition is satisfied, the program will exit the cycle and print Finish.

We can observe that the break statement is very useful to end a cycle as the example we just saw; there are other types of cases in which it could also be very useful. This break statement is considered a very essential tool when programming.

How do I know in which case to use a break type

statement? You might be thinking that they are used mostly for infinite cycles because it would make a lot of sense to break it, but in the program, we can get any kind of exception and this sentence would help us to break some unwanted error.

Continue statement: The continue statement is the one that, when evaluating if all the previous conditions are satisfied, is able to omit the rest of the instructions that are inside the cycle and then do another iteration. In short, we could say that this tool returns the program to the beginning of the loop while it is running.

A clear example of the continue sentence could be the following:

```
1   cycles= input("Please insert here the number of loops that are going to happend: ")
2   count= 1
3   while(count -1<int(cycles)):
4       x= count
5       count+= 1
6       if(a%2 == 0):
7           print("Error, please continue")
8           continue
9       else
10          print("This is not multiple of 2")
11      print(x)
12  print("End")
```

In this example we will have the case of a *while* cycle, in which the values that are multiples of 2 will be omitted, if these values are multiples, this will not print anything on the screen but will jump to the next iteration.

We begin creating a variable with the name cycles, which will be *input*, this will ask the user to enter the number of cycles to be performed in the program, and as is already known, the cycles are a string data.

Followed by this, we create the variable of integer type count; this variable is going to have the function of a counter; this way, we will have knowledge of the cycle in which we are.

Now we are going to create a *while* loop; this is going to indicate that the count variable is less than the cycle variable.

What does count -1 mean? Well, this is just to make sure that the program can do what we want and that our code works optimally. It is always recommended that every time we make a program of this type, we subtract a unit from it so that we can fulfill the number of cycles that correspond to our code.

Next, in the following line, we are going to declare a variable *x*, which will have the same value as the variable count since this will help us to know the current value that the cycle will have; in addition, this will increase one unit. (+=1)

Once this is done, we will go into the block of conditionals, which in this case will be that our variable "a"% == 0. What this means is nothing more that limiting the rest obtained from the division between *a* and 2, must necessarily be equal to zero so that this way, the *if* statement is executed.

The instructions of this statement are simple: first print on the screen the error that has occurred; followed by this, we will use the continue statement.

In a hypothetical case that the established condition is of the False type, the instruction found in the *else* block will be executed.

Once we have finished with our conditional blocks, the number of cycles will be printed on the screen in order to know the position of our program.

Finally, our program will print a message indicating that the program has finished.

Pass statement: The pass statement is considered a null expression since it has no effect on the code, but it does allow us to create a loop in its body, which will be empty (without code). In this way, this loop can be added later, and we can use it as a temporary filler (either to add some kind of delay or work more complex programs such as programming with processors.).

The pass statement can not affect in any way the behavior of our code and can be used anywhere on it, either for a cycle or even a function.

```
1    cycles= input("Please insert here the number of loops that are going to happend: ")
2    count= 1
3    while(count -1<int(cycles)):
4        x= count
5        count+= 1
6        if(a%2 == 0):
7            print("Error, please continue")
8            pass
9        else:
10           print("This is not multiple of 2")
11       print(x)
12   print("End")
```

Observing the last example, we can understand in a clearer way what this statement is about.

First, we have declared the variable cycles, and this variable is going to determine the cycles that the program will have when we order it, it is an *input* variable, as we already know, it is of the string type.

Next, we are going to create a counter (count); this one will have the function of indicating us in which position of the cycle we are.

Once this is done, we can start working with our cycle, that is the *while*, and the only function it must perform is that: count-1 must be less strict than the function int(cycles). Then we are going to declare the variable that is going to assign the value to count and this value will be increased by one unit so that in this way our program makes sense.

Now we must take care of the conditional, with the % operator our program will be able to verify if *x* meets the condition of being a multiple of 5, it is very important to take this into consideration and depending on this the result that returns will give a correct functionality to our program and lets remember that we have established that this must start in less than zero.

In the case that the established condition is satisfied, the program will print what we have indicated, and it will continue, with the pass sentence, we will add a delay to the program. If the condition were to be of the False type, this will automatically enter the *else* block, and it will only print out that the number entered is not a multiple of 5.

Once we have finished the conditional block, the program will not take into consideration if the condition is true or false, but will automatically print the current position of the cycle in which we are through print(x).

The program, at the end of the *while* cycle, will print us a string; in this case, we place an end to indicate that the program has finished correctly. With this example, we can see that adding a pass sentence is nothing more than adding a delay to our program.

For Loops

Cycle For: This is the other loop that we can get in Python, and this is responsible for repeating the code blocks a certain number of times, so they are extremely useful. Even on certain occasions can be supplanted a *while* loop controlled by counting, by a simple *for*.

One of the benefits of using the *for* is that it is not necessary to create a variable previously to enter in the *for*, the same will iterate within an element in which it can iterate, such as a list, a string or a range. Another noteworthy aspect is that it is not necessary to codify a sentence that increases the counter each time iteration ends.

To understand a little more this type of loop, we will proceed to see the following example:

```
loops.py    ✕

1    count=int(input("Number of cycles:"))
2    for i in range(count):
3        print("Cycle "+str(i+1))
4
```

As we can see in this example, the count variable is created, which is an integer, depending on the user's input. Later, we will create a *for*, which will be iterating from *i* to the counter range. But what does the range mean? The range returns a list that has a certain number of items, depending on the count, in this case; therefore, the variable *i*, will iterate as many times as count specifies. Finally, it will print on the screen the number of the cycle in which we are.

A very useful example of the use of the *for* is one in which we move over a list, as we can see below:

```
loops.py  ×

1    countries=["EEUU", "Italy", "Spain", "Venezuela", "Germany"]
2    for country in countries:
3        print(country)
```

In this example, we can see that we create a list, which has the names of different countries such as USA, Venezuela, Italy, Spain and Germany, then we enter the *for* cycle, which will have a variable that will iterate within the list countries; this variable will be country. Finally, in each iteration, an item will be printed within the list, which means that the name of a country will be printed.

Chapter 5: Functions

We define a function as a piece of code, which is reusable and is responsible for performing a certain task, according to our needs. This piece of code will have a name and it will be in charge of using some arguments as inputs, this function will follow a sequence of statements and steps, which will result in an operation that gives us a value or result, depending on what the function was supposed to do. One of the advantages of using Python is that it allows us to call any function whenever we want or need to.

Functions are considered a really important component for programming, mostly in the structured programming paradigm, since, as it has the benefit of reusing the same function in as many programs you want, you will skip and shorten some steps and lines of codes when programming. This also helps to make the code a long way easier and allowing us to use the functions of other people in our programs. Python has a lot of functions included by default; some of them are the following:

Some Python Functions

Function	Example
Print() function: This function will let us print an argument or result of any program on our screen	Print("Hello World") Will print: Hello World
Split() function: This function will let us separate strings to lists	A=(" This is an example") List=a.split() Will result in: List=['This', 'is', 'an', 'example']
Replace() function: This function replaces a string for another string	Text= ("This book is good") Text=Text.replace ("good","bad") Print(Text) Will print: This book is bad
Tuple() function: What this function does is to convert a string into a tuple	Word=tuple("Red pen") Print(Word) Will print: "R","e","d","p","e","n".
Upper() and lower() functions: This functions will convert	Name=("Steven") Name.upper() Print(Name)

all the letters on a string into upper or lower case	Will print: STEVEN Name.lower() Print(Name) Will print: steven
Join() function: This function will perform the action of putting two or more strings together through a "-"	List=['Spider', 'man']. Join(List) Will give us: Spider-man
Ord() function: This function will return a ASCII value type. (Whether it is a character or a string)	Let's suppose we assigned X=14 Print(ord('X')) Will print: 14
Type() function: This function will notify the type of data of the element we put on it.	X= 14; Y=("Hello") Print(type(X)); print (type(Y)) Will print: "int"; "str"
List() function: This function will create a list, using and argument on specific	Word=list("Book") Print(Word) Will print: "B", "o", "o", "k".
Str() function: This function will convert any integer data type	X=14 (A Number) A=str(X). print(A) Will print: 14 (A String)

into a string data type	
Range() function: This function will create a list of elements, determined by the programmer. This function is usually used in for cycles	X= range(5) Print(X) Will print: 0, 1, 2, 3, 4.
Float() function: This function will convert any value into a decimal type value (Float)	X=float("3.14") Print(X) Will print: 3.14
Min() and max() function: This functions will return the minimal and maximum value in an array of numbers	X=[15, 4500, 200] Print(min(X)); print(max(X)) Will print: 15; 4500
Sum() function: This function will add all the numbers in an array	Y= [10, 6, 9] Print(sum(Y)) Will print: 25
Int() function: This function will convert	X=int("19") Print(X)

any data type into an integer	Will print: 19
Len() function: This function will determinate the length of the characters contained on a string.	Len("I am a programmer") Will return: 17
Round() function: This function will round all the decimals numbers to its closest integer	Print(round(13.56)) Will print: 14

Rules to follow to define properly a function:

- The code that goes with the function will always start after the ":" character.
- It is really important to identify correctly our code and be very careful with its indentation (four spaces).
- The parameters that go with the function must be defined inside the parenthesis of the same.

A function will never be executed unless it is invoked, and this is nothing more than calling it by its name:

```
functions.py ×

1    def function(a, b):
2        #sentence 1
3        #sentence 2
4        #sentence 3
5        #.
6        #.
7        #.
8        #sentence n
9
10   funtion(x, y)
11
```

As we can see in this example, this is a way to define a function. Obviously, this function won't do anything, because it is just a demonstration of how the syntax is and how to call or invoke it. As you could see, we used the reserved word *def*, to then define the function. Then, inside the parenthesis, we have arguments or parameters of the function, which come to be the inputs, and lastly, the sentences and statements that define what our function will do.

After defining our function, we can call it whenever we want to.

How Can I Create My Own Function?

As we mentioned earlier, Python allows us to create functions; for that, we only have to make use of the *def* statement. After this, we will name it as we want (It is strongly recommended to use a name that is related to the program to avoid confusion).

Once created, how can I make use of it? In order to be able to call or use a function, all we have to do is to declare it at the beginning of our code. This is really important since if this is not done, the Python interpreter won't be able to identify it, so the function will not exist and will not work.

Parameters

We call parameters to all those values that are going to be used in a function; they will work as inputs. Functions can receive one or more parameters and they just have to be written correctly and separated by a comma, in order to be invoked.

For example:

```
1    def firstfunct(x, y):
```

With this, you could see how easy it is to define the beginning of a function. It is really, REALLY, important the use of the *def* word, since this is the one that will tell the Python interpreter that a function is being created.

Afterward, we name our function. In this case, we named it *firstfunct*. On it, we could observe that there are parenthesis around *x* and *y*, meaning that those are going to be the parameters that our function will use as inputs to work properly.

What are the arguments or parameters?

As we already know, the parameters are the values that the function is going to receive when it is defined. These values are going to be called arguments, and are classified as follows:

- **Argument by position**: When we send an argument to a function, this one receives it in an ordinated way, which was defined previously.

```
1   def Hello(name, age):
2       print("Hello" +name+ "i am " +age+ "years old")
3   x = input("My name is: ")
4   y = input("my age is: ")
5   Hello(x,y)
```

In this example, you can see that a function named "Hello" was created; its parameters are name and age. We have created this function to print a message on the screen saying the name and age that the user writes.

We also defined the variables *x* and *y*, which are strings that are related to the name and the age. It is important to do this because otherwise, the function will not be able to run.

Finally, we called the function "Hello", and we have put the arguments on a specific order so that the message that will be print on the screen makes sense. If we had written "Hello (y,x)", the message print on screen would have been like this:

"Hello 16, I am Matt years old".

- **Arguments by name**: When we call a function, it should have identified on its arguments the value that each parameter will have according to its name.

```
1    def number(x,y):
2          return y-x
3    c= number(y=15, x=10)
4    print(c)
```

You can see that we defined the number function; this will contain the parameters *x* and *y*. After we defined it, we added the sentence return and right after it a subtraction.

Later, we created the variable *c*, which will have the value of the return. To call this function, all we have to do is to write its name next to the values that it will have inside the parenthesis.

ERROR: Not enough arguments: This error happens when we call a function with defined parameters that are not present or written correctly.

Here, we will show you an example of a function that has no parameters.

```
1   def number():
2       print("number")
3
4   number()
```

As you could see, the function *number()* has no input parameters, hence, what it will do, is to simply print the message *number()*.

Return Statement

Until this point of the book, you may have noticed that Python's functions, on its majority, have return values, which can be explicit or implicit. We also know that the return statement is a keyword of Python; its purpose is to end the execution of a function in order to obtain a result value of it.

Lambda Function

We define a *lambda* function as a special function, this one is part of the default functions of the Python programming language, and it is an exclusive function.

What do we mean when we say that it is an exclusive function?

The *lambda* function has a special syntax and that is the reason why we consider it an exclusive function since it allows us to create any kind of function on a really fast way, without having to save it.

It is also capable of executing an expression and automatically return its result, this could also have some optional parameters on its structure, but the restrictions of this *lambda* function must always be respected.

Its syntax is really easy and simple, you only have to write the reserved word *lambda*, the arguments and finally the ":" character, like this:

```
1   sum= lambda a, b: a+b
2   x= sum(50,47)
3   print(x)
```

You can easily see the use of the *lambda* function. We have a *sum* function that we equaled to *lambda*, who is going to have two parameters, *a* and *b*, which are going to be added. Additionally, we have the x parameter, which will store the respective values of a and b in order to do the add.

The lambda function is used mostly to call functions that are needed in a program for a really short time, since, as it would be used so quickly and so little, naming it is not necessary. This function is commonly used with the *filter()* and *map()* functions.

Filter() Function

We define the *filter()* function as the one that has the task of filtering arguments, whether they are lists or iterators. As a result, this will always return an iterable with the elements that have already been filtered.

In this example, we will show you how it works. This will filter the people that will be able to enter a local for +18 people. We will define then, the *filter()* function and the iterable.

```
 functions.py ×

1   ages=[15, 18, 22, 10, 25, 21, 23, 17, 18, 22, 27]
2   def passfilt(ages):
3       if ages>18:
4           return True
5       else:
6           return False
7
8   result=filter(passfilt, ages)
9   for persons in result:
10      print("You can go with your age, which is "+ str(persons))
11
```

So, you could see how we created a list of the different ages of the people that want to go to the local. Then, we created the function *passfilt*, which will filter the data that is given, returning whether True or False. The next sentence will create a list with the people that approved the filter.

Lastly, we created a *for* loop, which will show us on the screen the obtained results, telling the user which ages were allowed.

Map() Function

This function will execute elements on a tuple or a list, in order to be able to return elements on the sequence, as the result of the operations. This function is used mostly to simplify the code and make it simpler, avoiding the creation of unnecessary loops or other resources.

```
functions.py ×

1    def sum(a,b):
2        return a + b
3
4    list1=[1, 2, 3]
5    list2=[4, 3, 2]
6    result=map(sum, list1, list2)
7    result=list(result)#[5, 5, 5]
8    list1=["Hello ", "are "]
9    list2=["how ", "you"]
10   result=map(sum, list1, list2)
11   result=list(result)#["Hello how ", "are you"]
12
```

In this example, you could observe that, at first, we defined the *sum()* function, which returns *a+b*. Then, we created the list1 and list2 lists, which has integers on it, put there as items. Later we created the result variable, which will have the value of the result of the *map* function. That value will be the addition of the items one by one of both lists. Then we used the *list()* function to convert that result into a list.

The second example, on the same image, was pretty much like the first one. The only difference is that instead of using integers, we used strings, and instead of adding, the function concatenates those strings.

Finally, we used again the *list()* function in order to get a list as a result.

What Is the Difference Between Def and Lambda?

As you may have noticed, creating a function with the *def* statement is the same as creating it with *lambda* since, in both cases, we will get the same result, and the difference is that the objective is reached in two different ways.

Sometimes, to get somewhere, we will find two different ways, one shorter and simpler and the other longer and harder; that is what happens here. *Lambda* would be the easy way since it allows us to use functions easily on our code.

When we create a *lambda* type function, this will be focused on a single line of code, reducing then the total line count of our program, while when using *def*, we have to define it in more than a single line.

At the moment of using the *lambda* keyword, we create an object or function which will not have to be defined with a name, unlike it happens with *def*, that has to be defined at the beginning of our code to be able to use it.

Despite being the *lambda* function better for saving lines of code, sometimes the *def* statement is easier to understand for those users that are getting started into programmers and even for those that already have some experience but not that much.

It is important when operating with a *lambda* function type, to assign a variable to it, since, if this is not done, it will only operate on the line on which it is defined.

Variables

As you might know, variables are those that store information, they can store different data types such as integers, floats, strings and they can be renamed and changed during your program and code by using the statements that you think are needed. Those variables will work on the main program. If you know a bit about the C programming language, those variables will be stored on the Main. But there are other types of variables, which can be very useful when it comes to programming.

Global Variables

These variables are really important since they will always be the same, no matter where on the code they are located. They will always have the same value and we will be able to use them all through the code.

A recommendation we can say about its use is that you must be really careful because you can make mistakes very easily.

```
functions.py ×

1    global vari
2    vari=0
3    def sum(a):
4        return vari + a
5    vari=sum(7)
6    vari=sum(15)
7    print(vari)
```

As you can see in the example, we declared the variable *vari* as a global variable, hence we can access them anywhere in the code.

Then, we defined the function *sum*, who will have as a parameter *a* and will return the add of the global variable *vari* plus the parameter entered on the function.

At last, *vari* will be equal to the *sum* of *vari* plus seven, in this case, *vari* would be seven, then *vari* would be equal to the of *vari* plus fifteen, and it will be equal to twenty-two.

Local Variables

This is another type of variable, which is very useful because they only exist inside a piece of a block of the program. After the block is ended, the variable is deleted. This type of variable is good and recommended when it comes to don't wasting memory. Here is an example:

```python
def sum(a,b):
    result=a+b
    f="HI"
    return result

a=sum(1,3)
print(a)
```

You can see that here, we defined the *sum()* function, which has two parameters, *a* and *b*. The next thing that was done was to create the result local variable that is equal to the sum of the parameters. Later, the local variable *f* is created, who is equal to the string "HI", and lastly, we ask the program to return the result variable.

After creating the function, we say that the variable *a* would be equal to the result of *sum* (1,3); then *a* would be equal to 4.

You might be wondering why we created the *f* variable. It is a local variable, so it does nothing outside the function we defined as *def*, so it doesn't affect the behavior of the code

Chapter 6: Modules

A module is defined as an object of Python, which has certain attributes, to which we can give an arbitrary name and also link them. A module allows us to organize the code, to make easier the understanding and use of our code to third party people and even to ourselves.

In other words, we can define a module as a simple file with a .py extension that is capable of defining functions, variables, classes and also include executable code.

Why Should You Use Modules?

Modules allow us to organize the elements and components inside our codes in an easier way, providing us with a big package of variables that are auto contained. Names that are defined on a superior level in a module file automatically will become an attribute of the object of the imported module.

Another advantage of using modules is that they let us reuse the code, using data services and linking individual files to broaden our program.

The main reason why we think that the modules are a very useful tool when it comes to programming is that they are really helpful to organize and reuse our code. This is very important when we talk about OOP (Object-Oriented Programming) since on that mode, the modularization and reusage are very popular. Since Python is a programming language oriented for that, it comes very user-friendly.

Imagine that you want to create an application or a program, more complex than what we have been doing until now. For it, you are going to need one of the previous codes to complement. Here is when you see the real benefit of the modules since you will be able to simply add one of the old codes to the complex application you want to do.

In modules, we will also have modularization. It is based on dividing our codes into several tiny pieces of codes, so that, at the moment of making the complex program or application, it won't have hundreds and hundreds of lines of codes that could be annoying and hard to read. Instead, the code will be separated into tiny files.

How Do We Create a Module on Python?

Creating a module is something very easy that anyone can do, all that needs to be done is to create a file with the .py extension, then, that file will be stored on a folder of your preference; this is known as import.

Python, on its default library, has a big amount of modules, we can observe them on the official manual. You can find it on the following link: http://docs.python.org/modindex.html.

In case we want to create a module of our own, you will have to do the following. We will make a program on which we will create a module that could be used later.

The module syntax is as follows:

```python
def calculator(a, b, option):
    if(option=="+"):
        return a + b
    elif (option=="-"):
        return a - b
    elif (option=="*"):
        return a * b
    elif (option=="/"):
        return a / b
    elif (option=="^"):
        return a ^ b
    else:
        return "Bad option"
```

As you could see, the syntax is really simple, since it is pretty much like creating a function. After we created it, we must be able to import it from another program, in order to do that, we will use the *import* statement.

Import Statement

A module is able to contain definitions of a function and even statements, which can be executable. With this, it is possible to initialize a module since they execute only when our module is on the import statement.

Modules are capable of importing other modules, that is why people use to put the import type statements at the beginning of each since with the names of our imported modules, they will locate on a space named global; function that modules have for importing.

With the help of the last example, we can manage to import the module created previously and use the functions that we defined there.

```
modules.py        examplemodules.py ×
1    from modules import *
2    op=input("Please enter the operation you want\nSum(+)\nSubtraction(-)\nMultiplication(*)\nDivision(/)
     \nEmpowerment(^)\nYour option:")
3    a=int(input("Please entre the number a:"))
4    b=int(input("Please entre the number b:"))
5    result=calculator(a, b, op)
6    print(result)
7
```

As you see in this example, we created the *op* variable, who takes the task of storing a string, which will specify the option that the users choose. Then, two variables would be initialized, *a* and *b*; they will store the value of the operators we are going to use to perform the mathematical operations.

Afterward, the result variable will store the value that the function calculator returns, according to the operators and the type of operation that the users want. The function calculator comes from the module that we have imported.

When the Python interpreter finds the *import* statement, it imports the module, as long as it is located on the full search path. The search path is nothing but a list where all the directories that Python accesses before importing any module are located.

How to Import a Module?

For being able to import a module, we just have to follow some instructions and steps that are performed at the moment of the execution:

We look for the module through the module search path, compile to byte code, and lastly, we execute the byte-code of our module to then build an object that defines it.

How can I search for a module through Search Path?

To search for a module, our search system compounds of the concatenation of paths; these can be seen on the directory "Home" of our program. After this, the environment PYTHONPATH will be located from left to right, and that is how we will find the directory of default libraries.

Namespaces in Modules

As you know, modules are files. Python creates a module object in which all the names that we assigned in that module-file will be contained. What does that mean? This means that namespaces are just places where all the names that later become attributes are created.

What Are the Attributes?

Attributes are the names that have been assigned to a value considered of a higher level on a module file, which does not belong to

a function or class.

Chapter 7: OOP (Object-Oriented Programming)

Object-oriented programming is a form of programming in which we can observe in a more real way than the things that occur to us at the time of programming. This is a paradigm, which refers to theories, models and methods that allow us to solve more quickly and efficiently any problem that may arise.

As its name implies, object-oriented programming is based on the object model, where the object itself is the main element that will contain all its characteristics and behavior, making it independent, but at the same time relating it to elements of a class.

This type of programming differs from structured programming since its main objective is that through some input data, produce an output.

Some of the benefits of working with OOP are:
We can maintain a certain uniformity in the code.
It allows the reuse of code, since it allows us, after

having created an object, to use that same definition, to create other objects.

It is a good practice when it comes to programs, not to say that it is one of the big pros of Python.

As we have seen before, object-oriented programming is a way of programming based on finding a solution to problems. This type of programming introduces new concepts, which complement and even overcome those we already know. But first, we should ask ourselves:

What Is a Class?

It is the way we can begin to create our own objects, since from there, we can add to each class its attributes that are nothing more than that class and its methods, which are something like the actions that the class can perform.

A clear example, to understand this, is that we have the computer class, which can have a mark, a color, a Ram memory, a ROM memory, a processor, among other things, being these the attributes of our class, then there are the actions that computers can do, such as navigate, turn on, turn off, sound, among others, being this the methods of our class.

In order to create a class, in this case, that of computers, let's see the following example:

```
classexample.py ×

1    class PC():
2        manufacturer="Dell"
3        ram="4 Gb"
4        rom="512 Gb"
5        processor="Intel I5"
6
```

As we can see in this example, we created the PC class, the brand is Dell, has 4 Gb of ram, 512 Gb of ROM and an intel i5 processor; this is the way we can create a class that only has attributes, but to make use of this class, we need to create an object, which will be explained below.

Object characteristics:

- Object: An object is an instance of a class, this entity is the result of a set of properties, attributes, behavior or functionalities in which they react to events that occur in the program.

- Method: A method is a type of algorithm, which will be related to an object or its class itself. The execution of an algorithm is triggered after receiving a message which indicates what an object can do, and even the method itself can generate changes between its properties.

- Message: We define a message as the direct communication to the object, this one is going to order itself to execute some of its methods with the parameters that it contains associated, according to be the event that generates it.

- Behavior: This will be defined by the messages or methods to which the object will know how to respond. What do we mean by this? This is nothing more than saying that the behavior will be the operations that can be performed with the object.

- Event: We define an event as an event that occurs in our program, either interaction of the user with the computer or a message sent by an object. Our program takes control of the event through a message to the target. How is this? In a few words, we can say that an event is a reaction that triggers the behavior of an object.

- Attributes: We define an attribute as the characteristic that a class is going to have.

- Components of an object: Objects are made up of attributes, identity, relationship and methods.

- Identification of an object: an object is identified through a table that is going to be composed by the attributes and functions that correspond to it.

After having explained some characteristics of the objects, we can create our first object, in this case, our first computer:

```python
class PC():
    manufacturer="Dell"
    ram="4 Gb"
    rom="512 Gb"
    processor="Intel I5"

myPC=PC()
print(myPC.ram)
```

As we could see in this example, specifically in the past one, we created the class, as we did previously, then we created our first object, with the myPC name, which is of the PC type. To verify that the ram of our computer is four gigabytes of ram, we use the *dot* property.

This property is used to access the attributes of our objects, and this is done by placing a dot, as previously seen, and then write some attribute of the object.

But this sounds a little repetitive since it seems that all computers are the same, but Python had already thought about this, for it, there are constructors so that we can make objects as the user wants and not in a predetermined way. In the following example, we are going to place constructors and methods in the same example, with the objective of making a complete example so that it is clear to the readers:

```
classexample.py ×

 1    class PC():
 2        def __init__(self, manufacturer, ram, rom, processor):
 3            self.manufacturer= manufacturer
 4            self.ram=ram
 5            self.rom=rom
 6            self.processor=processor
 7            self.state=False
 8
 9        def turnOn(self):
10            self.state=True
11            print("The PC is on")
12
13        def TurnOff(self):
14            self.state=False
15            print("The PC is off")
16
17    myNewPC=PC("Accer", "8 Gb", "1 Tb", "AMD")
18    myNewPC.turnOn()
19    print(myNewPC.processor)
20
21
```

In this example, we can see how to create a class, since it has its respective constructor, which uses the reserved word *self*, which is used to access an attribute from any method without any inconvenience, also to observe how the other modules were created, you could realize that they have been created using as arguments the word *self*, no matter what method it is, that word should always be there, and also, every time you want to access an attribute within the class, it is necessary to use the word *self*, you could also see how we added the behavior of turning the computer on and off.

The next act was to create an object called myNewPC, which is class PC, and also has the characteristics, whose brand is Acer, has 8 Gb of ram, 1 Tb of ROM and has an AMD processor. The next act was to turn on the pc, using the turnOn() method, using the methodology of the dot, and finally, we want to know which processor has our new computer, also using the nomenclature of the dot.

Already seeing the potentiality that this object-oriented programming has, we will be able to observe some very important properties of them:

Abstraction: They enhance the most significant characteristics of each object in an analog way that captures the behavior of it. These objects present a degree of abstraction since they allow to communicate with other objects of the same class even without needing to show their characteristics. Therefore, abstraction refers to an object being able to isolate itself from all others and only concentrate on its tasks.

Encapsulation: This is based on bringing together all the elements that are considered of the same essence that contains the same level of abstraction in order to make a better design of the structure of the components of the system.

Polymorphism: It is about the different methods or better said, behaviors associated with different objects that have the same name, because when the method is called, it will perform the behavior corresponding to the object that is required; an example of this, can be that a car is going to start, being this the method, then we also have that a motorcycle can start, being this a method of this class too.

Modularity: It responsible of dividing the program or the application in several stages, in this case, the modules; you can imagine it as an old equipment of diskettes, that the modules acted independently, where each one becomes independent modules of the others, allowing this way to run separately, but even so, these have connections with the other modules, but they do not depend on others to run, but that they could use the data of the other pieces of code.

Inheritance: This characteristic is very important, since it relates to several classes, so that they relate between them, generating a type of hierarchy, so to speak, the objects that have less hierarchy are going to inherit properties and attributes of the classes that have a greater hierarchy. In this way, polymorphism and encapsulation can be organized and facilitated, thus allowing objects with a smaller hierarchy to be created and defined as more specialized objects of the higher classes. Therefore, a small example could be that a computer being a fathering class, and a daughter could be a telephone, inheriting all the properties of the father class, with others a little more specific.

Now, in the case that an object inherits more than one class, this object has greater complexity, being a very specific instance.

Creating a class daughter: Already knowing the theory, we can see the following example, where we create a cell class because as we all know all modern cell phones are computers, but not all computers are cell phones, so let's see the following example:

```
classexample.py ×

1   class PC():
2       def __init__(self, manufacturer, ram, rom, processor):
3           self.manufacturer= manufacturer
4           self.ram=ram
5           self.rom=rom
6           self.processor=processor
7           self.state=False
8
9       def turnOn(self):
10          self.state=True
11          print("The PC is on")
12
13      def TurnOff(self):
14          self.state=False
15          print("The PC is off")
16
17  class cellphone(PC):
18      def __init__(self, manufacturer, ram, rom, processor, signal, battery):
19          PC.__init__(self, manufacturer, ram, rom, processor)
20          self.signal=signal
21          self.battery=battery
22
23      def call(self):
24          print("The cellphone is calling")
25
26  mycell=cellphone("Huawei", "4 Gb", "128 Gb", "ARM", "5G", "2000 mA")
27  mycell.call()
28  print(mycell.manufacturer)
```

As we could see in this example, a PC class is created, which we have seen previously how it was created, then we create the class daughter of PC, it has a constructor and has as inputs, all the arguments of the father class, plus the arguments *signal* and *battery*; then to initialize the constructor, we call the method of the father class __init__(), and then we will initialize the other two attributes as it is normally done, assigning to it the value of *self.signal* and *self.battery*, the corresponding values.

It also creates a *call()* method for the phone to call, and this method will show a message which will say that the phone is calling.

To instantiate a daughter class, what we do is to write a variable, which will be cellphone class, we insert the different arguments, such as Huawei brand, ARM processor, among other features. Then we will call the *call()* method so that our cellphone calls and finally we want to visualize which is the brand of our phone, which is Huawei

Chapter 8: File management

One of the advantages of Python is that it allows us to work at two different file levels: in one, we have the module, which facilitates the handling of what refers to the system files at the same level of the operating system. In the second level, we are allowed to manipulate the reading of the files; here we work reading and writing at the moment of working with the application since we would be working each file as an object.

When we work with files, these are manipulated in the following way: first, they are opened, we operate on them, and finally, we close them.

But... What is a Python file? What is meant by this?

We can define Python files as a set of bytes that will contain a certain composite structure.

Our file will look like this:

File header: These are the data that the file will

contain (name, size, type) of the file we are going to work with.

File Data: This will be the body of the file and will have some content written by the programmer.

End of file: This sentence is the one that will indicate that the file has reached its end.

How to Access a File?

There are two ways to access a file, which are very simple, one is using the file as a text file, where it will proceed line by line, the other way is treating the file as a binary file, where it will proceed byte by byte.

Open() Function

To open a file in Python, we will use the *open()* function, and this will take charge of receiving the name of the file and the way in which the file will be opened according to its parameters. If you don't enter a file opening mode, it will automatically open with a default mode, a read file.

It is important to note that the operations to open files

are limited, it is not possible to open a read file when it was opened for its writing, and we cannot write in a file which was only opened for reading.

There are two types of files in Python, one of them are text files and the other are plain files, so we must take into account when specifying which format the file will be opened to avoid any confusion and error in our code.

The *open()* function is based on only two parameters:
- Enter the path to the file you want to open.
- Enter the mode in which we want to open our file.

The syntax of the *open()* function is as follows:

```
1    func = open("file.txt","r")
2    func.read()
3    func.close()
```

Of which the following parameters have the following meaning:

File: This argument will provide us with the name of the file we are going to access through the *open()* function, this is what we will call the path of our file.

The file is considered a fundamental argument because it is the one that allows us to open the file, it differs from the rest of the arguments because when some of them can be optional, this one contains some that come from a predetermined way.

Mode: These will be the modes with which we are going to access and these are responsible for defining the way in which our file is going to be opened either for reading, writing, edition.

Next, we have all the ways to access a file:

w: This is the write mode, which will be responsible for opening a file only for writing; this mode will create a new file in case the file we are working with does not exist.

w+: This is still the same write mode, but its difference is that it has a plus, which also allows reading the file.

wb: This is still the same write mode, but its difference is that it opens the write file in a binary format.

wb+: This is still the same write mode, but its difference is that this file is opened in a binary format and also allows it to be a read file.

r: This is the read mode, which comes by default when opening any type of file. This mode will open the file for reading only.

r+: This is still the same read mode, but it has a plus, which allows it to open a file for reading and writing.

rb: This is the same read mode, which will open a read file in binary format only.

a: This is the add mode, which is in charge of opening a file to be added. This file starts being written from the end of the file itself and also takes charge of creating a new one in case the file we are working with does not exist.

ab: This mode is still the same as add, but opens in binary format. And it is in charge of creating a new file in case the file we are working with does not exist.

a+: This is still the same add mode, but its difference is that the same file also allows the reading of the file.

ab+: This mode is the same as add, but its difference is that besides being open in binary, it also allows the reading of the file.

Read a file in Python:

There are three ways to read a file:

1. read([n])

2. readlines()

3. readline([n])

It is important to note that the letter *n* enclosed between keys and parentheses will warn the file about the number of bytes that the file must read and interpret.

Read([ ]) Method

```
Ejemplos ▷  ❖ elif.py ▷ ...
1    func = open("D:\\filepython\\funcpythonfile.txt","w")
2    func.read()
```

If we want to add a certain amount of bytes to our file, all we have to do is to write the number of bytes to read inside the parenthesis.

For example, we want to add six bytes; then we write func.read(6)

Readlines() Method

Readlines method is responsible for reading only one line of our file; this way, he will be able to return in form of a string the bytes he has read. It is important to mention that this method is not capable of reading more than one line of code, even if the number "n" of bytes is higher than the bytes on that line.

Its syntax is very similar to the *Read()* method.

```
1    func = open("D:\\filepython\\funcpythonfile.txt","w")
2    func.readlines()
```

There are many types of attributes that we will face when opening our files and those help us to know more about the files.

File.name: This attribute returns the name of the file which we are going to work with
File.mode: This attribute returns the ways of access with which we have opened the file

File.close: This attribute returns a Boolean. It returns as True, if the file on which we were working on is closed, and a False if it is still open.

Close() Function

The *close()* function is the one through which we delete any information that has been written or stored on the memory of our program; this way, we can proceed to close a file properly. Even though there are other ways for closing files, like reassigning an object from a file to another, this function is the most common.

The syntax of the *close()* function is the following:

```
1   func = open("D:\\filepython\\funcpythonfile.txt","w")
2   func.readlines()
3   func.close()
```

What Is a Buffer?

A buffer is like a temporary file that will contain a fragment of the data (That composes the files of our operating system) on the ram memory. Usually, we make use of buffers when we are working with a file whose storage size is unknown.

If the size of our RAM memory is less than the size of the file that our program will occupy, the processing unit won't be able to execute the program properly.

It is really important to know the size of the buffer since it will indicate the storage size available at the moment of using our file.

The io.DEFAULT_BUFFER_SIZE function is the one that will show us the size of our file in a determined program

```
1    import io
2        print("Default buffer size: "io.DEFAULT_BUFFER_SIZE)
3        file= open("Funcfile.txt", mode="w", buffering=4)
4        print(file.line_buffering)
5    file_contents=file.buffer
6    for line in file_contents
7        print(line)
```

Errors

When working with files, we will have an optional string. That string will specify the way about how we will handle the errors of coding that may arise in our program.

Those errors can only be handled and managed on files .txt

Ignore_errors()= This control statement will ignore the comments that have a wrong format.

Stric_errors()= This control statement will generate a

subclass or an UnicodeError error type in case that there is any kind of fail, mistake or error at the code of the file we are working with.

Encoding

Now we'll talk about string encoding, which we often use when we're working with data storage. But what are data storages? This is just to say that they are the representation in characters of the coding; your system is based on bits and bytes in one common character.

The string encoding is expressed in the following way:

```
1    string.encode(enconding="UTF-8", errors= "strict")
```

Newline

When we talk about the newline mode we refer to the mode that controls the functionalities of creating a new line, these can be: '\r', " ", none,'\n', and '\r\n'.

Newline statements are universal, and newlines are universal and can be seen as a way of interpreting the text sequences of our code.

1.The end-of-line sentence in UNIX: "\n".

2.The end-of-line sentence in Windows: "\r\n"?

3.The end-of-line sentence in Max OS: "\r".

Handling files with the "OS" module

The management of files through the "OS" module gives us many benefits when performing certain operations that depend on the operating system, such as starting a process, listing the layers of our files and finalize processes. To do this, we will rely on a series of methods that make much easier the tools of file management; these are:

os.remove(file_name): The remove(file_name) method of the module will be in charge of removing a file from the program we are working with.

os.path.getsize(): The module path.getsize() method will show us the size of a file in bytes, based on a file that has been previously elapsed.

os.rename(current,new): The rename(current, new) method of the module will take care of renaming the file we are working with.

xlsx Files:

These files are those that allow us to work in spreadsheets as if we were working in a windows Excel program; if our operating system is windows, these files will have a much smaller weight to a file of type xlsx in another operating system.

This type of file is very useful when we work with databases, numerical calculations, graphics and any other type of automation.

To start working with this type of file, we will have to install the necessary library and this is done through the command "pip3 install openpyxl" in the Python terminal.

Once our command has been executed, the openpyxl module will be installed in our Python file.

Now we will create our first xlsx file:

```
from openpyxl import workbook
    def xlsxdoc()
    wb= workbook
    sheet= wb.active
    name= "docxlsx.xlsx"
    wb.save(name)
xlsxdoc()
```

In this example we can see that we have created our file by importing the *workbook* function, which belongs to the openpyxl module, then we have added our parameters such as: "wb" assigning the workbook function and declaring that it will be our working document, then we add the name and save the file.

Add information to the file with the xlsx module:

To add information to our file, we will rely on the append function

```
1   from openpyxl import workbook
2       def xlsxdoc()
3       wb= workbook
4       sheet= wb.active
5       message= ("Python","Document")
6       sheet.append = message
7       name= "docxlsx.xlsx"
8       wb.save(name)
9   xlsxdoc()
```

Now, to our document docxlsx.xlsx, we have added a tuple that contains words like Python, document. Once we have created this, the append function will allow us to add the information contained in the tuple in a message.

Here we can see that the main function of *append()* is to admit iterable data such as tuples.

Read documents in xlsx:

```
1    from openpyxl import workbook
2    name= "docxlsx.xlsx"
3    def xlsxdoc()
4        wb= load_workbook(name)
5        sheet = wb.active
6        file1 = sheet["A1"]
7        file2 = sheet["A2"]
8        print(file1)
9        print(file2)
10   xlsxdoc()
```

To read an xlsx file, we will only need to import the *load_workbook* class and know the name of the file we are going to work with. It is also very important that the files are in the same folder in which the program is stored; otherwise, an automatic error will be generated.

Once this is done, we will specify the object to work with, and we will ask for the information we need to read in order to finally print and compile it.

Handling PDF files

Now we are going to learn to work with "Portable Document Format" files, which have grown significantly over the years and have taken a place of great importance in educational and work environments, this due to their endless benefits that these have, allowing these types of files to add access keys in order to protect a very important document and even add their own watermark to prevent possible plagiarism in the future.

PDF files can be opened from any device (computer, tablet, smartphone), and their weight is much lower compared to the weight of a common txt document, as these pdf files are automatically compressed once they are created. Therefore, the ability to edit an already created PDF file is very complicated by its level of protection.

Other noteworthy data is that these documents can be viewed from any device, as it is not necessary to have a specific program; also the weight of the files is much lower because these texts are compressed unlike Word documents, which is why in this chapter we will only learn to create such files.

First, we will download the library with the command "Pip3 install fpdf".

```
1    from fpdf import FPDF
2    fpdfdoc = PDF()
3    pdfdoc.set_font("Arial", "B", 14)
4    pdfdoc.add_page()
5    pdfdoc.cell(10, 20, "PDF Document", 9, 8, "C")
6    pdfdoc.output("PDF Document", "F")
```

With this simple example, we can observe the level of difficulty of working with a PDF file. We observe that we need a lot of commands, we will start with the FPDF class of the fpdf library, we will create our pdfdoc object (it is recommended that the names have coherence to avoid confusion, but it can be of your preference), this will be our pdf document.

Once we have created this, we are going to customize what is format, size and font style through the *set_font* command.

Next, we will add a page with the command *add_page()*, this will be the page on which we are going to write since the function *fdpf* is not able to create a blank page by default. Here we are going to insert the information with the help of the *cell()* function; this will contain the width and height that our cell will occupy.

Finally, let's save our document with the command *output()* together with the arguments that accompany it to store our file with its name. It is important that it contains the ".fpdf" so that the program understands that we want a pdf file, and we end up with an F string.

Handling of BIN Type Files

As we have been learning, in Python, there is a great variety of file types, which are not exclusively text files, some are processed line by line and others are going to be processed byte by byte, giving a different meaning to the program. It is important that these files are manipulated in their correct format because otherwise, this will generate an error.

The files of the Binary format are nothing more than adding a *b* in the parameters of our mode.

```
1    with open("fileofpython", "wb") as f:
2        byte = f.read(7)
3        while byte:
4            byte = f.read(4)
```

When we are going to manage a file whose type is binary, it is very important that we have in mind that we must know very well the current position in which the data we need is, so that we can modify it correctly.

If we do not know the current position of the data, the *file.tell()* function will indicate the number of bytes that have elapsed since we started with our file.

If we want to modify the current position of our file, we will use the function *file.seek*(star,from) since this will allow us to move to a

certain number of bytes from the beginning to the end of the file.

Chapter 9: Exceptions

Exceptions can be defined as errors that occur during the execution of the program. When the syntax of the code is written correctly, and during its execution, something unexpected happens, an error that does not allow to execute the line of code where the error is manifesting and the subsequent ones.

An unexpected error in the line of codes could be considered important depending on how big is the program we are handling; if we have a program of hundreds or thousands of lines of codes, when the program starts to execute, the following happens, we already know that the execution flow goes in a top-bottom direction starting with the first line of codes and goes down with the code or the rest of the lines of code; if the execution flow finds in its way with a line of codes that generates an error that as we mentioned before we have not foreseen, what is going to happen is that the rest of the lines of code are not going to be able to execute.

In this case, the program will fail when reaching the code line where we get to the unexpected error.

And probably, the following lines are not going to be able to be executed, and they may have important information for our program, and therefore, we want it to be carried out. That is why it is important to know how to solve these exceptions that can be presented to us.

Several examples could be presented at runtime; below, we will mention the most commonly used to explain this type of errors:

```python
1   den=int(input("den="))
2   num=int(input("num="))
3   result=str(num/den)
4   print("Result="+result)
5
```

When seeing the code, there are several possibilities that an error may arise, since you can enter values that are not integers, therefore, the *int()* function could generate an error, on the other hand, there is the possibility that an error occurs in the division, because the denominator can be equal to zero, generating an error of division between zero.

What Is the Possible Solution to This Problem?

These problems can be solved by doing what is known as "Capture or exception control", which basically consists of telling our code to try to perform the instruction and in the case that it cannot perform it, that at least the rest of the program can be executed.

The line that has generated the error of the previous example is a line of codes that do not generate a division by zero, and this is an unexpected error. Perhaps this line will never be executed, but applying "capture or exception control", will allow us that the rest of the lines of code that follows after this one can be executed successfully.

The first thing we must do is discover where the error is and how it is called and this part is very important to determine, since, if we do not find the line of code where the error is being generated, we will not be able to apply the necessary instruction to solve the problem.

In the case of the example, it generates a division by zero, the description of the error would be: ZeroDivisionError: divisionbyZero, for example.

Once identified the instruction that generates the error, this instruction must be put inside a "Try" block that means "try", and is applied just before the instruction that generates the error, is there where we will introduce the word "try", followed by the instruction that generates the error and then the word "except", followed by the name of the error. Following with the previous serious example: "ZerodivisionError" and within this clause, we can add what we want the program to do, for example, we can add "can not be divided by zero", and after the error message what we want to return, return "erroneous operation".

In conclusion we can eliminate and solve the error, with "try", and in this way we are telling the system to try to make this division or the instruction that is generating the error, and if it does not succeed, it will execute what is inside the "except" that for this example is the message that says "cannot be divided by zero", this process is something similar to what happens with the sentences "if" and "else".

This way we control an exception, maybe we can't fix the error, but we will be able to keep executing the rest of the lines of code that follow after this error and execute the program.

```python
exception.py ✕

1    try:
2        den=int(input("den="))
3        num=int(input("num="))
4        result=str(num/den)
5        print("Result="+result)
6    except:
7        print("An error was obtained")
8    finally:
9        print("The program is over")
```

We can also capture several exceptions, that is, we can get with errors of the type division by zero as explained above, but also can happen other types of errors, for example, suppose that the program asks us to enter a numerical value and add a different value to a numerical one such as a text. Obviously it will throw us an error, and we are going to do the same as in the previous case and in this case we would be in the presence of an error "ValueError", and in this case we must capture several exceptions, we begin again locating the line that contains the error or lines of codes that originate this error of value.

The solution is to roll these two lines of code with another "try" block, "except", where we specify the error we want to capture, as it was done in the previous case, with the difference that now we are capturing two lines of codes and then we generate and execute the code.

For a code to be executed, we always have the alternative of introducing the code inside a "finally" clause, if an exception is captured or not when applying the "finally" clause, there is no need for there to be any "except".

Now, no matter what happens inside "try", the "finally" instruction will always be executed, whether something good happens or not.

Chapter 10: Other Topics

Python and Serial Communication in Electronic Devices

If you want to specialize in electronics, a topic that you must handle very well is serial communication, as it allows you to establish a communication between devices, through a set of logic signals, being a 1 a value of 5 volts and a 0 a ground value or 0 volts. The way to send data is sequential, bit by bit, they can only have two values, 0 or 1, as previously said.

There are several serial communication protocols, but in this case, we will focus on two, which are the most used at present. The RS-232 and the RS485. The first is used almost everywhere; moreover, all computers have an RS232 port, which has twenty-five pins and is designed to communicate a large amount of data at a short distance. On the other hand, we have the RS-485, mainly designed for industrial communications, over long distances and its technology is based on transmitting binary data, by bits, but by means of two wires, so as to inhibit the electromagnetic effects of large wires.

Some of the projects that you could do with serial communication and Python are device automation, equipment instrumentation, real-time measuring devices, image processing, among other things. Therefore, we can assure you that this tool is extremely useful for your professional life.

The library that we will use in this case is PySerial; for its installation, we use the console and the command:

Pip3 install pyserial

With this library, we will be able to do the serial communication, from configuring the communication ports to receiving and sending ASCII data through the ports.

For more information, visit the library documentation:

https://pyserial.readthedocs.io/en/latest/

Python and the Databases

Databases are widely used today, since they are everywhere, from the web pages to the data stored by banks, so this area is very important today, even more, is an area of study for computer engineers.

But you don't need to be an engineer to venture into this area, since you can imagine a database as an excel sheet, which will be filled, depending on the type of item you want to enter the database. For example, imagine that you need a database of soccer balls, since you have the balls of the World Cups of 2002, 2006, 2018, as well as several international tournaments, so you need a database to know the inventory of them.

Well, to design this, we need the knowledge of a very simple programming language, but a little new for us, as is SQL, which is responsible for programming the databases, but, in fact, the syntax is very simple, and to program this does not take much time, a few minutes I would say.

To make use of python databases, we recommend

using the PyMySQL library. To make use of it, use the following command in the terminal:

Pip3 install pymysql

After that, you will be able to design your own databases and work with them, either for your work or for your personal use.

For more information about this library and how to use it, visit the following link about your documentation:

https://pymysql.readthedocs.io/en/latest/

Python and Graphical Interfaces

This is another topic of vital importance for Python, since many times, you will imagine that it is not only to make a program and that the results are seen in the console, because sometimes it is necessary to make a program with a graphical interface, in such a way that the users are able to see a work a little more elaborated. An example of this can be to design a calculator and it cannot be just coded to show it in the terminal, because it is necessary to make an interface that shows the keys of the numbers, operations, the result because it is much easier for users to use that than a terminal. The same interfaces can have buttons, images, shapes, inputs, etc..

For this case of graphical interface design, there are many libraries, but the simplest is Tkinter, which has a cumulus of properties that allow us to make good and beautiful interfaces and if you are a little more advanced in the area of programming, you could use another library such as PyQT5, the same has some similarity to C++.

For the use of Tkinter, it is not necessary to import the library of them as in the other two previous items, but what you should use when making code is obviously import the module through the import sentence, as follows:
From tkinter import *

For more information, visit their official documentation page:
https://docs.python.org/3/library/tk.html

Already knowing all these topics that can cover Python, you can imagine the potential you have in your hands, we can only tell you that the limits are in your mind, get to work and program what you want.

Conclusion

Thank you for making it through to the end of *Python for Beginners: A Step by Step Crash Course to Learn Smarter the Fundamental Elements of Python Programming, Machine Learning, Data Science and Tools, Tips and Tricks of This Coding Language*, let's hope it was informative and able to provide you with all of the tools you needed to achieve your goal of becoming a programmer.

The next step is to start programming with all the tools we provided you in this book in order to keep improving your programming skills. As you could have seen, programming is not a very hard activity, but it is really important to practice since if this is not done, things can be forgotten.

If you have any doubts about anything, read it again and see the examples, imagine one of your own and code it in order to better understand the functioning of each statement and elements.

As you could see in the last chapter, Python can be used for a lot of things, it is almost used on everything, so, if you are good at a certain area or profession, now that you know how to code, you should be able to develop programs that make your daily activities easier. If you are an economist, you can make a program that calculates the taxes or fees of certain amounts of money, and if you are a doctor, you can make a program that calculates the amount of solution needed at the hospital. Those are just simple examples of what you can do and reach with this programming language

Finally, if you found this book useful in any way, a review on Amazon is always appreciated!

Linux for Beginners

An Introduction to Linux Programming Basics for Hackers, Its Operating System, Command-Line and Networking, Including Effective Strategies, Tips and Tricks to Learn How It Works

Jason Knox

Introduction

Congratulations on purchasing *Linux for Beginners:An Introduction to Linux Programming Basics for Hackers, Its Operating System, Command-Line and Networking, Including Effective Strategies, Tips and Tricks to Learn How It Works,* and thank you for doing so.

The following chapters will discuss all of the things that you need to know in order to get started with the Linux operating system. There are a lot of options out there for operating systems, but most of us are going to focus our attention on how to work with options like Mac and Windows. But while those are the most common options out there to work with, many people are starting to see the benefits of working with Linux. This operating system is more secure, easier to work with, and can provide us with the power that we need to get a lot of things done in the process. This guidebook is going to spend some time looking at how this will work for our needs, as well.

Inside this guidebook, we are going to take a look at the Linux system and how we are able to use this for some of our own needs as well. We will start out with a look at some of the neat things that come with Linux, the benefits of working with this one compared to some of the other options. This will help us to see what this is one of the best options to work with and will ensure that we are going to be able to get all of the benefits that we are looking for in no time at all.

Then it is time to move on to some of the things that we are able to do when we are working on the Linux system as well. We will explore first how to set up our own virtual box, and how this helps us to work with the Linux operating system, without getting rid of the traditional operating system found on our computers. While you can choose to just switch completely over to the Linux operating system if you would like many programmers are more comfortable with having this as an add-on and then working with their traditional operating system as well. This is what the VirtualBox can help us to accomplish.

We are also able to move on to some of the commands that are going to be so prevalent when we handle some of our work with Linux. We will spend a good deal of time looking at the basics of Linux and how we are able to use these commands to get a lot of things done in a short amount of time, as well. These commands will help us to create some of the files that we need, change them, and so much more, which can make the Linux system easier to use overall.

This is just a start to what we are going to look at when it is time to work with this guidebook and all of the neat things that are possible with the Linux operating system. We will look at how we can grant the right permissions to get this to work the way that we would like, how to handle some of the different shells that are present, and even a look at how to use the Fish shell. There are a lot of other options in shells that we are able to explore when it comes to using this kind of operating system. But when it comes to the ease of use that we are going to see, and all of the power that comes with it, you will find that Fish is one of the best options to choose from.

In addition, we are going to take a look at how to keep the security of your system intact, how to pick out the right text editor, along with some of the basics of using some of the most common text editors that we are able to focus on. And then, we will end the guidebook with a look at how the Linux system is able to work along with some of the hacking that you may want to practice to keep your system safe. There are a lot of reasons to work with Linux, but many people choose to work with this because it allows them to learn some of the basics of hacking in an easy and efficient manner.

There are a lot of great things that we are able to work with the Linux operating system, especially when it is compared to some of the other operating systems that are out there. But it is still not one that many people are familiar with, and that causes them to miss out on it quite a bit. With this in mind, make sure to check out this guidebook and learn a bit more about how the Linux operating system can work for your needs.

There are plenty of books on this subject on the market, thanks again for choosing this one! Every effort was made to ensure it is full of as much useful information as possible; please enjoy it!

Chapter 1: What is the Linux Operating System?

Before we are able to get into some of the cool codes and more that we are able to do with the Linux system, we first need to take a look at what Linux is. While this may not quite have the name recognition that we are going to find with some of the other operating systems out there, like Mac and Windows, you will find that Linux is creating its own niche and becoming more popular each day. That is why we need to spend some time learning more about this and what we are able to do with it overall.

From cars to smartphones, home applications and supercomputers, enterprise servers to home desktops, this operating system is going to be all around us. This is a newer operating system in some respects, and it came out around the mid-1990s. Since that time, it has been able to reach a big user-base that is found throughout the globe. In fact, we are going to find that Linux is found, in one form or another, all around us.

Linux is really versatile and a great option to work with, so you will find that it is going to be inside a lot of the options that you use on a regular basis. For example, many phones are going to have Linux inside of them. In addition, it is going to be found in thermostats, in cars, Roku devices, televisions, cars and so much more. And it is also responsible for running much of what we are able to find on the Internet, so that is a big plus as well.

But, outside of being one of the platforms of choice to help out with a lot of the work that needs to be done with embedded systems, servers and even desktops that are found throughout the world, Linux is actually going to have a lot of benefits that we are able to rely on as well. For example, when it is compared to some of the other operating systems that are out there, it is one of the most reliable, worry-free and secure options that you are able to choose.

With some of this in mind, it is time for us to go through and learn a bit more about some of the parts that come with this operating system, and how we are able to use these for our own benefit as well. Here is all of the information that you need to know as someone who is new to the Linux platform.

What is Linux?

The first thing that we need to take a look at is the fact that Linux is going to be an operating system. It is similar to the operating systems that we use like Mac OS, iOS and Windows. In fact, one of the most popular platforms that is found on the planet, Android, is going to be powered thanks to the Linux operating system.

To break this down, the operating system is simply going to be a type of software that is going to be able to manage all of the resources of the hardware that are associated with your laptop or desktop. To keep it simple, the operating system is going to help manage all of the communication that happens between the hardware and the software. If you did not have an operating system in place, then the software would not be able to function the way that you would like.

You will find that, just like some of the other operating systems that are out there, the Linux operating system is going to come in with a few different pieces that we need to work with. Some of these are going to include:

1. Bootloader: This is going to be the software that is able to manage the boot process on our computer. For most users, this is going to just be the splash screen that is going to pop up and then will go away when you are first booting up into the operating system.
2. Kernel: This is going to be the one piece of the whole that is called Linux. This is going to be the core of our system and it is responsible for managing the memory peripheral devices and CPU. The kernel is going to be the bottom level that we will find with our operating system.
3. Init system: This is going to be one of the subsystems that are going to bootstrap the user space, and then it will be in control of the daemons. One of the most widely used of these is going to be a system, which is also sometimes seen as the most controversial of them. This is going to be the system that is responsible for booting up the operating system, once the initial booting is handed over from the initial bootloader that we use.

4. Daemons: These are going to be some of the background services. It could include options like scheduling, sound and printing, but you can move them around to fit your needs. They are either going to start up when you do a boot of the system, or after you have had a chance to log into the desktop.

5. Graphical server: This is going to be the sub-system that will display all of the different graphics that you want on the monitor. It is going to be referred to as X or the x server.

6. Desktop environment: This is going to be the piece of the operating system that you are actually going to spend time interacting with. There are going to be a lot of options for this kind of environment that we are able to choose from, including Cinnamon, Pantheon Enlightenment and more. Each of these environments is going to include some of the applications that you need built-in, including the games, web browsers, configuration tools, file managers and more.

7. Applications: The desktop environment that you choose is not going to come with a ton of applications for you to choose from. Instead, it

is going to be necessary for you to go out and search for the software titles that you want, and then you can find them and install them for your needs. For example, Ubuntu Linux is going to have what is known as the Ubuntu Software Center, which is going to help you go through thousands of apps, and then install the ones that you like the most, from one centralized location.

Why Should I Use Linux?

This is one of the first questions that a lot of people are going to ask when they first hear about the Linux system overall. They may be curious as to why they should learn a completely new computing environment when the operating system that is already on their computer and was shipped to them when they ordered the device is working just fine. Would it really be worth their time to learn a new one and see how it works?

To help us to answer this question, it is important to answer a few other questions to give us a good idea of what the Linux system can do for us that our traditional operating system is not able to do. For example, does the operating system that you are currently using actually work just fine? Or are you constantly dealing with a lot of obstacles like malware, viruses, slowdowns, costly repairs, licensing fees and crashes all of the time?

If you find that these are things that you are dealing with on a regular basis, especially once you have had the computer for some time, then you may find that the perfect platform for you to use to prevent some of this is going to be the Linux system. It is one of the operating systems that has evolved to become one of the most reliable out of all of them. And when you are able to combine all of that reliability with zero costs, you will end up with the perfect solution for the platform that you need.

That is right, you are able to get the Linux system and all of the benefits that come with it all together for free. And you are able to take the Linux operating system and install it on as many computers as you would like, and use it as much as you would like, without having to worry about how much it will cost to use, how much the software is, and you also don't need to worry about server licensing.

We can also take a look at the cost of adding on a server in Linux compared to the Windows Server 2016. The price of the Windows option for a standard edition is going to be about $882 if you purchase it right from Microsoft and not from another part. This is not going to include any of the Client Access Licenses, and the licenses for all of the other software that you decide are important and need to be run in this as well, such as a mail server, web server and a database.

For example, the single user who works with the CAL on the Windows system is going to cost you about $38. But if you need to have a lot of users, that cost is going to go up pretty quickly. If you need to work with ten people on the server, then you are going to end up with $380 just to do that part. And that is just with the software licensing that you would like to get done.

But it is a bit different when we are working with the Linux server. For the Linux option, you will be able to get all of that for free and it is also easy for you to install. In fact, being able to go through and add in a web server with all of the features, including a database server, is just going to take a few clicks or a few commands to get done.

This alone, especially for some of the bigger businesses out there, will be enough to win others over to this operating system. But there are a few other benefits that are going to show up as well. This operating system is going to work and keep out the troubles, for as long as you choose to work with it. And it is often able to fight off issues of ransomware and malware and even viruses better than some of the others. And you will not need to reboot this all that often unless the kernel has to be updated, and this is often only done every few years.

If you have ever been frustrated with the operating system that you are working with and how it may not always do what you would like, that means it may be time for you to work with the Linux operating system. It is going to have all of the benefits that we want and will also be free to use, no matter how many computers you decide to hook it up to along the way.

Open Sourced

Another thing that we are going to enjoy when it is time to work with the Linux system is that it is open-sourced. This means that it is going to be distributed under this source license so that you are able to work with it in the manner that you would like. Open source is going to be useful for a number of reasons, but we will find that there are a few key tenants that we need to focus on, include:

1. You will find that you have the freedom to run the program, no matter what the purpose is.
2. You will find that you have the freedom to study and learn more about how this program works and what you can make any of the changes to it that you wish along the way.
3. You have the freedom to redistribute copies so that you are able to use it more than once for your own needs or to provide it to your neighbor who would like to use it as well.
4. You will find that you have the freedom to make some modifications to it in the manner that you would like, and then you can also distribute copies of these modifications to others.

There are going to be crucial points to understand when it comes to working with the Linux system and understanding more about the community that is going to work to create this kind of platform in the first place. Without a double, this is going to be an operating system that is by the people and for the people. These tenants are also going to be a big factor in why people are going to choose to work with this kind of operating system compared to some of the others. It is all about freedom, and freedom of use, and the freedom of choice, and the freedom to not have to worry about a bunch of crazy rules and other issues along the way.

What is a Distribution?

The next thing that we need to take some time to look at is the distribution part that comes with Linux. Linux is going to come with a number of versions that are going to suit the type of user you would like. Whether you are someone who is brand new to working with this or you have worked with programming and other similar things for a long time, you are sure to find the type of Linux that is going to be able to match all of your needs that you would like.

All of the versions that are available for Linux are going to be known as the distributions. And nearly all of these distributions that come from Linux are ones that we are able to download for free, burn over to a disk or a USB drive and install on as many different devices that we would like.

There are a ton of distributions of Linux that are popular, and it is often going to depend on what you are hoping to do with the operating system in the first place. For example, you could find Kali Linux, LINUX MINT, MANJARO, OpenSUSE, ELEMENTARY OS, SOLUS, FEDORA, ANTERGOS, UBUNTU and DEBIAN. And there are a lot of other options based on your own personal preferences along the way as well.

You will find that each of the distributions above is going to come with a different take on what the desktop should be doing during this time. Some are going to opt for some modern user interfaces, and these would include options like GNOME and Elementary OS. And then there are a few that are going to stick with a desktop environment that is more traditional and maybe closer to what we are working with in the past.

Of course, this doesn't mean that we need to leave the server behind here. For this arena, we have a lot of options like the SUSE Enterprise Linux, Centos, Ubuntu Server and Red Hat Enterprise Linux.

Now, some of the server distributions that we talked about above are going to be free. This may include the CentOS or the Ubuntu Server. And then there are going to be the other two that have a price with those. The main difference is that the ones that cost a bit are going to provide some support, so if this is important to you, then you should consider the pricing and go with those as well. You can get a lot of benefits out of Ubuntu and the free options as well, so do your research and figure out which one is going to meet your needs the best.

Which Distribution Is Best?

Before we end this, though, we need to take a look at which distribution is going to be the best. There are a lot of great ones out there that we are able to work with depending on what matters the most for our needs. And sometimes it is going to be based on the skills that we have, what we would like to do with this process and more. Some of the things that we need to consider when it is time to pick a distribution to work with will include:

1. How skilled are you at using the computer and working with some command-line interfaces rather than the graphical interface?
2. Do you find that you prefer a standard or a modern desktop interface?
3. Would you rather work with a desktop or a server?

If you would rather not work with anything that is too complicated when it comes to your computer skills, then you would want to pick out one of the distributions that are present that are meant to work well for newbies of Linux. Ubuntu, Linux Mint and Elementary OS are great options to work with. If you find that your skills in using the computer extend into the above-average range, then there are a few others that offer some more skills and features, including Fedora and Debian.

Of course, if you are someone who has spent a lot of time on computers and have been able to spend quite a bit of your time working on these along the way, then you can take it up to the next level. The best distribution for this is going to be Gentoo. And if you would really like to have some kind of challenge, you are able to go through and build up your own distribution of Linux and often working with Linux from scratch is a good option.

If you want to make sure that you are working with a server-only distribution option, you will need to decide if you would like to work the command line only option or if you would like to stay with the desktop interface. The Ubuntu Server, for example, is not going to install that GUI interface, so if that is something that you want to work with, then you will need to pick another distribution to make things work.

When you are working without the GUI interface, for example, then that means that you are not going to be bogged down with all of the graphics that need to load up when you are starting the server. But keep in mind that you have to work with the command line in Linux so that you can get into the parts of the system that you want. If you are not good with the command line or doing some of the codings that go with this, then you may want to consider going with another option as well.

The nice thing, though, is that if you would like to work with the Ubuntu Server, but you would also like to have the graphical parts there, then there is a GUI package that you are able to install to make it work for any programming that you would like. System administrators will also want to view a distribution while looking at some of the features that are going to come with it to ensure they are able to do some of the actions that they would like.

For example, would you like to work with a server-specific distribution that will offer you, right out of the box, all of the different features and parts that you need for your server? If this is something that sounds good for you, then you may want to go with an option like CentOS. Or, would it be better for you to work with a desktop distribution and then add in the pieces that you need as time goes on? If this is something that sounds more appealing to you, then Ubuntu or Debian may be better choices to go with.

As we can see, there are a lot of different parts that we are able to work with along the way when it comes to working on the Linux system. You will find that there are many ways that Linux is already being used in the world, even if we didn't realize it as much in the beginning. And we are able to take this and utilize it for some of our own needs with the help of adding this operating system to our computers and using it on a daily basis, or to help out with things like coding and hacking as we need. When you are ready to learn more about this great operating system, make sure to check out the rest of this guidebook to get started.

Chapter 2: How to Install Virtual Machines?

The next thing that we need to talk about is the use of a VirtualBox on our system to make sure that we can handle some of the work that we need to finish with Linux. VirtualBox is going to be one of the virtual machines that, first developed by the company of Sun Microsystems, is now under the ownership of Oracle. It is able to stimulate a separate computer and each virtual machine is going to come with its own operating system, applications and a lot of other things that you need to do for the coding.

VirtualBox is going to be a good option to work with when you would like to test out a lot of operating systems. For our needs, we are going to use it in order to add the Linux operating system on a Mac OS or Windows operating system. By using the Linux operating system in this manner, you don't need to make any permanent changes to the system that you are currently using. This makes it easier to use Linux just when you want to, and then switch over to one of the other options if that is what you would like to do.

Keep in mind you do have the option of using Linux as the main operating system on your computer if you would like. You can go through and take the other operating system off your computer if that works the best for your needs and can help you get things done. But many times, people want to work with Linux for some specific needs, so they will want to work with the VirtualBox to make this happen while keeping their traditional operating system in place.

With this in mind, we are going to spend some time looking at how we are able to install this VirtualBox program on our Windows or Mac system along the way. We are going to start out with installing it on our Windows system:

1. Go to the download page for VirtualBox and then look for the latest version that has been released at the time you visit. Click on this link.
2. When you are redirected to the next page, you want to look specifically for the file that is going to end in .exe and then download this. Pay attention to the location where you save this on your computer so that you can find it later on.

3. Once the installer has gone through the downloading process, you can go and find the .exe file and double-click on it. You can then follow the instructions on the screen in order to install this onto Windows. Keep in mind that when you are doing this that you may end up losing some of the network connections during this time because the virtual network adapters are being installed.

4. Now you need to go through the process of rebooting your computer. And when you do this, you will be able to find the VirtualBox in your own apps to use. From here, we are able to run this and install any of the other operating systems of our choice.

That is all that we need to do in order to get this whole program downloaded on our Windows system. But we are also able to do a similar process when it is time to work with doing this on a Mac operating system. The steps that we need to use to get this to happen includes:

1. Go to the download page for VirtualBox and then download the latest version of this app for the Mac.
2. Save the .dmg to a file location that you will easily be able to remember. You also want to make sure that you download the OS X hosts version.
3. When this download is done, you will want to locate the file and then install it with the help of the executable file.
4. When all of this is done, you are able to reboot your computer, and then it is time to use the VirtualBox.

Another thing that we are able to work with is how we can install this Linux operating system with the help of an image for VirtualBox. There are a few steps that we are able to use in order to get this to work in the manner that we would like. Again, we are going to work with the Windows system. After you have gone through the other steps that we did in the last part for downloading VirtualBox on Windows, it is time to work with downloading the disk image for Ubuntu Linux including:

1. First, if you do not have the BitTorrent client installed on your computer, you should take some time to install this right now. BitTorrent is going to be a P2P application that is going to allow us to have downloads from other users, which is going to really ease the loading that happens on the Ubuntu servers.
2. Now head to the Ubuntu release website and then make sure that you click on the latest release version to download it. You do not want to click on any of the links for a Desktop CD. You will find a full list of links that are at the bottom of this page, but you want to make sure to click on the one with the .iso.torrent extension. Download this somewhere that you are going to remember later on.
3. Then we can copy this to a bootable USB that we are able to use for our needs.

Something that we need to keep in mind here is that if you are working with an installation of WinRAR, it is going to automatically associate itself with the file that you downloaded and will ask if you would like to use this to help extract the contents. You DO NOT want to use this to extract the file, so don't do this.

Before we move on to the other steps that we need to use here, you need to make sure that we back up the contents of our hard drive somewhere that is safe. It is highly likely that you are going to lose everything if you do not go through and do this step. Then the other steps that we need to work with on this system will include:

1. You will want to open up the VirtualBox from the start menu before clicking on New. This is going to help us to open up the New Virtual Machine Wizard.

2. Click on Next and then provide a name for this virtual machine. Calling it something easy to remember is usually the best bet.

3. If you end up having more than 1 GB of RAM available to use on your computer, allocate one-quarter maximum to the machine that we are making. If you have less, then you will need to stick with the recommendations of VirtualBox here. Then click on Next.

4. When you are read, you will want to click on Create New Hard Disk before clicking on Next.

5. Click on Next another time and you will end up on a screen where you are able to set up the

type of hard drive that you would like to use. Our goal here is to choose Fixed-Size Storage.

6. If you intend to add in some software or you would like to install some really large files in this, then you will want to make sure there is some buffer here. Then click on Create.

7. Once we have been able to create the virtual hard drive, you will then need to add in the .iso image that we downloaded earlier. You can do this by clicking on Settings, then Storage and then on CD/DVD device.

8. Where there is the word Empty, there should be a folder icon that we are able to click on.

9. Choose the .iso that we went through and downloaded it already and then click on OK from here.

10. Now you can double-click on the virtual machine to get it to start up the way that you would like.

11. You will then be able to get a lot of instructions and warnings about using the guest operating system. You should take some time to read them and then mark them up so that they won't show up and interrupt again.

12. Give the system a bit of time to load up Ubuntu.

13. Before you are able to install Linux all of the ways, you first need to change up the BIOS settings on your computer. Usually, when you get the computer to start up, you will it the F1, F2, F12, Escape or Delete. You can restart your computer now and get into the BIOS settings and change up the boot option so that you boot from USB first.

14. Now it is time to plug the USB stick into the computer and do a reboot of the system again.

15. This is where we are going to see a screen that is blank, except for a few smaller logos on the bottom. Press on any key and a new screen is going to show up. Make sure to choose the language that you would like to work with.

16. Now we can click to Install Ubuntu. This is going to get the installer to start. Depending on the version, you may be asked to choose the language again.

17. This is where we will tick on the option so that we install the closed-source software as well.

18. Now you are going to be asked to connect back onto the Wi-Fi if this is not automatically done for you. You do not need to do this, and it honestly slows down the process that you are

doing, so skip it for now so that you can get it done.

19. This is where we are going to see three options. We want to click on the first one and then drag the slider to choose the sizes of the hard drive for both of these. This is going to help our drive be partitioned into two parts.

20. Then there will be a few questions that will show up on your screen. You can answer them to fit your needs.

21. Now we just need to wait a few minutes for Ubuntu to be installed, depending on the speed of your computer. This can sometimes take an hour to get it all done.

22. When this is done, you will need to reboot your computer and take the USB stick out of it. When you boot the computer up again, you should be in the Ubuntu environment as you would like.

If you went through and changed up the size of the partition that you were working within Windows, you are going to be asked to work on a disk check. This is not something that is necessary to work with, though. If you would like to do it, though, you can go back to Settings, then Storage and then CD/DVD and check that the entry is Empty again. This is going to help us out because it is going to eliminate any need for us to use the USB each time that we would boot up our computer.

From there, we are able to work with the Mac operating system and how we are able to go through this process as well. When you have finished up with the installation of the VirtualBox, it is time to download the iso to make this all work the way that we would like. The steps that we are able to use to make this happen includes:

1. First, we need to head to the download page and then click on the iso image for Mac. You will also want to choose your geographical location and then click on Begin Download. You want to make sure that you are saving the file rather than opening or mounting it.
2. When you get to this point, you will want to open up the VirtualBox and register it.
3. Now you are able to click on creating a new virtual machine. You can click on New to open up the wizard that you would like to work with, as well. Click on Next and then type in the name

that you would like to use for this virtual machine.

4. When you are asked, you will want to choose the Linux Ubuntu option for the operating system before licking on Net. Set the base memory as 384 MB and then click on Next.

5. When we are at this point, we need to click in order to create a new hard disk. This is going to be a disk that is going to take up some space on your existing drive. You need to make sure that there is enough memory for you to do this. Accept the default settings that are there and then click on Next.

6. At this time, the Create New Virtual Disk wizard is going to appear and you will want to click on the Next button. And then click on Dynamically Expanding Storage before clicking on Next again.

7. This is where we are going to choose where we would like to place the hard drive and how big we would like to have it. 2 TB is the maximum here, but for the most part, 8 GB will be enough. Click on Next when you are done with this and then on Finish.

8. When you get here, the framework is going to be ready, so you need to make sure that you have copied the iso to the bootable USB or DVD disk. Insert your USB or DVD. You can click on the CD/DVD and then tick for it to Mount this drive.

9. Click on your ISO Image File. Click on the folder beside the No Media and then drag your iso file onto it before clicking on Select and then on OK.

10. Click on Start, and then you will see a black screen show up. This is going to be the new session and everything you do now is going to happen on the virtual machine. If you would like to be able to change things back to Mac, you just have to click on the Command key on the left side of the space bar. Click OK.

11. When the Ubuntu screen shows up, you can double click to Install and then answer any of the questions that show up on the screen. When this is done, click on Forward and accept the default values that are there to make it easier before clicking on Forward.

12. Here we are able to input some of our own personal information, including a new password and a name for the machine. You can also

choose whether you would like to have this log in automatically or if you would like to have it protected by a password and then click on Forward.

13. Click on Install and then wait for a bit to give it time to load up.

14. When this installation is done, you will either be sent into it automatically, or you will need to use the password that you set up. This all depends on the way that you set it up in the beginning.

15. Ubuntu is going to spend some time checking for updates, so make sure to click on Install Updates and wait a few minutes. Then Reboot the Mac, and you are all ready to get things done.

Chapter 3: Understanding the Directory Structure of Linux

Now that we have more knowledge about how Linux is going to work and some of the steps that we need to take in order to set up the VirtualBox so we can get our own work done, it is time to take a look at some of the different parts of the directory of Linux. If you are planning on working with the Linux system and all that it has to offer, then we need to make sure that we understand some of the structure that comes with the directory of Linux.

If you are moving over to Linux from the Windows system, then you may find this directory a bit strange. There are also not going to be the drive letters because these will be replaced with other options. The FHS, or the File Hierarchy System, is going to define the file system structure when we are on Linux, but there are going to be a few other directories that have not been given their definition with this standard.

The first one is going to be the root directory. We are able to signify this with the (/) symbol. When you work with Linux, everything is going to be found under this directory, which is known as the root directory. This is going to be similar to what we find with C:/ in the Windows system, but there won't be the drive letters when you work with this.

Then we can go on to the /bin directory. This one is going to be known as the essential user binaries. This is a directory that is home to the programs or binaries that are going to be essential to the system being mounted in single-user mode. You would find that something like FireFox is going to be stored in the directory that is known as /usr/bin while some of the other system programs and utilities, like the bash shell, are going to be found in /bin. /

The /boot is going to be known as the static boot files. This is where the files that are needed to help make sure the system we are booting up will be found here. This could be the GRUB boot loader and the kernel files. The configuration files that you want to work with are going to be found in /etc. which will talk about further on in this guidebook.

Next on this list is going to be the /cdrom, which is the Mount Point for the CD-ROMs. This is a directory that we are not going to find under the standard of FHS but is still to be found in most of the operating systems. It is a temporary location for when you insert a CD-ROM into your computer.

/dev is the next option on the board, and this is going to be for the device files. Devices are going to be the exposed files that are on Linux, and this particular directory is going to come with several special files that are going to be representative of devices. These are not going to be the same kinds of files that we are used to working with, but they will look similar. For example, if you see the /dev/sda, it is going to be there to represent the initial SATA drive in your system. You will also find that there are a few pseudo devices that will come up here, which are basically going to be some virtual devices that are not going to hook up to any hardware in the process.

We talked about this one a bit before, but it is going to be the /etc. configuration files that we can use. This is where you will want to search when you are looking for your configuration files, and you will be able to do some editing with these on any text editor. However, we have to remember that only the configurations of the system are going to be found on this one. If you are going with some that are more user-specific, then you need to search for these on the home directory of the user.

The home folders or /home is where we are able to find the home folder for all of the users that we are working with. This is going to contain some of the data files, as well as the configuration files that are specific to the users on the system, and then each of the users will be the only ones who can write in these home folders. If you would like to make some modifications to the others, then you will need to become the root user so that you have the elevated permissions.

We can also work with the /lib directory, which is going to be the essential shared libraries. This is going to contain all of the libraries that the binaries are found in the /sbin and .bin need to work well.

Some of the other directories that we need to spend some time on when handling this kind of process will include:

1. /lost+found: These are going to be all of the files that are recovered. All of the file systems that you work with will have this kind of directory. If there is some reason that your system is going to crash, when you boot up again, a file system check will be done. If these corrupted files are found, they will be placed into this directory so that you are able to find them when needed for later.

2. /media: This is going to be the removable media. Here we are going to find all of the subdirectories, and this is also where some of the removable media is going to be mounted. For example, this will be where we find the USB, DVD or BD is going to be found. When each of these is mounted, you will find a new drive appearing, which allows us to access the media contents.

3. /mnt: This one is the temporary mount point. This is the place where the administrators are going to mount the temp file systems when they are in the process of using it.

4. /opt: This one is going to be for the optional packages. Here we are going to be able to find some of the subdirectories for the software

packages that you can optionally choose to work with. It is generally going to be used by the software that you are working with, but which is not going to follow the rules of the standard FSH.

5. /proc: This is going to be the Kernel and Process Files. This is going to be similar to what we find with the /dev directory because it is not going to have any files that are the standard. Instead of these standard files, it is going to have some of the special files that are going to be more representative of the process and the system information that we are working with.

6. /root: This is the root home directory. This is going to be the root user's home directory. Note it is not going to be located in something like /home/root, but instead, it is stored as just /root.

7. /run: This is going to be the application state files. This is going to be a bit newer, and it is going to provide us with a place for applications so that they are able to store their transient files, like the sockets and process IDs. These are not going to be stored in the file for /temp files

because this could delete some of the things that we need.

8. /sbin: This one is for System Administration Binaries. This is going to also contain some of the binaries that we need for the help of any system administration by the root user.

9. Selinux: You will find that this is going to be the particular Linux distro that you are able to use for security. The directory is going to contain all of the files that you need in order to work with SELinux. The directory is going to also hold onto all of the files that you need for this, as well. If you would like to work on the Ubuntu system and you see that this directory is there, remember that this is a bug in the program because Ubuntu is not going to use this, just Linux.

10. /srv: This is going to be some of the service data. This is a good place where we are able to find the data for some of the services that are provided by the system. If you were working with the server for Apache HTTP for the website you were creating, you would store all of the files for this website in this directory.

11. /tmp: This one is for the temporary files. This is where all of the temporary application files are going to be stored. When the system is ready to restart or reboot, these files are going to be deleted, and you will no longer be able to find them again.

12. /usr: This is going to contain the user binaries and some of the read-only data. Here you are going to be able to find files and applications that are going to be used by your users, rather than the system. For example, you may find some of the non-essential applications in this one, along with some of the binaries that are not necessary at this time.

13. /var: This is going to be for the variable data files. When you have the /usr as only readable, the /var is going to be writable. Here you are going to be able to find some of the log files and anything else that the user will be able to write out.

There are also a few different components that you are going to find when it is time to work with the Linux operating system. There are actually three main code bodies that are going to make Linux successful and will ensure that you are able to find some of the different codings that you would like to do with this process, as well. Some of the different components that we are able to see when it comes to working with the Linux system will include:

The kernel is first on the list. This is going to be the one that is in charge of the maintenance of all the abstractions of the Linux operating system, as well as the processes and the virtual memory that we are working with. This is going to be the center point for the operating system that we are working with, kind of like the spine of the system. Because of this, it is going to be the part that is responsible for the functionality that is required in order to run any process, as well as providing the system service that will give us some protected access to the hardware resources. Anything that is required for the operating system to run well will be done and handled by the kernel.

From there, we are able to work with what is known as the system libraries. These are going to be a set of functions that are important because they allow for some interrelation between the kernel and the applications. These are going to apply a lot of the functionality that we need with the operating system and it will not need to take away the rights or the privileges when it is time to handle the kernel code as well.

And finally, the third part that we need to focus on here is the system utilities. These are going to be the programs that we are able to use in order to execute specific managing tasks or the ones that are a bit more specialized. There are a few utilities that can be invoked just once in order to help initialize the features of our system and then configure them as needed. Others are going to be set up in a manner where they will run constantly, carrying out tasks like responding to the connections of the network, both the ones that come in and the ones that go out, accepting requests for logging on, or even taking the time to update all the necessary files and log records as well.

Chapter 4: The Commands You Need to Know in Linux

The next thing that we need to spend some time on when we work with the Linux system is some of the commands. The Linux system is going to work in a slightly different manner than what you will see when it is time to work with this operating system. Instead of having the graphics that you are able to work with and look through, you are able to work with this operating system with the help of the command prompt. This means that we need to know some of the commands and maybe a bit of coding, in order to get this set up in a manner that we are able to easily use.

That is why we are going to spend some time in this chapter looking at some of the more essential and basic commands in Linux, the ones that you will really need to learn more about in order to fire up this operating system and play along with it as well. As we go through the rest of this guidebook, you will find that knowing some of these commands can help you to get a better understanding of this operating system, and can make it easier to actually work with it when it is time. With this in mind, some of the different commands that we are able to work with when it comes to the Linux system includes:

The Listing Directories and Files

The first thing that we need to take a look at is the command of "ls." When you first get onto this operating system, you will find that you are on the home directory. This is going to come with the same name as you put into place for the username, and it is going to be where all of the subdirectories and personal files will be saved and easy to find. If you would like to be able to find out what the contents are of your home directory, you would just need to type in the following command to get it done:

% ls.

Now, it is possible that you will do this command; there will not be any files that are found in the directory. If there are none that are present there, then you are going to be returned right back to the prompt. Be aware that, using this command, you are only going to see the contents that are present but that do not have a name that starts with a dot.

In this operating system, if you have a file that starts with a dot, this means that the files are going to be hidden. This also means that there are going to be signs of important configuration information that is found in the file. The reason that they are hidden is that they are set up so that you should not touch them or mess with them.

If you would like to be able to see all of the files, including those with the dot, while still being found in the home directory, you will need to type in the following code to see these:

% ls -a

When we are able to use the coding above, you will find that all of the files, including the ones that are hidden up a bit, are going to be easy to see. Ls is going to be one of the commands that you are able to use for a lot of different things, and it is good for taking options and the above one is just a few of the options that you are able to work with. When you add on some of these different options, they are really going to change up how this command is able to work with.

Making Some Directories

The next command that we are able to work with is the mkdir option. To make a subdirectory of the home directory, which is able to hold onto the files that you want, you are able to work with the mkdir. We are going to make it simple here and just call it the linuxstuff. But to make this work for our needs, we need to type in the code that is below into the current directory:

% mkdir linuxstuff

If you would like to take it to the next step and see what directory we are working with, we will need to type in the following codes include:

% ls.

Changing Your Location to a New Directory

The next thing that we need to work with here is the command to change ourselves to another directory. We can do this with the cd command. This means that we want the system to change the directory from the current one to another directory of our choice. You can do this over to the directory that we created above. The code that we want to use to make this one happen would include:

% cd linuxstuff.

If you would like to see the content, which shouldn't have anything in it at this point since we have not gone through the process to add anything into that directory yet, we are able to type ls.

The Pathnames

Along with the same idea, we need to be able to spend some time with the command for pathnames, which is going to be pwd. This command is going to stand for the print working directory and it is going to use the pathname in order to let you work out exactly where you are located in the file system. For example, if you would like to know the absolute pathname that goes along with the home directory that you are working with, you would type in cd. This helps you to go back to what is known as the home directory. Once you are in the home directory, you would want to type in the code:

% pwd

When this is done, the results that you should see here is /home/its/ug1/ee51vn. And what this is going to mean here is that the home directory is going to be found as the subdirectory known as ug1. This is going to be located in the subdirectory that we called "its" which is going to also be located in the subdirectory of home, in the top level of the root directory that we are going to have named /.

This may seem like a lot of information to handle right now, but this is showing us that there are a few levels of things that we are able to work with at this time. You went from one level to the next, and down even further until you found the subdirectory that we wanted to handle right now. You will be able to take a look at the pathname in order to figure out how many times or subdirectories we need to go down in order to make this process work.

We need to spend a bit more time here looking at some of the pathnames and what we are able to do with them. If you are not currently in the home directory that is on our system, we need to get ourselves back there. We are able to type in the code below to help us get back over there:

% ls linuxstuff

This is going to spend some time listing out the contents that are found in the home directory. When we are found in this part of the code, we will want to type in the following code to help us get started:

% ls backups

At this point, you are going to get a message to show up, and it is going to say something like "backups: No such file or directory." Why does this happen? It is because you went through the process and created a directory with that name earlier on, but you didn't create it in the working directory. So, to get to the backups directory that we have, you either need to use the cd and then specify the directory that you have or you need to work with the pathname. A good code that we are able to use to make this happen will include the following:

% ls linuxstuff/backups

This is going to be the name of our home directory. We are also able to work with what is known as the tilde character (~)to help us refer ourselves back to the home directory and to make sure that we are able to specify a path that is going to start out with the home directory. So, if we stopped and typed out code like the following:

% ls ~ /linuxstuff

You would end up seeing a list of what is all in the linuxstuff directory. This is going to happen no matter where your current location is in that file system. This can ensure that you are able to see what you would like in the system, without having to click on a bunch of things or getting yourself lost.

Copying the Files

Another thing that we are able to work with is copying the files so that we can put them somewhere else or have them set up in the manner that we would like. The command that we need to work with here is "cp." If you would like to copy file1 that is found in the working directory, and then name it file2 instead, you would need to work with the following code to make it happen:

cp file1 file2

Removing a File or a Directory

The next thing that we need to consider working with
is removing a file or a directory when we no longer
what to work with this one at all. We would work with
rm to help remove the file and we can then work with
rmdir in order to remove the directory that we would
like to use.

To get a better idea of how this is going to work, we
are going to take a few steps and see how it can
happen for us. Let's make a copy of the science.txt
and then go through and delete it as well. To do this,
we need to go to the linuxstuff directory that we did
before and type in the code below:

```
      % cp science.txt tempfile.tx
% ls
% rm tempfile.txt
% ls
```

If you want to go through this process and get rid of
an entire directory along the way, we first need to go
and check whether there are files in it or not. We need

to have it free of all files and then we can work with the rmdir command. You can have a go at going onto your system and removing the directory that is there that is known as Backups. You will find that as it is right now, this is something that Linux is not going to allow because there is an item that is found in it. Once you remove that item, then the command will work.

How to Display File Contents on the Screen

The next thing that we are able to work with is how to display the contents in the file on the screen. This is going to need the help of the clear command to help it work. Before we move on with the rest of the things that we are able to do, we are going to spend a few minutes clearing out the terminal window of all the commands that are already typed in so that we can better understand the output of the next command as well. The code that we need to use to make this happen includes:

% clear

When you use this command, all of the text is going to be removed so that you end up with just a prompt left. This means that we need to move on to the next command. And this command is going to be "cat." This command is going to be used in order to concatenate and then display the content of the file on your screen. A good example of the code that we are able to use to make this happen is going to include:

% cat science.txt

You will find that when you dot this one, the file that you end up with is going to be bigger than the size of the window. This means that you will need to scroll through it to figure out what is all there and that makes some of the contents a bit harder to read through as well. This is where we are going to work with less command. This command is going to help us to write the contents of the file on the screen, doing it one page at a time. The code that you are able to use in order to make this happen to include:

% less science.txt

When you have this, all of the information is going to show up on its own page. You can press on the space bar if you would like to see the next page and do it a few times if there are more than two pages that you would like to work with. When you have had a chance to read through the information, and you do not need it any longer, then just type in q.

One thing to note here is that if you have some files that are long, you may want to work with something else. Working with the command of less rather than the cat command is going to be better when the files are really long because it can prevent some of the issues of taking up a lot of space.

Another command that we need to look at that falls into this category is going to be "head." This is the command that you are going to use when you just want the first ten lines of the file that you specify to show up on the screen. This can give you a kind of preview to see what is going on with the file and helps you to see if it is the right one for you. If you would like to work with this particular command, make sure to clear off the screen and then type in the following command:

% head science.txt

Rom there, you are able to type out the following:

% head -5 science.txt

Type that one in and see if it makes a difference in the output that you are going to get from this whole system. Then we are going to work with the tail rather than the head here. In contrast to what we are going to see when we work with the header command, this tail command is going to write out the final ten lines of the file that you specify on the screen. To work with this one, we will just want to work with the following code:

% tail science.txt

This one is a great option to help you see whether the file is complete or not. You get a chance to look at the final bit of the file that you have and you can read through it to see what is there, whether it is complete, and more.

How to Look Through the Contents of a File

Now it is time for us to take a look through some of the contents that are found in one of the files that we are working with. You will find that the less command is going to help with this one. Using this command, you are able to search for a pattern of keywords in a text file. For example, if you wanted to find all of the instances of the word science in this kind of file, you will be able to type in the code below:

% less science.txt

And then, staying with the less command, if you work to type in the forward slash, along with the word that you would like to search for, you can get the search all done. A good example of doing this is going to be below:

/science

All of the instances of the word that show up in that file are going to be highlighted. If you would like to find the next instance, though, and go through the file to see where all of these instances are, you would type in "grep." This is going to be one of the standard utilities that are found on Linux and it is going to be used to help us search for some of the specific words or patterns that we need in the work that we are doing. To make this one work, we need to clear off the screen and then type in the following command:

% grep science science.txt

Now, you should be able to see that the command of grep is going to print on all of the lines that have the word science in it. But is that the end of it? At this point, we are going to type in the code below:

% grep Science science.txt

What this shows us is that the original one did not find all of the instances. And this is because the grep search is going to be case sensitive. It is going to see that there is a difference between Science and science. If you would like to ignore the case sensitivity and make sure that all of the instances of science show up, whether they are in uppercase or lower case, you would want to add in the -i. For example, you would type in the following code to make this work:

% grep -I science science.txt

If you would like to search out a specific pattern or a phrase, this is possible, but you need to make sure that you are putting that all inside of some single quote marks in order to get it to work well. To search for a spinning top, you would type in the following code:

% gep -I 'spinning top' science.txt

There are a lot of other options that we are able to use to make this work for our needs, as well. Some of the other options that come with the grep command will include:

-v: This one is going to display for us the lines that are not going to match the specified text.
-n: This one is going to precede each of the matching lines with the correct line number that we are working with.
-c: This one is only going to print out the total number of matching lines that we want to work with.

Appending Files

The next thing that we are able to work with is how to append our files. We are able to work with the (>>) symbol in order to append the standard output to a file. So if we are working with this and would like to add in a few more items to our list1, we would be able to type in the code below to make this one happen:

% cat >> list1

When this is done, you would need to type in the names of the other fruits that you would like in the order that they need to be in when you do the file. Then, when the list is complete, you will click on CTRL + d to stop. To read the contents of the file, you can type in the code below:

% cat list1

You should now have two files. There is going to be one that will hold onto the six fruits that you are working with and then there is another list that is going to have four fruits. We will want to go through and combine together the two lists so that they are able to do the work that we want in no time. The cat command is going to help us to get all of this done and the coding that we are able to use to see this one work well will include:

% cat list1 list2 > biglist

This one is going to work out well because it is able to read the contents of both lists, in turn, and then will output the text from each so that it goes into a new file. Thanks to how we set this up, it is going to call the new file that we just created biglist. If you would like to be able to read through the contents that show up with the biglist, we need to type in the following command:

% cat biglist.

The Help Command

Another thing that we are able to spend some time here is the help command. There are a lot of manuals that you are able to find online that are going to provide you with some of the information that you need on these commands. The pages of these manuals can come with a lot of the information that you need when it comes to what the command is able to do, the options that it will take and how all of these options are going to be able to make some modifications to the command.

If you would like to read the page for one of the specific commands that we have, you would want to type in "man." For example, let's say that we want to go through and know a bit more about the command of wc. To do this, we could type in one of two codes including the two below:

% man wc

% whatis wc

This one is going to be useful because it is going to provide us with a small and quick description of the command. Keep in mind with this one, though, that it is not going to provide us with more information. You will not have any information about the options or anything else that goes with it. You would have to do some other topics in order to get things started and to gather up some more information as well.

As you can see, there are a lot of different things that we are going to be able to work with when it is time to bring out some of the commands that we will use in this language overall. You will find that handling all of these commands will work well when it is time to bring up different parts of the operating system, some of the files that you would like to work with and so much more. Make sure to take a look at some of the different commands that come with this, and see just how great this can be for your needs.

Chapter 5: Teach Yourself to Fish

The next option that we are able to work with is the idea of teaching yourself to fish. This may seem a bit silly right now, but as we go through this chapter, you will find that it makes sense and can really help us to do more when it comes to working with our Linux system. Keep in mind that all of the codes that we are going to work with will include https://fishshell.com

Fish is going to be a command-line shell that is similar to Bash, which is going to be really easy for the user to work with. You will find that it is able to handle a lot of the most powerful features, including things like tab completion, highlighting the syntax and autosuggestions. You will not need to worry about a ton of configurations along the way, and there is not a lot that you have to learn to do this work.

If you are trying to find a productive command line, one that is a lot of fun and more useful than some of the others that you may have used in the past, then fish is probably the method that will work the best for your needs. And we are going to spend some time looking at how to work with this command line and a lot of the neat things that we are able to concentrate on when it comes to this command line:

Learning Fish

The first thing that we need to work with here is how to work with the Fish command shell. We are going to make the assumption that you have gone through and worked with some of the shells and commands that are found with the Linux system, so you are ready to go. And now it is time to work more with Fish and how we are able to make this work.

To do this, we have to start out by downloading the fish shell and then we can get started. When it is downloaded, you can open up the Fish command line and then see a message that says something like "Welcome to fish, the friendly interactive shell." You are tenable to type for help in order to get some of the instructions that are needed on how to work with the fish program. The code that we need to make this one work will include:

you@hostname ~ >

Fish is already going to come with a default prompt in that it is going to show off all of your details when you do this. This means that things like your hostname, username and the current working directory that you would like to work with are going to show up when you do this. We will take a look at how we are able to make some changes to the prompt later on, but we are going to take a look at it this way for now.

Running Some Commands in Fish

We need to spend some time learning how to run commands in this command shell. Running some of the commands that you would like in fish is going to be the same as you are able to do with some of the other shells that are there. You will just need to type in the command, along with some of the other arguments that you need to go with it. The spaces are going to be the way that we are able to separate this out. This is going to be similar to some of the commands that we talked about earlier in this guidebook as well. Let's look at an example of this one below:

> ➢ echo hello world

And when we do this, we are going to get the output of hello world to help us out.

There are a lot of commands that we are able to work in order to really help us to get started with this option, and we are going to spend some time looking at how to make this work for our needs. To start, we are going to work with the Help command. Fish is going to include some of the best manuals and help pages that we are able to work with any time that we are questioning what we are doing or trying to figure out which steps to take next as well.

To get started, we simply need to run the help command, and it is going to open it up in a new web browser. Or you have the option of running man, and then the help file will open up for you in the man page. You are also able to find some help on the specific commands that you are confused about. So, if you would like to have a man set to see help in the terminal, you would want to work with the following code:

```
>  man set
```
Set – handle shell variables

Synopsis...

Another thing that we are able to work with when it is time to handle some of the commands in this shell is the idea of syntax highlighting. You may notice that just by spending a short amount of time working in Fish that it is going to be able to highlight the syntax that we are on when it is being typed out. If you see that you are working through this and you notice that it is being highlighted in red, then this is a good sign that the command is not valid.

This may be because the command is either one that does not exist or because you are writing out codes that re-referencing a file that we are not able to execute. When the command is actually valid, or you make the necessary changes to turn it into a valid code, then it is going to change colors.

Another thing that we need to work with is that some of the paths that are valid files are going to be underlined when we type them out. This is going to let us know that there is a file that is on our system that has that name. This can be useful when you are typing out the codes because it ensures that you are able to find what you would like.

We can also work with the wildcard as well because it is something that Fish is able to support. If you would like to look at all of the JPEG files that we have, you would type in something like the following:

> ls * .jpg
Leno.jpg
Moona.jpg
Sana margarita.jpg

It is even possible to go through and work with more than one wildcard based on what is going to work the best for some of the work that we are doing. From there, we are able to finish up with some pipes and redirections if those work out well with our code. This means that the Fish shell is going to support the use of the vertical bar, which is for our pipe command and you can use it for piping between the commands.

Autosuggestions are another thing that we are able to focus on here, as well. As you spend some time typing out the codes that you want to use in Fish, it is automatically going to get to work, suggesting commands. You will see that these suggestions are going to be shown to the right of the cursor and will be highlighted a bit in gray. You can choose whether you would like to work with these or not.

The Fish shell is also going to know a bit about the history of what you have done with coding in the past, which is going to be important and can save us some time and hassle as well. We are able to type in the command that we want to use. And then, when it is time to use it again, we can then start to type it all out again so that the full command is going to appear without having to worry about it the whole time or typing the whole thing out.

If you would like to accept the suggestion that it is given, you can press the right arrow key to let it come into the shell. If you just want one word of the suggestion, this is possible as well. If you just want to work with the one word, then you would hit the Alt + right arrow key. If the suggestion is, of course, and it is not what you want, you can ignore the suggestion and then move on to the next step to make this one work for your needs.

If you would like to be able to accept the autosuggestion, you can hit the CTRL + F to accept just the single word; you can work with Alt and right arrow. And then, remember to just ignore it if you do not want to work that particular autosuggestion at all.

Another thing that we are able to work with is tab completions. There are going to be a lot of tab completions in fish that work without any configuration whatsoever. To make this happen, we simply need to start by typing in an argument, path, or command, and then we are able to press on our tab key to get this to be complete. It is also possible to work with two or sometimes more suggestions. And this is a possibility; then we need to list them out in that manner as well.

The Variables

When it is time to work with any kind of coding language or shell, we need to work with the variables. As with other shells, the dollar sign is going to be used to perform some of the variable substitutions. It is also possible to do this with some double quotes if you would like, but never substitute these with single quotes, or it is not going to work the way that you would like.

However, we have to remember that there is not necessarily going to be some syntax that can be dedicated to setting this kind of variable. Instead, the Fish shell is going to use an ordinary command that we are able to call "set." This is going to take the name of the variable and then the value of the variable and use these in the manner that we need.

We always have to worry about the quotes. If they are not used, then you can put in one phrase with two words and they are going to be seen as two separate arguments, then we would have to worry about two lists of elements as well. In addition, when we work with Fish, the variables are not going to be split after we have provided them with a new substitution.

On the other hand, if you are in the Bash shell, you would end up with two directories when you are doing this. But in the Fish shell, we can get one and then we would pass any of the arguments that we are working with over to the mkdir.

The Lists

Another thing that we need to take some time looking at is the list. We have to remember before we get into this one that all of the variables that we work with are going to be classified as lists and they are going to contain no values or any number of values.

It is also possible that the variables we work with are going to come with just one value. And one of these is going to be the $PWD. Conventionally, we would talk about the value of that variable, but when we look at it in reality, it is the only value it has. Other variables have several values, like $PATH. During the expansion of the variable, you will be able to extend it out to more than one argument if you would like.

A list is not going to be able to contain any other list; there is no such thing as recursion here. A variable is going to contain a list of strings and that is all that you will find inside. If you would like to figure out what the length of the list is, you would need to use the count command.

You can append and add some more to the list by setting that list to itself and then adding in the extra arguments that are needed. In this example, we are going to append /usr/local/bin to the $PATH. The example of how we would work with this one includes:

> set PATH $PATH /usr/locale/bn

We will want to make sure that we are working with the square brackets to help us access all of the individual elements that are needed. Indexing is going, to begin with, 1 at the start, and then we want to work from the end, we would start with the -1 to make this all work. An example of how this is going to work will be seen below:

> echo $PATH
/usr/bn /bin /user/sbin /sbin /usr/localn/bin
> echo $PATH [1]
/usr/bin
> echo $PATH[-1]
/usr/local/bin

Fish also allows us to take this a bit further if we would like and we are able to access some of the slices in our code. This is going to basically be the range of elements. We are able to work with the options that are above but add in the different numbers that we are able to work with, or the range, rather than just one number.

And, similar to what we are going to see with any other kind of computer that we are working with, or even with other programming languages, we will be able to work with the "for loops" to make it easier to iterate over the list that we would like.

The Command Substitutions

The next thing that we need to take a look at here is the command substitutions. Command substitution is going to be when the output of a command is going to be used as an argument to a different command. Unlike some of the other shells that you may have spent some time working with in the past, there is not going to be anything like a backtick in Fish for this. Instead, we are going to work with the parentheses to show this off.

One of the most common of the idioms that are present in this shell is to use a variable in order to capture some more of the output from the command. But the command substitution that we are doing is not something that we want to expand out inside of some quotation marks. Instead, the quotes have to be closed for a bit and then we can add in the substitutions of the command when these are closed. When it is all done, we are able to re-open the quotes and all of this can be done in one argument.

While we are on the topic, there will be something known as combiners that we are able to handle in a lot of the different shells out there. However, there is not going to be one special syntax in the Fish shell that is going to help us to combine together the commands. Rather, we are able to work with three commands to make this work including or, and, and not.

Functions

Another thing that is important for us to work with when it is time to handle any of the codings that we want to do in the Fish shell is the idea of the function. When we are in the Fish shell, the functions are going to be the lists of commands, which sometimes will count as arguments and other times will not be. We are not going to pass the arguments as numbered variables here. Instead, we are going to pass them as single lists instead.

There are going to be a lot of different types of functions that we are able to work in order to help us out. The first type will be a built-in function. And in the Fish shell, they are going to be able to help us create some of the functions that we would like to work with.

In addition, we have to remember that there is not going to be a prompt or any kind of special syntax that is needed here and there will not be any aliases that show up. Functions are going to have their own unique place in his code, and you are able to use the functions keywords to make it easier to list out all of the names of the functions. Keep in mind that the Fish shell is going to come in with a large number of functions that we are able to work with. Unlike the other shells, though, Fish is not going to have a special prompting syntax or aliases that we use in the code because the function is going to take the place of all of these.

$PATH

The next thing that we need to spend some of our time on is the $PATH option. This is going to be one out of several environment variables that we are able to use here, and it is going to be the home of all of the directories that we will use for commands in the Fish shell. $PATH is not going to be delimited as a string, but it is more of a list. If you would like to prepend some of your paths to work with this, you would write out the code:

> set PATH /usr/local/bin /usr/sbin $PATH

You are able to do this with the help of config_fish, or you do get the option to modify the universal variable if you would like to make sure that you can automatically prepend the $PATH ahead of time. The major benefit of working with it in this second manner is that there isn't going to be the need to mess around with any of the files. All that you will need to do to make this one work is run the command once in the command line and then the changes will happen in both the current session that you are doing and in some of the ones that happen in the future as well.

One thing to keep in mind here, though, is that you do not add the code line over to the config_fish. If you do this, then the variable is just going to cause a mess because it grows in size each time that you do use this program, whether it is done in the right manner or not.

As we can see, there are a lot of different parts that we are able to work with when it is time to handle some of the parts of the Fish shell. This one is going to allow us to work with a lot of the same commands that we talked about before, which is going to make it so useful for a lot of the different needs that we have. With this in mind, let's take a look at a few of the other things that we are able to do with the Linux system and how we are able to expand this out for some of our own needs as well.

Chapter 6: How to Handle Your Editors

There are going to be a lot of text editors that we are able to work with when we handle some of the things that we want in Linux, so it is easy to become a bit confused when we need to put all of this together. We are going to narrow it down a bit to make life a little easier for someone who is just getting started with the Linux operating system for the first time. And this means that we are going to spend some time looking at the *nano* and the *vi* editors, which are two of the basic text editors that we need with Linux and will still provide us with some of the power that we are looking for.

Nano

Nano is going to be something that we find installed on a lot of the distributions of Linux already, and it is going to work well when we bring out Sudo. This is why we need to spend some time talking about it and seeing how we are able to work with this for our needs.

First, we need to take a look at how to run Nano. There are two main ways that we are able to run this text editor to get it up and working the way that we want. The first one is that when the command prompt gets started, we just need to type in "nano." The second one is that we are able to input the command of "nano/name of file" and that will do it. You can insert the name of the file and then nano will take the time to look for it. If this file is found, then Nano is going to open it up. If your editor is not able to find it, then you will get the empty bugger that has the same name as the filename.

At this point, we can look at the top of the screen, and we are going to see some information there about the file that we are working with. If we are not currently in a file for this one, then it is going to say, New Buffer. Following that is going to be all of the content of your document in the form of text. Then there will be some information in the system that will provide us with the necessary data on how to get things started.

The first thing that we are going to work with on this one is some of the shortcuts that we are able to focus on. These shortcuts are going to be program functions like saving and exiting, and we are going to be able to look near the bottom of the screen to see some of these when we are in Nano. You will not need to use SHIFT when you want to work on the shortcuts, and they are going to be in lowercase and an unmodified number format.

To start here, we will look at how to save a file. Doing this is going to be known as "writing out," and you are able to do this with the CTRL + O. Next, you will be asked for the name and the shortcuts that will change to show you what we are able to input to finish the command.

If we would like to be able to insert the contents that are needed from another file into the one that we are working with, we can type in CTRL + R and help us cancel both of these commands, then we just need to press on CTRL + C. If you have any trouble with this key, then you can just press on ESC two time. And if you see some commands that are going to ask you to work with what is known as the Meta key, then the Alt key is going to be fine. And we are able to work with the CTRL + X to help us exit out of what we are doing at the time.

There are a few other methods that we are able to use in order to navigate one of the text files that we want to handle. In order to navigate this kind of file, you are able to use a few keys, including the array key, page down and page up, end keys and home. If you would like to use those, you will be all set, but there are a few other shortcut keys that we are able to use to make ourselves more efficient at the work that we are doing in our editor. Some of the other keys that we need to know how to work with if we choose include:

1. CTRL + F: This one is going to move the cursor forward.
2. CTRL + B: This one is going to move our cursor to go backward.
3. CTRL + P: This one is going to move the cursor to go up by one line.
4. CTRL + N: This one is going to move the cursor so that it goes down by one line.
5. CTRL + A: This one is going to take the place of the Home key that you would like.
6. CTRL + E: This one is going to take the place of the End key that you may have used in other options.

7. CTRL + V: This one is going to help us to move down just one page.

8. CTRL + Y: This one is going to help us to move up one page.

9. CTRL + SPACE: This one is going to make it easier for us to move forward just one word at a time.

10. ALT + SPACE: This one is going to make it easier for us to move backward one word at a time.

11. CTRL + C: This one is going to indicate where the cursor is located at any given time when you need it.

Working with Vi

Now that we have had some time to look over how to work with the Nano version of this, it is time to look at the command line editor that is known as Vi. This is going to be a really powerful command-line editor that you are able to choose, but it is going to be plain, similar to the Notepad that we are able to find on Windows. And to use it, we have to rely simply on the keyboard, rather than the mouse. For some people who are just getting started with all of this, that may seem a bit awkward, but it ensures that you are going to get the most out of this.

Vi is going to come with two main operating modes that we are able to focus on. These are going to include the Insert of the Input mode and the Edit mode. In the Insert mode, you are able to insert content into the working file that is current and then when we are in the Edit mode, you are going to spend your time navigating around the file, performing things like copy, delete, search, replace, save and more.

Setting up the Vi command-line editor and making sure that it is running the way that you would like is going to be pretty simple. You just need to type in one command-line argument that is going to contain the file name that you are hoping to edit with this. An example of how we would get the Vi editor up and running includes:

Vi <name of file>

If you want to get started with this without having to specify a filename, you are able to go through and open it up from within. Just keep in mind that it is much easier to must close Vi down and start it up again. But the choice on how to handle this is up to you.

Like with the other option, we need to take a moment to look at some of the steps that we should take in order to navigate with this command-line editor. These commands are going to be a bit different compared to what we are used to with some of the others, and it is even a bit different compared to what we did with Nano before.

For this one, we want to make sure that we are able to open up a file to work with again and then get ourselves into the insert mode. You will need to enter in a few paragraphs here, the content does not really matter we just need to have something there and then click Esc so that you are able to get yourself back into the editing mode from before.

To help you go through and navigate around the file that you are using, you will need to work with some of the following commands. Do some of these in real-time so that you are able to see how they work and get a real-life look at the things that they will use when it is time to handle your document or your file:

1. You can first work with the arrow keys. These will help you to just move the cursor around as needed.
2. J: This one is going to move the cursor to go down.
3. K: This one is going to move the cursor to go up.
4. H: This one is going to move the cursor to the right.
5. L: This one is going to move the cursor to go to the left.
6. $: This one is going to move the cursor so that it ends up at the end of whichever line you are on right now.
7. ^: This one is going to help us to end up back at the start of the line that we are on.
8. nG: This one is going to move us over to what is known as the nth line. For example, if you are writing out 6G, it is going to take you to the 6th line in the file.
9. G: This is going to move us over to the final line that is in the text that we want to work with.

10. W: This one is going to move us to the start of the next word, based on where we are right then.

11. Nw: This one is going to help us to move forward a certain number of words. For example, if we are working with 4c, then this means that we want the program to move us forward by four words.

12. B: This one is going to ask that the program takes us to the start of the last word.

13. Nb: This is going to take us back to the word that we specify out in the code.

14. {: This one is going to ask the command-line editor to take us back by a paragraph.

15. }: This one is going to ask the command-line editor to take us forward by a paragraph.

As we can see here, both of these text editors are going to be useful for what we would like to do in some of our codings. But often, it depends on what we are hoping to get out of the process and what results we think we can get from both. There are also some other command-line editors that you are able to work with, so before you decide on the right one, do some research, see which features are available for each one and then work from there to choose the best one for your needs.

Chapter 7: The Necessary Permissions

Another thing that we need to consider when we are working with all of these is the permissions we want to give out. This can include both the files and the directory. You most likely, for security reasons, do not want to provide full access to the files and directories to each person who is going to come by, and this is why we need to go through and come up with some of the best file and directory permissions right from the beginning.

That is why this chapter is going to spend some time looking at the steps that are needed to set up these permissions. These permissions are important because they are going to be used in order to specify what the user can and can't do with a particular file or a directory. This is going to help us make sure that any of the working environments that we have are as secure as possible. You don't want to allow someone to mess around with the files and then causing some issues, so we will work with the Linux system to add in permissions and keep it all safe.

Permissions are going to dictate what you and others are able to write, read and execute when it comes to the directories and the files. We are able to look at these and see that there is a single letter that goes with each one. So, *r* is going to be the permission to read, which allows the users to read the contents of a file. Then there is *w* for write, which allows the user to go through and edit some of the contents that are in a file. And *x* is going to be the process of executing, which is going to allow the user the permission to run files as if there were a program or a script.

For each of the files that we are working with, we will notice that there are three users that we can define. Knowing these can give us a better idea of the different options that are there and the permissions that each one is going to work with. For example, there is the owner, who is the person who is the owner of the file. Often this is the person who was responsible for creating the file in the first place, but this is not always the cause. Then there is the group, which you will find that each file is going to belong to one of its own groups. And then there are others, which is going to catch anyone who isn't going to fall into the two sets that we had above.

So, we are going to find that there are three main types of permissions that we are able to work with, and then there are three users. And these things are going to be the summary of these permissions and how we are able to work with them. But with this in mind, we need to go through and take a look at the steps that are needed in order to edit them.

Viewing Permissions

If you would like a chance to view the permissions that are on a file, you will need to work with the ls command and make sure that it is going to have a long-lasting option that comes with it. We can take a look at how this code is going to look below:

Ls = l [path]\
Ls – l /home/ryan/linuxtutorialwork/frog.png
-rwxr – x 1 harry users 2.7K Jan 4
07:32/home/ryan/linuxtutorialwork/frog.png

When we take a look at this example, we need to take a look at some of the first ten characters that are going to help us see the permissions that are allowed as an output. For example, the first character is going to tell you what the type of file is. If it is a *d*, then that is the directory and it is an ordinary file that we can work with here.

Then we can look at the next three characters to see what the permissions of that file are for the file owner. A letter tells you that there is going to be some permissions in place and then will identify which one. We will see that the (--) is going to tell us that there are not permissions here. In the example that we worked with above, the owner of this file has the permissions to go through and do anything that they would like to this file, including reading, writing and executing the file.

The next three are going to tell us which permissions the whole group is going to have. For this example, the whole group is able to read through the file if they would like, but they are not able to write on it or execute it. You should note here that the permissions are always going to end up in the same order with reading, write and execute.

And finally, we are at the last three characters. These are going to be where we will find the permissions for everyone else, or for the others. For this one, the only permissions for the others are to execute the file, rather than being able to write it or read through it.

Changing the Permissions

If you have done some of the steps above, but then you find that you would like to change up the permissions of the file or the directory, then you need to work with the command of chmod. This is going to stand for change file mode bits, something that is a bit long, but all that you need to remember is that the mode bits because these are going to be the indicators that we need for the permissions. A good code that we can look at for this one includes:

Chmod [permissions] [path]

The permissions arguments that we are able to work with on this command have been set out in three main components that we are able to work with. For example, the first one is who the permission is being changed for. This could be the users, the owner, the group, others, and all depending on what you are trying to do here. Then we are letting it know whether we are granting or taking away the permission we will see the + or – sign in order to see this. And then finally we are going to put in information about which permissions are being set here. Remember that we are able to work with reading, write or execute so stick with those.

Shorthand to Set the Permissions

While the methods that we have been talking about above are going to be easy to use and will make it possible to work on some of the permissions that we would like, it is going to end up being a bit long if we need to go through and set up some specific permissions for specific files on a regular basis. The good news here is that we are able to work with a somewhat shorter version of this if we would like.

To understand this method, though, and how it is meant to work for us, we need to really get into the number system in Linux. The normal number system is going to be all about the decimals, with a base 10 number. And it usually goes from 0 to 9. We also have the octal number system, which is going to be a base 8 system and goes from 0 to 7. There are also three permissions that come up with this one, and each is either going to be on, or it is off, and as such, there will be 8 combinations that we are able to work with.

It is also possible for us to go through and work with binary in order to represent these numbers. When it is time to handle binary, we get two options, the 0 and the 1. The following will show us how some of the octal numbers are going to be mapped out when we work with the binary numbers:

0000
1001
2010
3011
4100
5101
6110
7111

What your mind find a little bit interesting here is that we can just use three of the binary values in order to represent the 8 octal numbers each time that we work with each possible combination of the 0 and 1 in our work. So, there are going to be three bits and there are also three permissions that are allowed. You can use 1 to represent on in this, and then 0 can represent off, and that means that one octal number can be used in order to represent permission set for the users that you choose. If we work with all three of the numbers, then we can represent the permissions of all three, including the owner or users, the group and others while we are there.

Basic Security to Follow

While we are on the topic here, we need to spend a little bit of time looking at the basic security that is needed in our Linux directories. Your space on the Linux system is going to be the home directory and it is going to be your responsibility in order to make it stay safe and secure all of the time. Some users are going to choose to give themselves the full permission that is necessary to read, write and execute, but will not provide any permissions for others or for the groups. And some will allow for a few permissions to the others and the groups. Each owner will need to set it up to work the best for their needs.

To get the best security on the directory you are using, you should not give the group, or any of the others, the right to access your own home directory. But you can provide them with some execute permissions so that they can still use it as needed, without adding on the read permissions. If you choose to do this, other users are going to be able to access your home directory, but they will not be able to see what is there. A good example of this one is going to be your own personal web pages.

Some systems are responsible for running web servers and give each of their users a webspace all to their own. The most common of these is to create a directory that is found in the home directory and call it public_html. This allows the server to read it and then to display what is found inside of it as well. However, because we will find that the web server we are working with is not going to be the same user that you are, it is not able to get in and it won't be able to read the files. In this kind of situation, it is going to be necessary for permission to execute to be given on the home directory before that happens.

If you provide this permission, it is going to allow the webserver user to get to the resources that they need. But all of this is going to be up to you and what you would like to see done with the whole system as well. Sometimes the information is not that sensitive or you don't mind if a few of the groups or other people are able to get some access to change it. And sometimes the information needs to be left secure so that only you are able to make the changes as well. It is all going to depend on what your directories are about and how secure you need to keep that information as well.

As you can imagine here, there are a lot of parts that come with providing permissions when you work with the directory that you are in. Being careful with the permissions that you are allowing is going to make a big difference in how successful this process is going to be, and will ensure that we are able to really keep our information safe and secure overall as well.

Chapter 8: Looking at the Variables of Your Environment

The environment variables are going to be some of the objects that are given names and will be able to contain the data that will be used by a minimum of one application, though there is usually more than one application that is relying on it. To keep it simple, the environment variable is just going to be a variable that has both a name and a value that is attached to it.

This means that the environment variable values could be the default that the editor has given to it, or it could be something else as well. Newbies who have not had much time working with Linux may find that it can turn into something that is a bit cumbersome, but the environment variable is still a good way for us to share the settings of configuration between more than one application and process in the meantime.

Utilities

The first thing that we are going to take a look at here is known as the utilities. The package that is known as coreutils is going to be home to the *env* and the *printenv* programs that we are going to need at this point. If you would like to be able to go through and list out all of the current environment variables that we can access, and that also has some value right now, we would need to type in the following code:

$ printenv.

Some of the variables that we are going to work with are kind of user-specific. And there may be times when we will want to check on these and see if they are the right option for us, or at least check that they are still providing us with the information that they need. We can do this when we compare the output that we get as the normal user and then checking it again when we are the root user. If they are the same, then we can see that they are not user-specific in the first place.

In addition, the utility that we are going to call *env* is going to be used to help us run some of the commands that we would like in the environment that was modified for some reason or another. The code that we are going to have below is going to help us run the *xterm* with the help of the EDITOR, the environment variable, and it is going to be set to *vin*. This is going to have absolutely no effect on the global version that we are able to get of this same variable. The code that we are talking about here will include:

$ env EDITOR = vim xterm.

How to Define the Variable

There are going to be a few methods that we are able to use when it is time to handle our variables. First on the list is the global variables. Most of the distributions that you are able to use of Linux is going to ask you to change or add the variable definitions in the path of/etc/profile, or to some other location that makes the most sense to what you are trying to do.

However, before you just do this without thinking, we have to remember that there are going to be a few of our configuration files that have to stick with certain packages or they will not work well. And when this is necessary, these environment variables may have some settings that they need to focus on and remain with as well.

These variables, in particular, have to be managed and maintained, and you need to pay some special attention to all of the files that could be found with that environment variable as well. With just the principle here, any of the scripts that utilize a shell are able to initialize an environment variable. But if we are working with some conventions that are a bit more traditional, then we have to remember that these statements should not be found in all of the files, but only in a few of them.

More to Learn Here

Now that we have had some time to look at a few of the different parts that we are able to work with there here, there are a few terms and topics that we need to know as well, before we can really get through some of the work that we would like to accomplish on the Linux system. Some of the other topics that we need to follow through with include:

1. DESKTOP_SESSION: This is going to be similar to the DE that we talked about before, but it is going to be used inside of the environment of LXDE as well.

2. PATH: This is going to be the home to a list of directories that we have and they are all going to be separated by colons. And this is where our system is going to head through to look for any files that we are able to execute. When the shell is able to go through a command that is seen as regular, such as the ls that we talked about before, it will start to take a look at any executable file that has the same name as the command that is in the listed directories, and then it is going to execute it as well. If you are doing this process and you would like to run some of the executables that have not been put into this PATH, you need to use the path that is absolute and then pick out a specific executable to make it work.

3. HOME: This is where we are able to find the exact path that is going to lead over to the home directory where the user is logged in a. This can be used by more than one application in order to associate some of the configuration files with the user that is already running that particular variable.

4. PWD: This is where we will be able to find the right path in order to lead to the working directory, as well.

5. OLDPWD: This is where you will find the path that is able to lead to the previous working directory. This means that the value of the PWD had before the last execution of cd.

6. SHELL: This is where we are going to be able to find the right path that can lead us over to the shell that the user prefers to work with. This may not be the shell that they are currently using, depending on some of the preferences that you have as well. No matter which method, the variable is going to be set with the Bash shell when you get it started up.

7. TERM: This is going to contain the type of terminal that you are running at this time. This is going to be used the most often by the program that is going to run in the terminal and the need capabilities that are going to be specific to the terminal that you handle.

8. PAGER: This is going to be one of the commands that will run the program, which is in use to list the contents of the file if you would like.

9. EDITOR: This is going to be the command that we are able to use for running the light programs of file editor. For example, you could write a switch that is more interactive between nono or gedit under X.

10. VISUAL: This is where we are able to find out the command that will run the full editor and it is used for some of the more demanding tasks like mail editing.

11. MAIL: This is the place where we are going to be able to find the location of any incoming mail. The setting that we will often use for this one is going to be /var/spool/mail/$LOGNAME

12. BROWSER: This is where we are going to find the path that will lead us right to our web browser. It is useful to work with when we would like to come out with an interactive configuration file that is set for the shell because it can be altered in a more dynamic manner, depending on how available our graphic environment is in the first place.

13. MANPATH: This is the place where we are going to be able to find out a whole list of directories and we are going to separate them out with

some colons. This is also where the man will search for man pages.

14. INFODIR: This is going to be the list of directories, which is also separated out with a colon and this is where the command is going to spend some time looking for info pages when needed.

15. TZ: This one is going to be used when it is time to set some of the time zones, especially when you need it to be different from the one that is on the system. If you take a look inside of the usr/share/zoneinfo, you will be able to see the zones that we are able to see as our references.

As we can see, there are a lot of different things that we are able to do when it comes to working in the Linux system and getting it all set up for some of our own needs. Even a little bit of this can ensure that we are able to use this in the right manner and that we will be able to get the whole system set up in the manner that we would like in no time.

Chapter 9: Linux and Hacking

The last thing that we are going to spend some time on is looking at how we can work with the Linux system to help us complete some of the ethical hacking that we would like to do. While we are able to do some hacking with the help of Windows and Mac, often, the best operating system to help us out with all of this is going to be the Linux operating system. It already works on the command line, which makes things a bit easier and will have all of the protection that you need as well. And so, we are going to spend a bit of our time taking a closer look at how the Linux system is going to be able to help us out with some of the hacking we want to accomplish.

There are a lot of reasons that hackers are going to enjoy working with Linux over some of the other operating systems that are out there. The first benefit is that it is open source. This means that the source code is right there and available for you to use and modify without having to pay a lot of fees or worry that it is going to get you into trouble. This open-source also allows you to gain more access to it, share it with others and so much more. And all of these can be beneficial to someone who is ready to get started with hacking as well.

The compatibility that comes with Linux is going to be beneficial for a hacker as well. This operating system is going to be unique in that it is going to help us support all of the software packages of Unix and it is also able to support all of the common file formats that are with it as well. This is important when it comes to helping us to work with some of the hacking codes that we want to do later on.

Linux is also designed to be fast and easy to install. If you took a look at the second chapter in this guidebook, you might have noticed that there are a number of steps that we had to go through in order to get started. But when compared to some of the other operating systems this is not going to be that many and it can really help you to get the most out of this in as little time as possible.

You will quickly notice that most of the distributions that you are able to do with Linux are going to have installations that are meant to be easy on the user.

And also, a lot of the popular distributions of Linux are going to come with tools that will make installing any of the additional software that you want as easy and friendly as possible too. Another thing that you might notice with this is that the boot time of the operating system of Linux is going to be faster than what we see with options like Mac and Windows, which can be nice if you do not want to wait around all of the time.

When you are working on some of the hacks that you would like to accomplish, the stability of the program is going to matter quite a bit. You do not want to work with a system that is not all that stable, or that is going to fall apart on you in no time. Linux is not going to have to go through the same periodic reboots like others in order to maintain the level of performance that you would like and it is not going to slow down or freeze up over time if there are issues with leaks in the memory and more. You are also able to use this operating system for a long time to come, without having to worry about it slowing down or running into some of the other issues that the traditional operating systems will need to worry about.

For someone who is going to spend their time working with ethical hacking, this is going to be really important as well. It will ensure that you are able to work with an operating system that is not going to slow down and cause issues with the protections that you put in place on it. And you will not have to worry about all of the issues that can come up with it being vulnerable and causing issues down the line as well. It is going to be safe and secure along the way, so that you are able to complete your hacks and keep things safe, without having to worry about things not always working out the way that we would hope.

Another benefit that we will spend a bit of time on is how friendly the Linux network is overall. As this operating system is an option that is open source and is contributed by the team over the internet network, it is also able to effectively manage the process of networking all of the time. And it is going to help with things like commands that are easy to learn and lots of libraries that can be used in a network penetration test if you choose to do this. Add on that the Linux system is going to be more reliable and it is going to make the backup of the network more reliable and faster and you can see why so many users love to work with this option.

As a hacker, you will need to spend some of your time multitasking to get all of the work done. A lot of the codes and more that you want to handle in order to do a hack will need to have more than one thing going at a time, and Linux is able to handle all of this without you having to worry about too much going on or the computer freezing upon you all of the time.

In fact, the Linux system was designed in order to do a lot of things at the same time. This means that if you are doing something large, like finishing up a big printing job in the background, it is not really going to slow down some of the other work that you are doing. Plus, when you need to handle more than one process at the same time, it is going to be easier to do on Linux, compared to Mac or Windows, which can be a dream for a hacker.

You may also notice that working with the Linux system is a bit different and some of the interactions that you have to take care of are not going to be the same as what we found in the other options. For example, the command-line interface is going to introduce us to something new. Linux operating systems are going to be specifically designed around a strong and highly integrated command-line interface, something that the other two operating systems are not going to have. The reason that this is important is that it will allow hackers and other users of Linux to have more access and even more control, over their system.

Next on the list is the fact that the Linux system is lighter and more portable than we are going to find with some of the other operating systems out there. This is a great thing because it is going to allow hackers with a method that will make it easier to customize the live boot disks and drives from any distribution of Linux that they would like. The installation is going to be fast and it will not consume as many resources in the process. Linux is light-weight and easy to use while consuming fewer resources overall.

The maintenance is going to be another important feature that we need to look at when we are trying to do some ethical hacking and work with a good operating system. Maintaining the Linux operating system is going to be easy to work with. All of the software is installed in an easy manner that does not take all that long and every variant of Linux has its own central software repository, which makes it easier for the users to search for their software and use the kind that they would like along the way.

There is also a lot of flexibility when it comes to working with this kind of operating system. As a hacker, you are going to need to handle a lot of different tools along the way. And one of the best ways that we are able to do this is to work with an operating system that allows for some flexibility in the work that we are doing. This is actually one of the most important features in Linux because it allows us to work with embedded systems, desktop applications and high-performance server applications as well.

As a hacker, you want to make sure that your costs are as low as possible. No one wants to get into the world of ethical hacking and start messing with some of those codes and processes and then find out that they have to spend hundreds of dollars in order to get it all done. And this is where the Linux system is going to come into play. As you can see from some of our earlier discussions of this operating system, it is going to be an open-source operating system, which means that we are able to download it free of cost. This allows us to get started with some of the hacking that we want to do without having to worry about the costs.

If you are working with ethical hacking, then your main goal is to make sure that your computer and all of the personal information that you put into it is going to stay safe and secure all of the time. This is going to be a command-line to keep other hackers off and will make it so that you don't have to worry about your finances or other issues along the way, either. And this is also where the Linux operating system is going to come into play to help us out.

One of the nice things that we are going to notice when it comes to the Linux operating system is that it is seen as being less vulnerable than some of the other options. Today, most of the operating systems that we are able to choose from, besides the Linux option, are going to have a lot of vulnerabilities to an attack from someone with malicious intent along the way.

Linux, on the other hand, seems to have fewer of these vulnerabilities in place from the beginning. This makes it a lot nicer to work with and will ensure that we are going to be able to do the work that we want on it, without having a hacker getting. Linux is seen as one of the most secure out of all the operating systems that are available and this can be good news when you are starting out as an ethical hacker.

The next benefit that we are going to see when it comes to working with the Linux operating system over some of the other options, especially if you are a hacker, is that it is going to provide us with a lot of support and works with most of the programming languages that you would choose to work on when coding. Linux is already set up in order to work with a lot of the most popular programming languages. This means that many options like Perl, Ruby Python, PHP< C++ and Java are going to work great here.

This is good news for the hacker because it allows them to pick out the option that they like. If you already know a coding language or there is one in particular that you would like to use for some of the hacking that you plan to do, then it is likely that the

Linux system is going to be able to handle this and will make it easy to use that one as well.

If you want to spend some of your time working on hacking, then the Linux system is a good option. And this includes the fact that many of the hacking tools that we are working with are going to be written out in Linux. Popular hacking tools like Nmap and Metasploit, along with a few other options, are going to be ported for Windows. However, you will find that while they can work with Windows, if you want, you will miss out on some of the capabilities when you transfer them off of Linux.

It is often better to leave these hacking tools on Linux. This allows you to get the full use of all of them and all of the good capabilities that you can find with them, without having to worry about what does and does not work if you try to move them over to a second operating system. These hacking tools were made and designed to work well in Linux, so keeping them there and not trying to force them into another operating system allows you to get the most out of your hacking needs.

And finally, we are able to take a quick look at how the Linux operating system is going to take privacy as seriously as possible. In the past few years, there was a lot of information on the news about the privacy issues that would show up with the Windows 10 operating system. Windows 10 is set up to collect a lot of data on the people who use it the most. This could bring up some concerns about how safe your personal information could be.

This is not a problem when we are working with Linux. This system is not going to take information, you will not find any talking assistants to help you out and this operating system is not going to be around, collecting information and data on you to have some financial gain. This all can speak volumes to an ethical hacker who wants to make sure that their information stay safe and secure all of the time.

As you can see here, there are a lot of benefits that are going to show up when it is time to work with the Linux system. We can find a lot of examples of this operating system and all of the amazing things that it is able to do, even if we don't personally use it on our desktop or laptop. The good news is that there are a lot of features that are likely to make this operating system more effective and strong in the future, which is perfect when it comes to doing a lot of tasks, including the hacking techniques that we talked about in this chapter.

Conclusion

Thank you for making it through to the end of *Linux for Beginners:An Introduction to Linux Programming Basics for Hackers, Its Operating System, Command-Line and Networking, Including Effective Strategies, Tips and Tricks to Learn How It Works*, let's hope it was informative and able to provide you with all of the tools you need to achieve your goals whatever they may be.

The next step is to get started with some of the work that we want to be able to work with when it is time to bring out the Linux operating system. In many personal computers, other options like Windows and Mac are going to be the main operating systems that we are able to work with. But there are many other applications out there that are going to rely on Linux and all of the neat features that come with this option as well. It is free to use, comes with fewer problems than some of the other operating systems and can really help us to get things done without worrying about viruses, malware and even ransomware along the way. With this in mind, we are going to spend some time in this guidebook looking at what the Linux system is able to do for us and why it is such a powerful option to rely on.

This guidebook spent some time going through the basics of the Linux system. There are so many things that we are able to do when it comes to working with this operating system and we are going to discuss the benefits of working with this, why the costs are so low compared to other operating systems and some of the different distributions that we are able to work with as well.

But that is just the beginning to help us get our feet wet in the process. We are also going to spend some time looking at more about this as well. To start with, we are going to spend some time creating our VirtualBox so that we can use Linux when we would like, while still maintaining some of the other operating systems that we would like to use. Then we moved on to learning more about some of the commands that we can use in Linux, how to handle the Fish shell and even how to handle some of the protection and more that need to happen in order to make sure that your files and directories are not going to be corrupted in the process.

To finish off this guidebook, we spent a bit of time looking at a few other important things that can help us to get our work done as well. We spent some time looking at how to handle the text editors that we are able to work with, including some information on Nano and Vi so that you can write out some of the commands that you would like. And then, there was a discussion on how we are able to use the Linux operating system as our number one tool to handle most of the work that we want to do with hacking.

There are a lot of great operating systems out there that we are able to work with as well. Windows and Mac can provide us with some great options as well. But if you are looking for an option that is going to have a lot of power and great features and will be open-sourced and not cost what the others do, then the Linux operating system is the best option for you to choose from. When you are ready to learn more about the Linux system, make sure to read through this guidebook to help you get started.

Finally, if you found this book useful in any way, a review on Amazon is always appreciated!

Kali Linux

A Comprehensive Step-by-Step Beginner's Guide to Learn the Basics of Cybersecurity and Ethical Computer Hacking, Including Wireless Penetration Testing Tools to Secure Your Network

Jason Knox

Introduction

Congratulations on purchasing *Kali Linux: A Comprehensive Step-by-Step Beginner's Guide to Learn the Basics of Cybersecurity and Ethical Computer Hacking, Including Wireless Penetration Testing Tools to Secure Your Network,* and thank you for doing so. The book covers the numerous tools in Kali Linux that you can use for performing penetration tests. You will also be able to learn the operations of the various utilities in this Debian distribution. To use this book effectively, you will require prior knowledge of basic Linux administration, computer networking and the command utilities but on a minimum. This will help you to comprehend the various subjects that have been covered herein.

You will get to know how hackers are able to gain access to your systems and the methods they use to steal information. Furthermore, you will also learn the countermeasures required to safeguard yourself against the numerous hacking techniques. To this end, the books cover topics that include: an Introduction to Kali Linux, The Basics of Kali Linux, The Hacking Process, Wireless Network Hacking, Uses and Applications of Kali Linux, Introduction to Cybersecurity

Network Scanning and Management and some basics on Web Security you will need to know in your journey to be a professional hacker.

By the time you flip the last page of this book you will have mastered both theoretical and practical concepts on the basic techniques that you require to become a hacker. You will have the techniques needed for penetration of computer networks, computer applications alongside computer systems. Let me say that we have numerous books that cover this topic, but you have decided to pick this one up. Many thanks for that. No efforts have been spared in ensuring that the content in this book is relevant and refreshing to you. Have fun reading!

Chapter 1: Introduction to Kali Linux

In this chapter you will be introduced to a diverse area of ethical penetration testing. It is also referred to as ethical hacking and is defined as a technical procedure and methodology which gives professional hackers a platform to simulate the techniques and actions that real-life hackers would use in the exploitation of an information system or a computer network. We are going to learn the steps that are usually followed by the penetration tester right from the understanding and analysis of a select target to the actual break-in. The book also covers topics dealing with the numerous tools that are used in the penetration testing exercise. These are briefly introduced in this chapter but will be covered in depth in chapter 4. The reader will get to understand the practical applications of Kali Linux in the real world besides knowing how to download and install this distribution of Linux. So, let us get into it without further ado.

History of Kali Linux

Offensive Security is the company behind this wonderful distribution. Kali Linux is the company's latest release. Kali is a live disk security distribution having over 300 penetration testing and security tools. If you have prior experience with the operating system, you may have noticed that the tools have been categorized into groups that are commonly utilized by penetration testers and any other entities doing the assessment of information systems. Kali Linux utilizes Debian 7.0

distribution as its base, unlike the earlier distributions that were released by Offensive Security. The operating system is of the same lineage as its predecessor, Backtrack Linux. It is worth noting that it is also supported by the same team.

The name change to Kali Linux, according to Offensive Security, implies that this operating system is a total rebuild of the Backtrack distribution. The major improvements that were made meant that it was not just a new version of Backtrack but a new operating system altogether. Going down memory lane, you will remember that Backtrack itself, just like Kali, was an upgrade that was derived from White Hat and SLAX, abbreviated as WHAX alongside Auditor. Technically speaking, Kali is the most recent incarnation of the information security industry penetration and auditing assessment tools.

Tool categories in Kali Linux

Kali Linux comes prepackaged with plenty of tools we can use for carrying out penetration testing. As we have said previously, the tools in Kali Linux are categorized in a fashion that helps with the penetration testing exercise. Below are the broad categories:

1) **Information gathering tools:** In this category, we have numerous tools that are used in the information gathering process. Normally, a penetration tester would be interested in information about DNS, operating systems, IDS/IPS, SSL, network scanning, routing, voice over IP, SMB, e-mail addresses, VPN, and SNMP.

2) **Vulnerability assessment tools:** Here, tools that are used in the scanning of vulnerabilities, in general, are located. We have tools that are

utilized for the vulnerability assessment of the Cisco network and database servers. We also have several fuzzing tools in this category.

3) **Web applications:** Just like the name, tools in this category relate to web applications. They include database exploitation, content management system scanner, web vulnerability scanners, web crawlers, and web application proxies.

4) **Tools for password attacks:** Tools that you can use to carry out both online and offline password attacks are found under this category.

5) **Exploitation tools**: You will find tools for the exploitation of the vulnerabilities unearthed from a selected target environment. Here, you will get exploitation tools you can use for databases, the Web, and the network. Also, under this category, you will find tools for carrying out social engineering attacks. The tools will give the user information about the exploits carried out too.

6) **Tools for sniffing and spoofing:** The tools here are used for sniffing web traffic and the network traffic. We also have network spoofing tools, for example, Yersinia and Ettercap.

7) **Tools for maintaining access:** A penetration tester will use the tools found here to maintain their access to a target machine. Obviously, you require the highest level of privilege to install tools located in this category. We have tools that can be used for backdooring web applications and the operating system. Tools used for tunneling are also found in this category.

8) **Tools for reporting:** Tools that are used for documentation of the penetration testing methodology and the obtained results and recommendations are found in this category.

9) **System services:** We have numerous services which are necessary during the penetration testing exercise in this category. Examples include: the Metasploit service, Apache service, SSH service, and MySQL service.

10) **Wireless attacks:** Here, we have tools for carrying out attacks on wireless devices, RFID/NFC and Bluetooth devices.

11) **Reverse engineering:** Tools in this category are normally used for debugging programs or carrying out disassembly of executable files.

12) **Stress testing**: If you want to carry out stress testing of your network, VOIP environment, wireless and Web, you will find all the tools relevant in this category.

13) **Hardware hacking:** If you are interested in working with Arduino and Android applications, all the tools you need are found here.

14) **Forensics:** The forensics category contains numerous tools normally utilized in digital forensics. Examples of forensics include the acquisition of hard disk images, carving of files and, more importantly, analyzing the image retrieved from the hard disk. To do these tasks properly, a user is required to go to the Kali Linux Forensics menu then select the No Drives

or Swap Mount from the booting menu. This way, the operating system will not automatically mount the drives. This implies that the integrity of the drives will be maintained.

Hold onto this information for now as we will look at some of it in chapter 5.

The Lifecycle for Penetration Testing

Today, we have various lifecycle models of penetration testing that are being used. So far, the lifecycle and the methodology defined and used by the EC-Council Certified Ethical Hacker program is the one that is widely used. This penetration testing life cycle is made up of five phases, including Reconnaissance, Scanning, Gaining Access, Maintaining Access and finally Covering Tracks in that order. Later in the book, we will look at each of the stages above in detail.

General Penetration Testing Framework

We have said before that Kali Linux provides us with the versatility we need in the process of penetration testing and security assessment from the numerous tools it possesses. A penetration tester who does not follow a proper framework is likely to get unsatisfactory results emanating from unsuccessful testing. This means that it is therefore essential for managers and technical administrators to ensure that the security testing is in harmony with a structured framework: the goal of the test is to provide useful findings.

What you are going to learn here is a general testing framework that is normally used by both the white box and black box approaches. From it, you will get an elementary understanding of the typical phases that a penetration tester or a security auditor should progress. The frameworks, however, need to be adjusted appropriately basing on the target being assessed. The following are steps that need to be followed so that the assessment procedure is successful.

- Scoping of the target
- Gathering Information
- Discovery of the Target
- Target Enumeration

- Mapping out Vulnerabilities

- Social engineering

- The exploitation of the Target

- Escalation of Privilege

- Maintenance of access

- Reporting and Documentation

1. Scoping of the Target

This is usually the first step prior to beginning the technical assessment of the security. It is essential that observations are carried out on the target network environment so that the scope is well understood. It is also possible to define the scope for a given set of entities or a single entity that is given to the auditor. Examples of typical decisions normally made in this step include;

- What element requires testing?

- How will it be tested?

- What are the parameters that will be applied when conducting the test?

- What are the limiting factors of the test process?

- How long will the test take?

- What objectives are intended to be achieved?

For any penetration testing exercise to be successful, the tester must have a good understanding of the technology being assessed, its basic operations together with the way it interacts with the network environment. What this means is that an auditor's knowledge is what determines the success of the penetration testing procedure.

2. Information gathering

After scoping has been done, the next phase is the reconnaissance phase. Here, the penetration tester will make use of resources that are available publicly to get a better understanding of their target. One can get valuable information from sources on the Internet, which include:

- Social networks
- Articles
- Forums
- Blogs
- Bulletin boards
- Commercial or non-commercial websites
- Newsgroups
- Search engines, for example, MSN Bing, Google, among others.

Additionally, Kali Linux has several tools that you can use to get a target's network information. The tools use crucial data mining techniques for gathering information from DNS servers, e-mail addresses, traceroutes, phone numbers, Whois database, personal information, and user accounts. Chances of having a successful penetration test increase with the amount of information that is gathered.

3. Target discovery

Here, key activities are the identification of the network status of selected targets, its OS and, if possible, the target's network architecture. Such information gives a penetration tester a comprehensive outlook of the interconnected devices or current technologies in the network. That means that they will be able to enumerate the numerous services running within the network. It is possible to do all this (determination of hosts on the network that are live, the running OS on the hosts and the characterization of each of them based on their roles in the network system) using the Kali Linux advanced network tools. The detection techniques employed by these tools can either be active or passive. This is done on top of network protocols and can be manipulated in a fashion that will yield useful information. An example of this information is the OS fingerprinting.

4. Target Enumeration

This phase advances the previous efforts by finding open ports on the systems being targeted. After the identification of open ports, enumeration of the ports will be done for the running services. Employing port scanning techniques like stealth, full-open, and half-open scan can assist a hacker, or a penetration tester checks the visibility of ports. This is possible for hosts that are behind an Intrusion Detection System or a firewall. To help penetration testers or hackers discover existing vulnerabilities in a target network's infrastructure, an investigation of the services which are mapped to the open ports can be done. This means that we can use target enumeration as a platform for unearthing vulnerabilities present in the various devices on the network. Through the vulnerabilities, one can penetrate the network. A security auditor can utilize Kali Linux's automated tools to do target enumeration.

5. Vulnerability mapping

By now, we will be having enough information about the target network.

We will now need to analyze the identified vulnerabilities basing on the services and ports we have discovered. We have automated vulnerability assessment tools for applications and the network in Kali Linux that can help us achieve the objectives of this phase. It is also possible to do vulnerability mapping manually. The only downside is that it requires expert knowledge and consumes plenty of time. The best approach to this is to combine the two so that a security auditor can have a clear vision that will enable them to investigate vulnerabilities that are either known or unknown in the network systems.

6. Social engineering

Social engineering is a type of attack which uses human beings as attack vectors. In most information security configurations, human beings are regarded as the weak link through which an attacker can gain access to a system. An attacker can penetrate a target network and execute a malicious code that will do some damage and, in some cases, create a backdoor for future use. All this will have been made possible through deceiving the people in charge of or those using a given network. Social engineering can be of different forms. For instance, an attacker using a phone can pretend to be a network administrator prompting a user to disclose their account information. Another form of social engineering is an e-mail phishing scam, which is used by malicious users to steal the account details of your bank. Physically, a person can imitate a legitimate user to gain access to a physical location. This is also social engineering. From these examples, we can see that the possibilities for achieving a required goal are immense. To make any penetration testing exercise successful, it is important that the tester or attacker takes time to understand human psychology as it is a skill that will help them improvise accordingly in their targeting. Note that most countries have laws regulating this, and as such, it is good to know the laws before attempting anything lest you end up in jail.

7. Target exploitation

After we have studied the vulnerabilities we have uncovered, we can go ahead and penetrate our target based on the available types of exploits. Most of the time, modifications or additional research on existing exploits are needed to ensure the exploits work as intended. The task is, of course, daunting. However, Kali Linux comes prepackaged with advanced exploitation tools that can help in the simplification of the exercise. Further, a tester is at liberty to employ client-side exploitation tactics in addition to some little social engineering to enable them assume control of a target system. A keen reader should, by now, see that this phase concentrates more on the process of target acquisition. Target exploitation encompasses three key areas. These are pre-exploitation, exploitation, and post-exploitation activities.

8. Privilege escalation

After target acquisition, the penetration exercise will be deemed successful. The penetration tester or auditor will now be able to roam in the system freely based on their access privileges. Using local exploits matching the environment of the system, a tester can escalate these privileges. Once these exploits are executed, a hacker or a penetration tester will now be able to get system-level or super-user privileges. From here onwards, a tester can carry out additional attacks on the local network systems. Based on a target's scope, this process can either be non-restricted or restricted. It is also possible to get more information regarding a compromised target through cracking passwords to various services, network traffic sniffing, and employing spoofing tactics on local networks. This implies that the main objective of privilege escalation is to enable one to acquire the highest-level access to the targeted system.

9. Maintaining access

A penetration tester, in some instances, can be requested by a client to maintain their access in the system for a specified period. This can be used as a demonstration to the network managers to show how illegal access to the system can be done without the need for a penetration process again. Also, it serves to save resources, time and cost that is spent in gaining access to the system for purposes of assessing its security. One can choose to use secret tunneling methods that utilize proxy, protocols, or end-to-end connection strategies. This way, a tester can create backdoor access, which will assist them in maintaining their presence in a target system for as long as they are required to. This technique of accessing the system gives us an indication of how an attacker can keep their presence in a targeted system without raising suspicion.

10.   Reporting and Documentation

A penetration testing exercise will not be complete if a presentation of disclosed vulnerabilities is not done. Verified and exploited vulnerabilities should be well documented, reported and presented. Ethically speaking, this is crucial as it will help the network and system administrators and managers to direct their resources towards sealing any security loopholes present in their infrastructure. The reports will have different outlooks based on the needs of the different contracting organizations. The customizations of the report will help technical staff and businesses get to know and analyze points of weaknesses existing in their IT infrastructure. In addition to that, the reports can be used in the comparison of the integrity of a target system after and before the penetration process.

Let us look at the Ethics

To ensure that everything remains legal, we have rules of engagement. These must be adhered to by the auditors and other information security professionals.

These rules describe the way the penetration testing should be given, the way testing is to be performed, the determination of legal negotiations and contracts, definition of the testing scope, test plan preparation, the process the test should follow, and the management of a reporting structure that is consistent. A keen examination is required to address each of these areas. The making of formal procedures and practices need to be adhered to throughout the engagement period. These rules include but are not limited to, the following:

1. The test schedule should be chosen in a way that does not affect or interrupt the normal operation of a business. It is prudent to create a schedule that does not cover the typical working hours.

2. The rules governing the test process clearly outline a set of steps to be followed during the

testing exercise. The organization's managers and technicians participate in the formulation of these rules for purposes of restricting the testing process with its environment and people.

3. It is forbidden to provide testing services to a client after hacking their systems prior to coming up with any formal agreement. This is akin to unethical marketing, and in some cases, it may lead to failure of the normal business operations and can cause one to face excruciating legal repercussions based on the country's rules and laws.

4. It is strictly prohibited to conduct a penetration test past the scope of testing or breaching the set limits without a clients' express permissions.

5. A legally binding contract should be agreed upon by parties involved so that it limits the liability of a job unless there is evidence of illegal activity. It must clearly state the conditions and terms of the test procedure, the

emergency contact information, the description of work, and any conflicts of interest if present.

6. The scope of the penetration test should be clearly defined, indicating the contractual entities and any restrictions that have been imposed on them during the procedure.

7. On completion of the testing, reports and results must be presented in a consistent and clear fashion. It should include all the vulnerabilities that are known and unknown. Furthermore, it needs to be confidentially delivered to authorized personnel only.

Terminologies

In this book, we are going to encounter commonly used terms in the field of penetration testing. The terms are normally understood differently by members, technicians and professionals in the same field, and that is the reason we need a working definition to avoid any misunderstanding. Below are the terms and associated definitions we shall be using.

Penetration Testing

We define it as the process, methodology and procedures that are used in the attempt to bypass the safeguard mechanisms of the information systems, including overcoming the integrated security set up of that system. Normally, the entire process follows approved and specific guidelines. Penetration Testing is concerned with examining the administrative, technical, and operational controls and settings of a system. The testing assesses the security of a particular information system exactly as it is configured. The system administrators and staff of the targeted network may or may not know that such an exercise is happening.

Ethical Hacking

This is a professional penetration tester whose main job is to carry out an attack on the computer or network systems for an organization or a particular owner of the information system. In this book, you will note that Ethical Hacking and Penetration Testing are used interchangeably.

White Hat

This terminology is synonymous with computer security professional or an Ethical Hacker who is specialized in the security testing of information systems so as to provide security where it is lacking or improve it where it is possible.

Black Hat

This is a terminology used to describe a person who uses his IT skills for bypassing the security of information systems without permission. The intention of black hats is normally to commit computer crimes. Red Team members, together with Penetration Testers, normally employ techniques used by Black Hats in their work. This is to simulate the malicious fellows in security testing while they are carrying out legitimate tests or exercises.

Grey Hat

In life, we have the good guys, the bad guys and those who lie in between. In hacking, grey hats are those in the middle. Normally, they will try to circumvent the security features of an information system in most cases without prior permission. They do this normally to bring to light the discovered weaknesses to the system administrators. In most cases, they are not after profit. What makes them illegitimate is the fact that they do not seek prior permission from the owners before carrying out their activities.

Vulnerability Assessment/Analysis

This is an exercise done to evaluate the security configurations of a system. The forms of the assessments that can be carried out comprise the evaluation of security patches that have been applied to a system and those that are missing. The team that carries out Vulnerability Assessment can either be external or it can be part of an organization's IT team.

Malicious User Testing

In this scenario, the assessor will act as if they were an insider acting maliciously. Of course, being an insider makes them a trusted entity. What happens is that the assessor will be given legitimate login credentials belonging to an authorized user; this will be a test account. They will then go ahead and use the credentials to try and circumvent laid down security measures. They can do this by modifying settings that are not supposed to be changed, viewing settings and documents that the account is not authorized to and escalating their permissions and privileges beyond the level the test account should have. In summary, a malicious user test attempts to simulates actions that a rogue insider can carry out using their trusted credentials.

Phishing

In this type of attack, attempts will be made to get the targeted entities to reveal personal information such as passwords, account numbers, and user names. Normally, this is done by the use of authentic-looking emails that are fake. The emails can be from customer support staff, banks and corporations. A different type of phishing attack is where users are prodded to click on phony hyperlinks. This will make it possible for malicious codes to be installed on the target system without the owner's knowledge. Once this has been done, the malware can be used to attack other computers or for obtaining data stored on the computer. Phishing attacks are by nature, not directed to a specific target. Targets can be all the people in a mailing list or those whose email addresses have a specific extension, such as those with a "@kali.com" extension.

Spear Phishing

This is a type of phishing attack whereby the targets are specific. For instance,

An attacker can perform reconnaissance to discover email addresses of top-level management of an organization. They can go ahead then to carry out the phishing attack on only these individuals.

Dumpster Diving

In this technique, the penetration tester will make attempts to filter through a systems' discarded trash. This trash might be from any of the users and the system administrators. Any information obtained here will be of great help in understanding a particular target. A penetration tester might recover information detailing network diagrams, system settings and configurations, the hardware components and the software versions that are being used. On a good day, one might even get user credentials such as passwords and user names. Dumpster Diving is a term used to explain the process of entering a large trash container. Also, garbage cans from small offices normally have some lucrative information.

LiveOS, Live Disk, Live CD

The terms above are used to refer to an optical disk containing a complete operating system. Live disks are a crucial asset to penetration testers and assessors since it is possible to modify them to suit the needs at hand. One can customize them to have specific settings, tools and software components. Many of the live disks in distributions are normally Linux based, although, over the years, we have had numerous Microsoft Windows versions being released. In most assessments, it is sufficient for an assessor to only bring with them a live disk. The systems under assessment can be directly booted to the live disk, effectively turning the information systems assets against the system itself.

Chapter 2: The Basics of Kali Linux

Downloading Kali

In the introduction, we pointed out that Kali Linux is a Linux distribution and can be downloaded as an ISO file. You will be required to download it from a different computer, after which you will burn it onto a disk before installation. You can download this interesting distribution of Linux from this link http://www.kali.org/downloads/. To know how to install it, you can get the documentation for configurations, advanced operations, and special cases on http://www.kali.org/official-documentation/. If you need any additional help, we have an active community where you can make any inquiries or you can help other members solve their problems. Offensive Security manages these community boards, and new users are required to register to enable them to obtain access.

The security company is the makers of Kali Linux. Occasionally, Offensive Security will provide messages pertaining to their products, community information and updates. When downloading Kali Linux, ensure that you select the proper architecture for your computer (either amd64564-bit or i386532-bit). I do not wish to talk about the images of Kali Linux in this book since that information is well captured in the links I have provided. Tap on the correct link to select and download the image. For those of you that are using Microsoft Windows, you will need to burn the image using the Burn ISO or any other application (I can think of Rufus). Proceed with the burning process until it is complete. Similarly, Linux users can use a disk burning application (say K3b) to convert the ISO image.

Installation of Kali Linux on the Hard Drive

You are going to learn how to do a graphical and textual installation of this operating system. The graphical interface has been designed to be as simple as possible. You will be required to configure your Basic Input Output System

(BIOS) to boot from the optical disk you have created. First, load your optical disk or flash drive containing

Kali onto the computer and start. For advanced users, there is an option of using virtualization technology like Oracle's VirtualBox or VMware's Player.

First Time Booting of Kali Linux

The screenshot below shows a computer that has successfully booted to the Kali Linux disk. 64-Bit Kali Linux version 1.0.5 has been used in this book. With time, you will observe that versions of Kali Linux that are downloaded at different times will appear different, albeit slightly. That aside, graphical installations are similar.

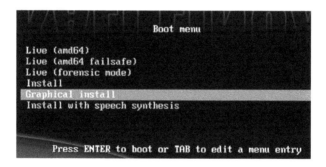

At http://www.kali.org/, you will find up to date guides for all the latest releases of Kali Linux. As such, it is important to check out this site before you carry out an installation. Kali Linux, besides being installed on a computer's hard drive, it can be run straight from the disk having the converted image. This is what we call a Live CD. This enables the operating system to boot. The tools that come with Kali will also execute. The only thing to note here is that the operating system from the live CD is nonpersistent. This terminology is used to mean that upon shutting down the computer, any memory, documents, saved settings and any other essential research or work is likely to be lost. A great way to learn Kali Linux is by running it in a nonpersistent state. Additionally, your current operating system will not be affected in any way. You can see that we have an option for installation with Speech Synthesis. We will not be going into the intricate details for that, but you should know that it is a recent upgrade feature to the Debian operating system and Kali. Users can control the installation procedure vocally if their hardware can support speech synthesis. How exciting! Like I have said before, let us concentrate on the graphical installation for

now. Using the directional keys, scroll and highlight Graphical Install and bang the Enter key.

Setting the Defaults

You will be required to select default settings for your location, keyboard layout, and language in the next few screens. After you have made the appropriate selections, click on continue to proceed to the next step. You will notice various bars denoting progress on your computer's screen throughout the installation as the computer begins the actual installation of Kali. Picking the default settings is a good choice for most of the selection screens.

Initial Network Setup

See the image below. In this stage, you will be required to do a basic configuration and an initial setup of your primary network interface card. Select a Hostname. Do this simply by typing in the provided box and hit the continue button to proceed. Make sure you pick a unique hostname to avoid having different computers with similar hostnames on the same network.

That will help to minimize networking complications. Once you are done choosing a hostname, hit the Continue button to proceed. On the next screen, you are going to provide a fully qualified domain name, FQDN. For most lab environments, this is not necessary unless you wish to join a domain environment. Let us leave it blank for now. We will click on the Continue button to move ahead.

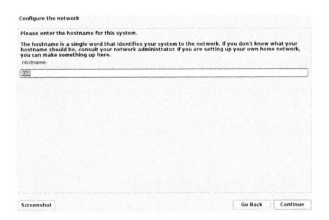

Setting Up Passwords

The next screen that comes up will prompt you for a root-level password. In Kali Linux, the default password is toor. I recommend that you create a new password that is strong, have no traceability to the user and that it should not be easy to guess. On keying in the password twice, tap the Continue button to move on to the next step. Are you still with me? Let us now configure the system clock.

Configuring the System Clock

You will be prompted to select a time zone of your choice, as shown in the figure below. Choose appropriately and then press the Continue button to proceed onto the next installation step.

Configuration of the clock.

Partitioning Disks

We have several ways of configuring partitions for setting up a Linux OS. We are going to focus on Guided Partitioning, which is the most basic installation. The figures below display the settings that are normally highlighted by default. You do not have to select anything till you reach the figure under partition disks - 5. All you need to do is click on the continue button until partitioning is complete. Let us take some time and understand what is happening at each step of the installation wizard.

Below, you will see the various options that you can choose for partitioning your computer's hard drives during the installation.

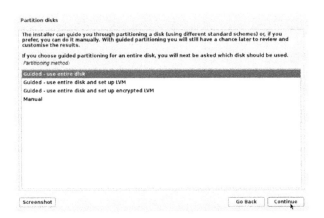

Partition disks - 1.

For laptop SD card or thumb drive installation, it is not recommended to use Logical Volume Management (LVM). Advanced users normally use LVM for managing many hard drives. The option that you should select is "Guided - user entire disk." Hit the Continue button to move onto the next step of the installation process. The figure below will indicate which drive has been picked for installation. Click on Continue to proceed.

Partition disks - 2.

If you are a new Kali Linux user, select the option "All files in one partition (recommended for new users)." This is the best option for you. Hit the Continue button to proceed with the installation.

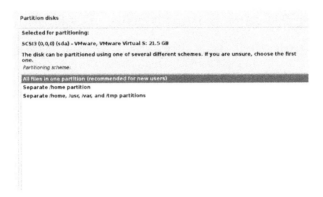

Partition disks - 3.

Keep clicking on the continue button to advance the installation.

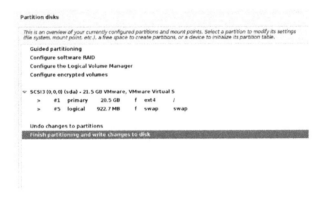

Partition disks - 4.

The wizard will take you through the above steps and present you with a screen for your review. Now, a partition having all the system, scripting, and user files, known as the primary partition, will be created as a single partition. A second partition will be made for swap space. This is a virtual memory in the system that is used for paging files to and from the computer's random-access memory and the central processing unit. It is recommended that all systems running Linux have a swap area. The common practice is to configure the swap area be one and a half times or even equal to the amount of the computer's installed physical random-access memory (RAM).

You will come to a screen looking like this.

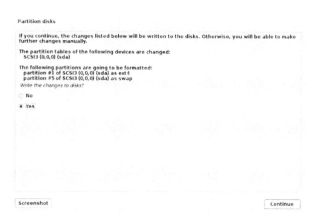

Partition disks - 5.

From the figure above, you will be asked to "Finish partitioning and write changes to disk." Pick the Yes option and click on the Continue button to proceed with the installation process. Take note that that will be the last chance you will have to review your partitioning options prior to the installation of the operating system on the hard drive. Should a need to amend the sizes of the partition arise in the future, it is still possible to do that. However, changing the partition sizes can destroy your operating system if it is not carried out properly.

Installation in progress.

The partitioning of the hard drive and installation will begin after you click continue (at the figure at partition disks – 5). The installation can take an hour or even a few minutes depending on your computer's hardware.

Setting Up the Package Manager

This is the update repository where your operating system will derive its security patches and updates from. As such, the package manager is very important in the functioning of the operating system. You can use the network mirror, which comes together with the Kali Linux image. It is recommended to use it since it contains the latest for package management sources. A "YES" option will be picked for you by default, as shown in the figure below. Proceed with the installation process by clicking on the Continue button.

Configuration of the package manager.

Suppose you are utilizing a proxy; you will need to input the configuration information on the next prompt the installation wizard will bring up. You can leave it blank as below. Hit the Continue button to proceed to the installation of the GRUB loader.

Configure the package manager

If you need to use a HTTP proxy to access the outside world, enter the proxy information here.
Otherwise, leave this blank.

The proxy information should be given in the standard form of "http://[[user][:pass]@]host[:port]/".

HTTP proxy information (blank for none):

Screenshot   Go Back   Continue

Configuring a proxy.

Install the GRUB Loader

GRUB is an abbreviation for Grand Unified Bootloader, and it is the main screen you will see each time you start the computer. GRUB provides a platform where a user can verify specific settings during the booting up, make changes where it is necessary and adjust settings prior to the loading of the operating system. GRUB is highly recommended for most Linux installations even though there are advanced users who do not necessarily need it. The figure below indicates that "YES" has been picked for you to install the GRUB. To advance to the next installation stage, click on the Continue button.

Installing the GRUB loader.

Completing Installation for Kali Linux

Your installation will now be complete. Take out the optical disk or flash drive from the computer and reboot. The computer will prompt you to reboot. Select the Continue button to complete your installation. See the figure below. Upon rebooting, you will be met with a welcome screen requiring you to log in. Use the credentials you set up earlier. That will be it. Welcome to Kali Linux!

Completing the installation.

Why You Should Use Kali Linux

As we have said before, Kali Linux comes with just about every tool pre-installed that can be used for any of the above purposes. It is for this reason that Security Auditors, Forensics Investigators, Penetration Testers and Researchers prefer it.

Kali can be used in the breaking of WiFi networks, to hack websites and networks, to run Open Source Intelligence on an entity, among others. Kali Linux possesses tools that can be used for forensic investigation besides ethical hacking. This is becoming an equally essential branch of security that primarily collects evidence, analyze it and uses the results to backtrack Cyber Criminals. Forensic Investigation makes it possible to locate and eradicate malicious effects emanating from malicious activities. It also comes in handy in the calculation and management of loss that occurs after a Cyber Attack. A key feature in Kali is the stealth Live mode mostly used in forensics and that it does not leave traces (fingerprints and footprints) on a host's system.

The Terminal

The very initial step in using Kali is to open the terminal, which is the command-line interface we'll use in this book. In Kali Linux, you'll find the icon for the terminal at the bottom of the desktop. Doubleclick this icon to open the terminal or press CTRLALTT. The terminal opens the command line environment, known as the shell, which enables you to run commands on the underlying operating systems and write scripts. Although Linux has many different shell environments, the most popular is the bash shell, which is also the default shell in Kali and many other Linux distributions. To change your password, you can use the command passwd.

Basic Commands in Linux

To begin, let's look at some basic commands that will help you get up and running in Linux.

- Finding Yourself with pwd

The command line in Linux does not always make it apparent which directory you're presently in, unlike that in Windows or macOS. To navigate to a new directory, you usually need to know where you are currently. The present working directory command, pwd, returns your location within the directory structure. Enter pwd in your terminal to see where you are:

kali >pwd
/root

In this case, Linux returned /root, telling me I'm in the root user's directory. And
because you logged in as root when you started Linux, you should be in the root user's directory too, which is one level below the top of the filesystem structure (/). If you're in another directory, pwd will return that directory name instead.

- Checking Your Login with whoami

In Linux, the one "all-powerful" superuser or system administrator is called root, and it has all the system privileges needed to add users, change passwords, change privileges and so on. Of course, you do not want just anyone to have the ability to make such changes; you want someone who can be trusted and has proper knowledge of the operating system. As a hacker, you usually need to have all those privileges to run the programs and commands you need, so you may want to log in as root. A Linux user can see which user they are logged in as using the "whoami" command as below:

kali >whoami
root

Here, the user is logged in as root.

- Navigating the Linux Filesystem

Navigating the filesystem from the terminal is an essential Linux skill. To get anything done, you need to be able to move around to find applications, files and directories located in other directories. In a GUI-based system, you can visually see the directories, but when you're using the command-line interface, the structure is entirely text-based and navigating the filesystem means using some commands.

- Changing Directories with cd

To change directories from the terminal, use the change directory command, cd. For example, here's how to change to the /etc. directory used to store configuration files:

kali >cd /etc

root@kali:/etc#

The prompt changes to root@kali:/etc, indicating that we're in the /etc. directory. We can confirm this by entering pwd

root@kali:/etc# pwd

/etc

To move up one level in the file structure (toward the root of the file structure, or /), we use cd followed by double dots (..), as shown here:

root@kali:/etc# cd ..

root@kali:/# pwd

/

root@kali:/#

This moves us up one level from /etc. to the /root directory, but you can move up as many levels as you need. Just use the same number of double dot pairs as the number of levels you want to move:

- You would use .. to move up one level.

- You would use .. .. to move up two levels.
- You would use .. .. .. to move up three levels, and so on.

So, for example, to move up two levels, enter cd followed by two sets of double dots with a space in between:

kali >cd .. ..

You can also move up to the root level in the file structure from anywhere by entering cd /, where / represents the root of the filesystem.

- Listing the Contents of a Directory with ls

To see the contents of a directory (the files and subdirectories), we can use the ls (list) command. This is very similar to the dir command in Windows.

```
kali >ls
bin  initrd.img      media      run      var
boot  initrd.img.old  mnt       sbin     vmlinuz
dev  lib            opt       srv     vmlinuz.old
etc  lib64           proc      tmp
home  lost+found      root      usr
```

This command lists both the files and directories contained in the directory. You can also use this command on any particular directory, not just the one you are currently in, by listing the directory name after the command; for example, ls /etc. shows what's in the /etc. directory. To get more information about the files and directories, such as their permissions, owner, size and when they were last modified, you can add the -l switch after ls (the l stands for long). This is often referred to as the long listing. See the example below:

```
kali >ls -1
total 84
drw-r--r--    1    root    root    4096    Dec    5    11:15    bin
drw-r--r--    2    root    root    4096    Dec    5    11:15    boot
drw-r--r--    3    root    root    4096    Dec    9    13:10    dev
drw-r--r--   18    root    root    4096    Dec    9    13:43    etc
--snip--
drw-r--r--    1    root    root    4096    Dec    5    11:15    var
```

- Getting Help

Nearly every command, application or utility has a dedicated help file in Linux that guides its use. For instance, if I needed help using the best wireless cracking tool, aircrack-ng, I could type the aircrack-ng command followed by the --help command:

kali >aircrack-ng --help

Note the double dash here. The convention in Linux is to use a double dash (--) before word options, such as help, and a single dash (-) before single letter options, such as –h. When you enter this command, you should see a short description of the tool and guidance on how to use it. In some cases, you can use either -h or -? to get to the help file. For instance, if I needed help using the hacker's best port scanning tool, Nmap, I would enter the following:

kali >nmap -h

Unfortunately, although many applications support all three options, there is no guarantee of the application you are using will. So if one option refuses to work, please try another.

Finding Files

Until you become familiar with Linux, it can be frustrating to find your way around, but knowledge of a few basic commands and techniques will go a long way toward making the command line much friendlier.

The following commands help you locate things from the terminal.

- Searching with locate

Probably the easiest command to use is locate. Followed by a keyword denoting what it is you want to find, this command will go through your entire filesystem and locate every occurrence of that word. To look for aircrack-ng, for example, enter the following:

```
kali >locate aircrack-ng
/usr/bin/aircrack-ng
/usr/share/applications/kali-aircrack-ng.desktop
/usr/share/desktop-directories/05-1-01-aircrack-ng.directory
--snip--
/var/lib/dpkg/info/aircrack-ng.mg5sums
```

The locate command is not perfect, however. Sometimes, the results of locate can be overwhelming, giving you too much information. Also, locate uses a database that is usually only updated once a day, so if you just created a file a few minutes or a few hours ago, it might not appear in this list until the next day. It's worth knowing the disadvantages of these basic commands so you can better decide when best to use each one.

- Finding Binaries with whereis

If you're looking for a binary file, you can use the whereis command to locate it. This command returns not only the location of the binary but also its source and main page if they are available. Here's an example:

```
kali >whereis aircrack-ng
aircarck-ng: /usr/bin/aircarck-ng /usr/share/man/man1/aircarck-ng.1.gz
```

- Finding Binaries in the PATH Variable with which

The which command is even more specific: it only returns the location of the binaries in the PATH variable in Linux. For example, when I enter aircrack-ng on the command line, the operating system looks to the PATH variable to see in which directories it should look for aircrackng:

```
kali >which aircrack-ng
/usr/bin/aircrack-ng
```

Here, which was able to find a single binary file in the directories listed in the PATH variable. At a minimum, these directories usually include /usr/bin, but may consist of/usr/sbin and maybe a few others.

- Performing More Powerful Searches with find

The find command is the most powerful and flexible of the searching utilities. It is capable of beginning your search in any designated directory and looking for several different parameters, including, of course, the filename but also the date of creation or modification, the owner, the group, permissions and the size.

Here is the basic syntax for find:

find directory options expression

- Filtering with grep

Very often, when using the command line, you may want to search for a particular keyword. For this, you can use the grep command as a filter to search for keywords. The grep command is often used when output is piped from one command to another.

```
kali >ps aux | grep apache2
root 4851 0.2 0.7 37548 7668 ? Ss 10:14 0:00 /usr/sbin/apache2 -k start
root 4906 0.0 0.4 37572 4228 ? S 10:14 0:00 /usr/sbin/apache2 -k start
root 4910 0.0 0.4 37572 4228 ? Ss 10:14 0:00 /usr/sbin/apache2 -k start
--snip--
```

In the above example, the command will display all the services that are running and then pipe that output to grep. What grep does is it will search the received output for the keyword we asked it to look for. In our case, the keyword is apache2. Grep will go ahead and output only the relevant results. This command saves time.

Modify Files and Directories

After finding the directories and files you were looking for, you may need to carry out several operations on them. We are going to learn the creation of directories and files, copy files, rename files, plus delete the files and directories.

- Creating Files

There are many ways to create files in Linux, but for now, we will look at two simple methods. The first is the cat, which is short for concatenate, meaning to combine pieces (not a reference to your favorite domesticated feline). The cat command is generally used for displaying the contents of a file, but it can also be used to create small files. For creating bigger files, it's better to enter the code in a text editor such as vim, emacs, leafpad, gedit or kate and then save it as a file.

- Concatenation with cat

The cat command followed by a filename will display the contents of that file, but to create a file, we follow the cat command with a redirect, denoted with the > symbol, and a name for the file we want to create. Here is an example:

kali >cat > kalilinux
Hacking with Kali Linux!

- File Creation with touch

The second command for file creation is touch. This command was initially developed so a user could touch a file to change some of its details, such as the date it was created or modified. However, if the file does not already exist, this command creates that file by default. Let's create newfile using the touch command:

kali >touch newfile

Now when I then use ls –l to see the long list of the directory, I see that a new file has been created named newfile. Note that its size is 0 because there is no content in the newfile.

- Creating a Directory

The command for creating a directory in Linux is mkdir, a contraction of make directory. To create a directory named newdirectory, enter the following command:

```
kali >mkdir newdirectory
```

To navigate to this newly created directory, do enter this:

```
kali >cd newdirectory
```

- Copying a File

To copy files, we use the cp command. This creates a duplicate of the file in the new location and leaves the old one in place. Here, we are going to create the file oldfile in the root directory with touch and copy it to /root/newdirectory, renaming it in the process and leaving the original oldfile in place:

```
kali >touch oldfile
kali >cp oldfile  /root/newdirectory/newfile
```

Renaming the file is optional and is done simply by adding the name you want to give it to the end of the directory path. If you don't rename the file when you copy it, the file will retain the original name by default. When we then navigate to newdirectory, we see that there is an exact copy of oldfile called newfile:

kali >cd newdirectory
kali >ls
newfile oldfile

- Renaming a File

Unfortunately, Linux doesn't have a command intended solely for renaming a file, as Windows and some other operating systems do, but it does have the mv (move) command. The mv command can be used to move a file or directory to a new location or to give an existing file a new name. To rename newfile to newfile2, you would enter the following:

```
kali >mv newfile newfile2
kali >ls
oldfile newfile2
```

Now when you list (ls) that directory, you see newfile2 but not newfile, because it has been renamed. You can do the same with directories.

- Removing a File

To remove a file, you can use the rm command, like so:

kali >rm newfile2

If you now do a long listing on the directory, you can confirm that the file has been removed.

Removing a Directory

The command for removing a directory is similar to the rm command for removing files but with dir (for directory) appended, like so:

```
kali >rmdir newdirectory
rmdir:failed to remove 'newdirectory': Directory not empty
```

It is important to note that rmdir will not remove a directory that is not empty but will give you a warning message that the "directory is not empty," as you can see in this example. You must first remove all the contents of the directory before removing it. This is to stop you from accidentally deleting objects you did not intend to delete. If you do want to remove a directory and its content all in one go, you can use the -r switch after rm, as shown below:

kali >rm -r newdirectory

Just a word of caution, though: be wary of using the -r option with rm, at least at first, because it is straightforward to remove valuable files and directories by mistake. Using rm -r in your home directory, for instance, would delete every file and directory there, that is certainly not what you were intending.

Searching for tools/packages

Before you download a software package, you can check whether the package you need is available from your repository, which is a place where your operating system stores information. The apt tool has a search function that can check whether the package is available. The syntax is straightforward:

```
apt-cache search keyword
```

Note that we use the apt-cache command to search the apt cache or the place it stores the package names. So if you were searching for the intrusion detection system Snort, for example, you would enter the command shown below.

```
kali >apt-cache search snort
fwsnort - Snort-to-iptables rule translator
ippl - IP protocols logger
--snip--
snort - flexible Network Intrusion Detection System
snort-common - flexible Network Intrusion Detection System - common files
--snip--
```

As you can see, many files have the keyword snort in them, but near the middle of the output, we see snort – flexible Network Intrusion Detection System. That is what we are looking for.

Adding Softwares

Now that you know the snort package exists in your repository, you can use apt-get to download the software. To install a piece of software from your operating system's default repository in the terminal, use the apt-get command, followed by the keyword install, and then the name of the package you want to install. The syntax looks like this:

apt-get install packagename

Let us try this out by installing Snort on your system. Enter apt-get install snort as a command statement, as shown below.

```
kali >apt-get install snort
Reading package lists... Done
Building dependency tree
Reading state information... Done
Suggested packages:
snort-doc
The following NEW packages will be installed:
snort
--snip--
Install these packages without verification [Y/n]?
```

The output you see tells you what is being installed. If everything looks correct, go
ahead and enter Y when prompted, and your software installation will proceed.

Removing Softwares

When removing software, use apt-get with the remove option, followed by the name of the software to remove. An example is listed below.

```
kali >apt-get remove snort
Reading package lists... Done
Building dependency tree
Reading state information... Done
The following packages were automatically installed and are no longer
required:
    libdaqo libprelude2 oinkmaster snort-common-libraries snort-rules-default
--snip--
Do you want to continue [Y/n]?
```

Again, you will see the tasks being done in real-time, and you will be asked whether you want to continue. You can enter Y to uninstall, but you might want to keep Snort since we will be using it again. The remove command does not remove the configuration files, which means you can reinstall the same package in the future without reconfiguring. If you do want to remove the configuration files at the same time as the package, you can use the purge option, as shown below.

```
kali >apt-get purge  snort
Reading package lists... Done
Building dependency tree
Reading state information... Done
The following packages were automatically installed and are no longer required:
    libdaqo libprelude2 oinkmaster snort-common-libraries snort-rules-default
--snip--
Do you want to continue [Y/n]?
```

Enter Y at the prompt to continue the purge of the
software package and the configuration files. To keep
things small and modular, many Linux packages are
broken into software units that many different
programs might use. When you installed Snort, you
installed several dependencies or libraries with it that
Snort requires so that it can run. Now that you are
removing Snort, those other libraries or dependencies
are no longer needed, so they are removed, too.

Updating Packages

Software repositories will be periodically updated with
new software or new versions of existing software.
These updates do not reach you automatically, so you
need to request them to apply these updates to your
system. Updating is different from upgrading:
updating updates the list of packages available for
download from the repository, whereas upgrading will
upgrade the package to the latest version in the

repository. You can update your system by entering the apt-get command, followed by the keyword update. This will search through all the packages on your system and check whether updates are available. If so, the updates will be downloaded. See the example below.

kali >apt-get update
Get:1 http://mirrors.ocf.berkeley.edu/kali kali-rolling InRelease [30.5kb]
Get:2   http://mirrors.ocf.berkeley.edu/kali   kali-rolling/main amd64 Packages
[14.9MB]
Get:3 http://mirrors.ocf.berkeley.edu/kali kali-rolling non-free amd64 Packages
[163kb]
Get:4   http://mirrors.ocf.berkeley.edu/kali   kali-rolling/contrib amd64 Packages [107kB]
Fetched 15.2 MB in 1min 4s (236 kB/s)
Reading package lists... Done

The list of available software in the repository on your system will be updated. If the update is successful, your terminal will state Reading package lists... Done, as you can see above. Note that the name of the repository and the values, time, size and so on might be different on your system.

Upgrading Packages

To upgrade the existing packages on your system, use apt-get upgrade. Because upgrading your packages may make changes to your software, you must be logged in as root or use the sudo command before entering an apt-get upgrade. This command will upgrade every package on your system that apt knows about, meaning only those stored in the repository, as shown below. Upgrading can be time-consuming, so you might not be able to use your system for a while.

```
kali >apt-get upgrade
Reading package lists... Done
Building dependency tree... Done
Calculating upgrade... Done
The following packages were automatically installed and no longer required:
--snip--
The following packages will be upgraded:
--snip--
1101 upgraded, 0 newly installed, 0 to remove and 318 not upgraded.
Need to get 827 MB of archives.
After this operation, 408 MB disk space will be freed.
Do you want to continue? [Y/n]
```

You should see in the output that your system estimates the amount of hard drive space necessary for the software package. Go ahead and enter Y if you want to continue and have enough hard drive space for the upgrade.

Chapter 3: The Hacking Process

In short, Ethical hacking, performed by white hat hackers, is a term used to describe defense hacking for companies and organizations, which involves the identification of potential threats on a computer or network.

Like all good projects, ethical hacking also has a set of distinct phases. It helps hackers to make a structured ethical hacking attack.Different security training manuals explain the process of ethical hacking in different ways, but in my experience, the entire process can be categorized into the following six phases:

1. Reconnaissance.
2. Scanning.
3. Access Gain.
4. Maintain Access.
5. Clearing your Tracks.
6. Reports.

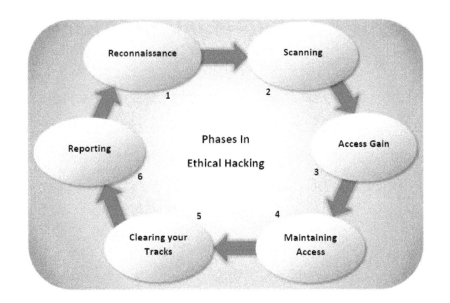

Reconnaissance

What is Reconnaissance? From the dictionary meaning, it is a preliminary survey that is carried out to obtain information. An example is the exploratory surveys that militaries conduct on the territory belonging to the enemy. When it comes to cyber-security, Reconnaissance is a way of gathering information on a target using different techniques. When performing this exercise, there are three main information that is of interest to an ethical hacker;

1. The Network.
2. The Host.
3. Users/People involved.

Steps in Performing a Reconnaissance Exercise.
In ethical hacking, the first step is normally meant to help a penetration tester better understand their targets. This is done under a category that is collectively known as Information Gathering. Hereunder, we have something known as Reconnaissance, which we define as being a set of techniques and processes that are utilized in the discovery and collection of crucial information about a target. They include Scanning, Enumeration and Foot-printing. In an exercise meant for Reconnaissance, an ethical hacker tries to gather as much information about a target system as possible, following the seven steps listed below;

1. Collecting first information.
2. Determine a network's range.
3. Identification of active machines.
4. Discovering of Access Points and open ports that are available.
5. Operating System Fingerprinting.
6. Scanning for services running on various ports.
7. Network Mapping.

Reconnaissance is categorized into two major parts.

1. Active Reconnaissance: Active reconnaissance involves direct contact with your target's computer system to gain information, and information gotten directly is actually accurate. There is the risk of being caught in the process of active reconnaissance without permission. But most hacking activities require active recon.

2. Passive Reconnaissance: In this process, you will not be directly connected to a computer system. This process is used to gather essential information without ever interacting with the target systems.

Enumeration

Enumeration, in the actual sense, is the complete listing of things in an orderly manner with regards to items in a collection. Enumeration is the act of making a list of policies, user accounts, shares and other resources. This step happens just before vulnerability assessment and after scanning. This helps the attacker put together the best strategy for gaining access. Enumeration can be used to gain information on:

1. Users and Groups
2. Networks and shared paths

3. Hostnames

4. Route Tables

5. Service Settings

6. SNMP port scanning

7. DNS Details Applications and Banners.

Enumeration can be done with the following tools. In the Windows Operating System, the use of many tools is done to enumerate NetBIOS names with commands like:

• Net accounts,

• Net config server,

• Net config workstation,

• Net view.

Scanning

This is a procedure that is used in the identification of services, active hosts and the ports that are used by the target application. Let us say you wish to unearth the vulnerabilities in a system, what you will need is a point you can attack in the System. In ethical Hacking, Network Scanning is employed to find out these points. These are points that Black Hats use to penetrate a system. After discovering these points, the relevant teams will then direct their efforts to improve the system. We know that all organizations have networks. They can either be internal or even connected to the internet. To hack these networks, you must first find a vulnerable point within them so that you can use it to carry out exploits. Network Scanning is the method we employ to help us discover such points within a network.

Network Scanning Objectives

1. It helps in the discovery of open ports, live computers or hosts and the IP address of the victim.
2. Network scanning makes it possible to identify the services which are running on the host computer.
3. It also aids in the discovery of the system architecture and the operating system of the target.
4. Scanning Live hosts enables us to unearth and mitigate vulnerabilities.

How is Network Scanning different from Reconnaissance?

To help you understand the difference between the two, I am going to use this analogy. Assume that you are commander in the army and you have been tasked together with your team to go and carry out an attack on a terrorist camp. We are going to assume that you already have an idea of the camps' location and the details about the vicinity of the camp. Now, this is information normally obtained through Reconnaissance. You will still be required to identify an entry point to the terrorist camp so that you can launch your attack. This is now what we are calling Network Scanning. We can confidently conclude that Reconnaissance is a technique you will use for gathering information to help you know more about your target. On the other hand, Network Scanning is a technique you will employ to help you locate possible vulnerable points within the network. It is through these points that one can penetrate a targeted network. Based on the information revealed by the scan, Network Scanning can be divided into two main categories:

- Port Scanning
- Vulnerability Scanning

Port Scanning

From the name, we can deduce that Port Scanning is a way of identifying active ports on the network. A Port Scanner works by transmitting requests from a client to the range of ports located on a network that they are targeting. The details about the ports will be saved and then a response will be transmitted back. This, good readers, is how active ports are found. Upon acquiring a target's IP address (through scanning a victim organization's UDP and TCP ports), the hacker will proceed to map the organization's network under his/her grab.

Types of Port Scanning

SYNScan: In this mode of scanning, the TCP three-way handshake technique is not completed. Here, a hacker or penetration tester will send a victim the SYN packet. In case the response of an SYN/ACK frame is received, a connection will be completed by the target and the port will be able to listen. Receiving an RST from the target can mean that the port is not activated or it is closed. This type of scan has an advantage in the sense that only a few IDS systems will log this as a connection attempt or an attack.

XMASScan: The scan transmits a packet containing PSH (push), URG (urgent), and FIN (finish) flags. Suppose we have an open port; we do not expect a response; the target will respond with an RST/ACK packet if the port is closed. (RST=reset)

FINScan: This scan is almost similar to an XMAS scan with one exception. FINScan transmits packets with just the FIN (finish) flag. The scan does not have the other two flags (URG and PSH flags). The response is similar to that of XMAS scans. Also, the two scans have similar limitations.

IDLEScan: This kind of scan utilizes a spoofed IP for the transmission of a SYN packet to the target through the determination of the responses from the port scan together with the IP header sequence number. The port is considered opened or closed based on the response of the scan.

Inverse TCP Flag Scan: In this case, a hacker will transmit TCP probe packets with a TCP flag (FIN, URG PSH) or with no flags. If there is no response, then it indicates that the port is open and RST means the port is closed.

ACK Flag Probe Scan: In this type of port scanning, an intruder will transmit TCP probe packets to a point where an ACK flag is set to a remote device that is used for the analysis of the header information. This information comprises of WINDOW and the TTL field. To know if the port is open or closed, one uses the RST packet. You can also use this scan for checking a target's filtering system.

Vulnerability Scanning

Essentially speaking, this is a type of Network Scanning that we use in our search for a network's weak points. Vulnerability Scanning unearths the vulnerabilities which can arise because of a misconfiguration of the network or due to poor programming. Before we go far, let us have a look at a few tools used for Network Scanning.

Tools for scanning networks and ports

Nmap: is utilized in the extraction of information, for instance, operating systems, type of packet filters/firewalls, live hosts on the network, services and the operating system versions.

Angry IP Scanner: this tool can be used to scan for IP addresses on systems available in each input range.

Superscan: this is a powerful tool developed by Mcafee. Besides being a TCP port scanner, it can also be used for pinging.

ZenMap: this scanner has a very powerful Graphical user interface tool that can help one detect the type of OS version, port scanning, OS, ping sweep, etc.

Net Scan Tool Suite Pack: this refers to a collection of different utilities and tools that are used for performing web rippers, port scans, mass emailers and flooding. Note that the tool is a trial version, but paid versions are also available.

Omnipeak and Wireshark are famous and powerful tools that are used for listening to network traffic. Both tools can be used as a network analyzer.

Countermeasures against scanning

1. System administrators can set up IDS and firewalls not only detect, but also block any probing attempts.

2. Employing custom rules which will lock down the network and bar any ports not wanted.

3. A user can run tools for port scanning so as to ascertain if the firewall detects any port scanning activities accurately.

4. Security Experts are required to make sure that there is a correct setting up of anti-spoofing and anti-scanners rules.

5. System and network managers need to ensure that the firewall firmware IDS and routers are up to date.

Gaining Access

Gaining access is by far the most critical phase of an attack. I am talking in terms of potential damage. Malicious actors do not always require to have access to a system to cause damage. For example, a denial-of-service attack can be carried out remotely with the potential to cause an abrupt termination of the services that are actively being executed on the target or in some cases, exhaust available resources. To stop a service, one can kill processes. This can be accomplished by the use of a logic/time bomb. Also, a reconfiguring and crashing of the system can achieve similar results. Network resources can be exhausted locally via the filling up outbound communication links. Such exploits can be done over a LAN or the Internet, locally, or offline as a deception or theft. Let us list some examples of these below:

- Session hijacking
- Buffer overflows that are Stack-based
- Denial-of-service and distributed denial-of-service

Sophisticated attackers normally carry out spoofing so that they can exploit a target's system by way of pretending to be different systems or strangers.

Using this approach, they can transmit a malformed packet having a bug. This bug will attempt to exploit vulnerabilities that are found in the target system.

A technique known as packet flooding can be employed to remotely stop the availability of essential services. We have a different type of attack known as smurf attacks. These attacks attempt to elicit a response from the available network users. Their legitimate addresses will then be used to flood the victim. The success of gaining access to a target system by an attacker is heavily dependent on the following:

- The initial level of access gained.
- The level of skill of the attacker and
- The configuration and architecture of the target system.

The most damaging type of denial-of-service attack is the distributed denial-of-service attack. This happens when an attacker employs the use of zombie software that is spread over many machines on the Internet to initiate a coordinated large-scale denial of services.

Maintaining Access

After a hacker gains access to his target system, he/she will need to dedicate their efforts to ensure their boat remains afloat, metaphorically speaking. The attacker can decide to exploit the hijacked system while being in stealth mode, use it as a launching pad for attacks such as DDoS or spam campaigns or use it for scanning and exploiting other systems. All these actions can be damaging. Let me show you a practical example. A hacker can create a sniffer to help them intercept all network traffic (both inbound and outbound). Part of the traffic can include the telnet sessions with other systems and file transfer protocols to enable them to send the captured data to any destination. Those who do not wish to be detected will be required to take steps that will help to conceal their presence. We have many techniques to do this. The preferred method is where the hacker installs hidden infrastructure based on covert channels, rootkits, Trojan horses and backdoors to enable them to have unfettered access to those systems.

Tools and Methods

A Trojan or backdoor is one such way to establish quick access to a system that has already been breached. A Trojan horse allows a hacker application-level access. The downside to this is that the Trojans need to be installed locally on a target system. In systems running Windows, it is possible for Trojans to install themselves as a service. After that, they will have administrative access. This means that they can run as a local system. A malicious individual can use these Trojans to steal credentials, passwords and any other sensitive information on the system. As the case with remote access Trojans, the backdoors attackers normally install come with inbuilt download and upload functionality. This technique relies on port 80 in the case of HTTP, 443 for HTTPS and port 53 for DNS for covering up their traffic.

A Covert Channel

This is a scenario where secret communication tunnels are used for transmitting data. Examples of such paths include HTTP tunnels, DNS tunnels, ICMP tunnels and VoIP. Take note that the covert channels we have mentioned can be used for transporting encrypted data as well. Detection of covert channels is possible. Only that it requires substantial efforts on the victim's part. There are indicators of anomalies in the traffic going out, such as protocol analysis, network signatures and flow data analysis. These require special tools to come across. Take note that the detection of a covert channel is one thing, but blocking it is a different ball game. You can employ one or more of the following measures.

- Barring outbound ICMP at the corporate information border;

- Blocking requests that are DNS related to servers outside corporate networks. The requests can be allowed for internal DNS servers;

- HTTP tunnels disposing through the leveraging of Web proxies;

- You can schedule a delay in the delivery of voicemails in cases of exfiltration tunneling using VoIP RTR. This will allow for sending the voicemail to an audio processor for the examination of every packet to find any encoded data in the same way an antispam software works.

Rootkits

This is a malware that is highly adept at concealing itself from a computer system. It is this feature that distinguishes rootkits from other malware types. Their heightened capability to hide gives them the ability to circumvent security measures that have been put in place on the computer. The main idea behind their creation is the very fact that they are not easily detected by normal malware detection software. Normally, Trojan horses are used to load rootkits beginning with "user" level access on the platform that is being targeted. Once in the target system, the rootkits will spy on login details such as passwords so that they can get "administrator" level access. Keen readers will say this is privilege escalation. That is correct. Despite this, the real specialty of the rootkits is to maintain access.

Rootkits will tend to hang around a targeted system slowly and progressively undermining it. This is unlike the norm with ordinary viruses that are designed to cause maximum damage in as little time as possible. The keyword here is 'secrecy.' For instance, keyloggers possessing rootkits are purposely built to capture all the words an unknowing victim keys in using their keypad. It will collect sensitive information for as long as it remains undetected. This makes identity theft highly probable. A good analogy is a parasite which, through various means, enters the body. It will stay dormant for a very long time. After it has mustered up enough energy to surmount over the body's immune system, it will now go ballistic.

A computer system can be broken down into three basic layers. These are the operating system, the kernel and the hardware level. The kernel is the backbone of the operating system, essentially speaking. Many a time, low-priority processes are used by user-level rootkits to compromise the software tasked with safeguarding a computer. A dangerous and stealthier rootkit is the kernel-level rootkit. This is majorly due to the following reasons:

- Time and again, the removal of boot-level and kernel-level rootkits have been proven to be difficult.
- The rootkits that have made a residence in the kernel memory do not leave any traces on the hard disk normally. Additionally, these rootkits normally change parts of the disk, files and sometimes modify the kernel to enable them to become "reboot resistant."
- Rootkits can camouflage their presence in cases where they make the addition of their code to sectors of the kernel;
- Kernel-level rootkits can run even before the operating system starts;
- This category of rootkits can bypass encryption through the creation of secret channels to allow them unfettered access to the compromised system.

Rootkits that are installed at the kernel level will acquire complete administrator access to the targeted systems. Rootkits normally create an access path right to the operating system level, unlike Trojan horses.

Removing rootkits

The typical security measures, for instance, antivirus software, cannot sufficiently deal with rootkits on their own. Alternatively, we have purpose-built programs such as Malwarebytes Anti-rootkit, TDSSKiller, Sophos Anti-Rootkit, and GMER that you can use to eradicate rootkits from your system. Note that, in some cases, the rootkit cannot be removed from your system for good. The programs above can only reduce the adverse effects that the rootkit leaves all over your system. In addition to using software to deal with rootkits, a user can also opt to initiate the clean slate procedure. Here, the important files are backed up, and a clean re-installation of the operating system is done. Normally, this will ensure that the rootkit is removed from your system. Again, this is not a guarantee that the removal will be 100%. We have BIOS-level rootkits, which are rare but can survive the re-install. We will always have signs indicating a presence of rootkits in any system, no matter how hard they try to hide. This is major because they are designed to keep an ingress path for an attacker from outside.

Data Exfiltration

This can be described as an unauthorized transfer of data to an external device or system. The data can originate from IT servers or a computer system. The process can either be manual (copy-pasting) or automatic (through malware). Back in 2015, the security organization, McAfee, reported that the majority of the data exfiltration cases (Around 60%) were carried out through direct electronic means. The remaining 40% happened via physical media, for example, stealing a laptop or using a USB drive to download data. Interestingly, a significant portion of that 40% involved mobile phones. The data categories which were most exfiltrated were personal health information, personally identifiable information, financial data and intellectual property. Different kinds of tunneling protocols, file transfers, web protocols or email transfers are used in the electronic exfiltration of data. We know that the file transfer protocol is a standard network protocol meant to help us transfer files. It can also come in handy in data exfiltration campaigns.

Peripheral devices on the targets and other components such as microphones and webcams can be rigged to enable the monitoring of the target's activities. To stay anonymous, the hacker can use the Tor network or make use of HTTP file transfers. To prevent hackers from exfiltrating your data and staying safe from Advanced Persistent Threats, early detection is what will make the difference. It is important that organizations possess a working threat intelligence mechanism that will aid in the identification of suspicious activities relating to data exfiltration. Linking the local threat intelligence system to the global threat intelligence network will help in keeping abreast of the latest trends in the security realm. Let me list some notable indicators of data exfiltration. These can be used as a platform to launch a comprehensive investigation. They are:

- Port activities that are not approved/sanctioned.

- Multiple email transmissions to non-corporate domains

- Excessive email sending by hosts

- Above normal DNS queries

- Web upload activity by the users. The uploads will normally be directed to non-corporate sites.

As I conclude this sub-topic, you have learned that for an attacker to obtain meaningful information, they will have to linger around their targets for some time. That implies that "Maintaining Access" is a key cycle of the hacking process which you will be required to master. This is easier said than done. Kali Linux comes with plenty of tools that can help you maintain access to a targeted system. Maintaining access is like getting into somebody else's house without their permission. You will quickly realize that getting inside the house is just one part. Maintaining your presence without being detected is another. It may be even more difficult than the former task.

Clearing Tracks

In this step, we will be learning about how hackers cover their tracks with the objective of erasing any digital signs they may have left behind. It is obvious that this as an unethical activity. Simply put, it is concerned with the deletion of logs of the activities which took place during the hacking process. I am going to be very detailed in the covering of this sub-topic since it is of immense importance to the readers who seek to be professional hackers. There is one more process after clearing tracks, that is report writing, which is mostly paperwork. To know if a system has been targeted, we can carefully examine digital signs left behind by an intruder. It is in a hacker's interest to clear any traces of such activity that can lead to them. You may have noticed that in the previous phases, a penetration tester or hacker successfully avoided detection by intrusion detection systems and firewalls. In this phase, however, the objective is to conceal any hints that are likely to disclose the nature of the hacker's deeds.

The key components of covering/clearing tracks are:

1) Anti-Incident Response – these are measures that are meant to prevent real-time detection and,

2) Anti-Forensics – these are measures aimed at thwarting the collection of digital evidence during a possible post factum inquiry.

Anti-Incident Response

The main objective of Anti-Incident Response is to disrupt, confuse and out-maneuver the incident response team at work in the company, which was targeted. Additionally, activities falling under this category make it possible for a hacker/penetration tester to obtain a long-term foothold within their target even after they have been detected. Crucial tasks that can be carried out under anti-incident response include:

- Deployment of backdoors secretly
- Configuration of infrastructure to allow for agility in lateral movement
- Constantly updating the number of infected hosts. Also, their numbers should not be too large.
- Using a wide variety of malware on the network.
- Preventing investigators or responders from keeping up with what is going on by way of picking up the pace yourself.

- A perfect cover for internal hop-points can be provided by busy servers
- You can also use busy file servers as avenues for data staging.
- Using a VPN for communication in some cases may circumvent some measures put in place for network monitoring.
- Camouflaging the origin of malware transmission

The actions are undertaken in the prevention of immediate detection of an ongoing, or a continuous cyberattack is what matters when it comes to the working of an anti-incident response. The deliberate measures undertaken by hackers or penetration testers to destroy any evidence present and lead to a digital investigation to die out during the initial stages, anti-forensics, on the other hand, is designed to handicap the investigators' ability in obtaining adequate digital evidence that will be submitted before a court of law during later stages. This, therefore, implies that activities under anti-incident response are urgent since a large portion of the action occurs on a live, running system in real-time. The countermeasures that the incident responders are likely to take are presumably much more time-constrained as compared to those by investigators in a potential digital investigation in the future.

Anti-Forensics

Before we start devouring this topic, let us first understand what forensics is. We define computer forensics as a discipline whose main objective is to enable the acquisition, preservation, analysis and presentation of digital evidence in a court of law by forensic experts. We define anti-forensics as a discipline that encompasses all the existing means and tools for purposes of deleting, modifying, or hiding digital evidence. The main objective of anti-forensics is the destruction, erasure, or manipulation of digital evidence. Anti-forensics has also been described by some as the "Attempts made to negatively compromise the quality, amount, and the existence of evidence from a crime scene or to complicate the examination and analysis of evidence so that it is impossible or difficult to conduct." One can tell from the name that this is involved with the techniques or actions that are supposed to create obstructions to an eventual digital investigation and to reduce both the quantity and quality of digital evidence. Cyber terrorists, hackers, counterfeiters, online pedophiles and other cybercriminals are among the typical users of anti-forensic techniques and tools. It is obvious that their intentions are to erase any existing traces capable of incriminating them.

Deleting Evidence

There are those of us who are so paranoid to the extent that they have invested resources on privacy protection tools and commercial disk cleaners solely to wipe data they do not wish others to lay their eyes on. It is believed that these tools can permanently delete everything from the hard disk. The specific information that can be deleted include:

- Web browsers history and cache
- Instant messengers chat logs including Skype and others
- Giving users a "secure delete" option with which they can wipe files
- Carry out the cleaning of these: registry items, thumbnails, jumplists, Skype chatsync and so on.

A forensic expert can use specific forensic tools to outsmart many of these clean-up programs. For example, pictures of interest to a forensic expert can be recovered. This is because even with the erasure of the original image, Windows Thumbnails will still have a smaller version of this picture. Even with the removal of the thumbnail, forensic can restore it by doing what we call file carving. Jumplists can also give information pertaining to pictures, applications, documents and numerous other types of files that the user has interacted with. The jumplists are normally created even for externally accessed files.

They will stay intact, regardless of whether there has been an erasure of the original file or that the external device has been removed. These lists will typically have a MAC address, the name, the path to the file being accessed, the application used to view the file, the computer name, alongside the time and date that the item was accessed. This implies that jumplists can be used as an excellent proof of access. Deleting Skype history manually will not clean internal data stored in the "chatsync" folder. The folder's content can be used to unearth bits of user conversations. Despite the methods imperfectness (Deleting), when it is done properly, it can dispose of evidence irreversibly, leading the forensics experts to come out empty-handed.

Hiding, Moving, Renaming or Altering Files

This may sound naïve even though some of the wrongdoers can use this method to evade detection. The method used to cover tracks here can include renaming files, moving files containing conversation histories or changing file extensions. This, my friends, is not an easy task. There exist programs which can be used to break large files into small partitions. These partitions can be concealed at the end of other files. Using specialized programs, a hacker can use the unused file space, which is known as slack space, for hiding crucial information from plain sight. Additionally, a hacker can conceal a file inside another (You may have heard of stenography). This method works fine with executable files.

Timestamping

Many a time, the investigators do not normally examine all the files in a computer system. In most cases, they sort the information chronologically so that they can prioritize their search for potentially relevant information. They will want to view the information just at the time an attack occurred in cases where it is known. Criminals will typically attempt to counter this approach through the modification of the metadata belonging to the files they require. Usually, they alter the times and the dates when each file was last accessed, last modified and when it was created. This anti-forensic technique is known as time stamping. Once the modification or transformation of a file has been done, the computer or device will think that the file is a different one. For instance, renaming an mp4 file to make it look like a .gif file.

Despite this, forensic investigators will normally depend on their experience and skills to find moved or renamed files. Also, we have methods for information forensics that can assess hard drives for suspicious discrepancies automatically. An example of such a method is data carving. This is a method that is used for carrying out a comprehensive and sequential scan of media. Data carving is effective in the sense that it can directly read low-level data from the media. It does not depend on the manner in which the file locations and names appear on the file system. For instance, an mp3 file is identified based on the contained actual data stream that is inherent to mp3 files and not based on the file's name.

Finally, encryption is a wonderful security measure a hacker can use. As far as digital forensics is concerned, encryption is a nightmare. Utilizing a strong encryption algorithm can result in the data being unreadable and will, therefore, be useless to the investigators.

Log Tampering

In computers running Windows, log files are typically kept in the event viewer. You can easily find it using the "Search" bar. The logs are stored in the/var/log directory in most Linux/UNIX operating systems.

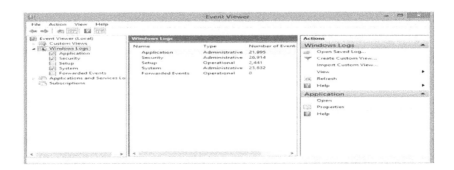

System administrators can view any malicious activities that have occurred in their systems simply by examining the log files. We have two types of log files, the application generated and the system-generated log files. In log manipulation, a hacker normally has two options. One way is to completely delete the logs and the other way is to modify the contents of the log files. Here, a hacker can also replace the system binaries with malware such as Trojans to make sure that any evidence of cyber intrusion will not be detected. Deleting log files is not normally a good idea as it will create a gap in the logs files and this will raise suspicion. The log files can be used in the detection of malicious activities. They can be used as a warning system on the health and the actual state of a system. Any discrepancies in the logs will likely draw unwanted attention. A wise attacker will likely carry out his attacks when the probability of viewing the log data is minimal say on weekends or during nighttime. An attacker will need to have root privileges to tamper with the information on log files. After escalating their privilege, a hacker can modify the log data associated with their activities within the log file itself. Any scrutiny by a system administrator will, therefore, not display any unusual activity.

Prudent system administrators normally set up their system in a way that they will send all the log files to a remote server.

In summary

One precondition for success is being stealthy. Therefore, preventing detection during the hacking process is not enough. The process should continue even after the actual attack has been carried out. Any missteps will likely set off the radar detection and the forensics team will be quickly brought in to identify the attacker. This implies that the final step of covering tracks is of immense significance and should not be underestimated. If you wish to break into sophisticated systems, maintaining a low profile is a key skill that you will be required to have. We can say that covering tracks is a fail-safe technique that hackers employ to keep them out of trouble. The trouble can be immediate or after some time, say during an investigation.

Chapter 4: Wireless Network Hacking

Wireless Hacking

There are many advantages to using wireless networking. However, this kind of technology comes with a host of threats and vulnerabilities that hackers can take advantage of. Since information is sent over the air via radio frequencies, it is easier for hackers to intercept it compared to wired connections. This is more so when the information being sent is not encrypted or the encryption algorithm is weak.

Wireless networks consist of for basic elements:

- A wireless access point that connects to the network
- Data being transmitted via radio frequencies
- The Client device used, such as a laptop, tablet, etc.
- The users

Every one of these elements can be targeted by a hacker to compromise at least one of the three major objectives of a secure network: availability, integrity and confidentiality.

Wireless Network attacks

1. Accidental association

It is possible for a wireless network to be hacked accidentally. In some cases, one wireless network overlaps with another, thus enabling any user to jump into another unintended network accidentally. This may seem benign, but a malicious hacker can take advantage of this and gain access to information that should not have been exposed in such a manner. If the overlapping networks belong to organizations, then the link can be used to steal proprietary data.

2. Malicious Association

This occurs when malicious hackers gain access to a private network using their own device rather than through the legitimate access point (AP). A hacker can create a "soft AP," which can be a laptop with software that makes its wireless network card appear to be a genuine access point. This allows the hacker to steal passwords, attack computers or send users Trojan horse programs. A hacker can effectively have full control of every computer that joins the fake network.

3. Ad-hoc Networks

These are networks between two wireless computers with no access point separating them. Such networks can be attacked quite easily since they rarely have adequate protection.

4. Non-traditional networks

These include Bluetooth devices, wireless printers, handheld PDAs and barcode readers. These kinds of networks are rarely secured by IT personnel since all the focus is usually on laptops or access points. This makes them fair game for malicious hackers.

5. MAC Spoofing

This is a form of identity theft where a hacker monitors network traffic to identify which computer has network privileges. The aim is to steal the MAC (Media Access Control) address of that computer within the network. Many wireless systems have a MAC filter that allows only specific computers with specific MAC addresses to access and use the network. A hacker may get software that is able to "sniff" the network to find these authorized computers and their IDs and then employ other software that allows the hacker's computer to use these stolen MAC addresses.

6. Man-in-the-middle Attacks

This occurs when a malicious hacker sets up their laptop as a soft access point and then lures other users to use it. The hacker then connects the soft access point to a genuine access point using a different wireless card, thus forcing users to go through the fake AP to reach the real one. This enables the hacker to sniff out whatever information they want from the traffic. This type of attack has been made easier by software such as AirJack and LANjack. Wireless Hotspots are a great place to launch this kind of attack since there is hardly any meaningful security on such networks.

7. Denial of Service Attacks

This is where a hacker continuously sends numerous requests, commands and messages to a specific access point until the network crashes or just to prevent genuine users from getting onto the network.

8. Network Injection Attack

A malicious hacker injects counterfeit networking re-configuration commands into an access point that does not filter traffic. These fake commands bring down the entire network or switches, routers and hubs, forcing a reboot or reprogramming of every networking device.

Wireless Network Authentication

Wireless networks are designed to be accessible to anyone who has a wireless-enabled device. For this reason, most networks are protected using passwords. There are two common authentication techniques used: WEP and WPA.

WEP

This stands for Wired Equivalent Privacy and was developed to provide users with the same level of privacy as wired networks. It adheres to IEEE 802.11 WLAN standards. WEP encrypts data that is being sent over a network to prevent eavesdropping.

WEP vulnerabilities

There are significant flaws in the design of this type of authentication technique:

1. It uses Cyclic Redundancy Check 32 to verify the integrity of packets. The problem with CRC32 is that a hacker only needs to capture two packets to crack into the network. They can also modify the checksum and encrypted stream to force the system to accept the packet.

2. It uses an RC4 encryption algorithm to make stream ciphers composed of a secret key and an Initial Value (IV). The IV length is fixed at 24 bits, but the secret key can be 40 to 104 bits in length. If a secret key of a lower length is used, the network becomes easier to hack.

3. Since it is a password-based authentication technique, a hacker can successfully deploy a dictionary attack.

4. It does not have a central key management system, thus making it very difficult to change keys in big networks.

Due to the numerous security flaws, WEP has fallen out of favor and replaced by WPA.

How to crack WEP networks

Exploiting the numerous security vulnerabilities on a WEP network is possible either through passive attacks or active cracking. If a passive attack is launched, the network traffic is not affected until WEP authentication has been successfully cracked. This makes it harder to detect. Active cracking tends to increase the load on the network, thus making it easier to detect, though it is also more effective.

The tools that can be used for cracking WEP include:

Aircrack — This is also a network sniffer and can be downloaded from www.aircrack-ng.org/

Kismet — This multi-purpose tool can sniff network packets, detect invisible and visible networks and even identify intrusions. It can be downloaded from www.kismetwireless.net/

WEPCrack — This open-source tool can crack secret keys and can be downloaded at www.wepcrack.sourceforge.net/

WebDecrypt — It cracks WEP keys using a dictionary attack and generates its own keys. Get it at www.wepdecrypt.sourceforge.net/

WPA

WPA is an abbreviation for Wi-Fi Protected Access. It was primarily developed to mitigate the weaknesses of WEP. WPA uses greater IV than WEP, 48 bits to be precise. Packets are encrypted using temporal keys.

WPA vulnerabilities

1. Hackers can easily overcome it using denial of service attacks.

2. Its keys rely on passphrases and if weak passphrases are used, a dictionary attack can be successfully launched.

How to crack WPA networks

Since WPA uses passphrases to authenticate user logins, a well-coordinated dictionary attack makes it vulnerable, especially if short passphrases are used. The tools for cracking WPA include:

Cain and Abel — It is used to decode files that have been sniffed by other programs like Wireshark.

CowPatty — This is a brute force attack tool that cracks pre-shared keys. Download from wirlessdefenc.org/Contents/coWPAttyMain.htm

How to crack network WPA and WEP keys

You are going to need the right software, hardware and patience in order to crack the keys to a wireless network. However, successfully doing so is dependent on the activity levels of users within the network you have targeted.

Backtrack is a great security operating system that is based on Linux. It contains many well-known tools that are very effective for collecting data, evaluating weaknesses and exploiting networks. Some of these tools include Metasploit, Ophcrack, Wireshark, Nmap and Aircrack-ng.

Cracking network authentication keys requires the following:

- Wireless network adapter able to inject packets.
- Backtrack OS, downloadable from backtrack-linux.org/downloads/
- Proximity to the network radius.
- Adequate knowledge of Linux OS and how to use the scripts in Aircrack.
- Patience, as there are factors that you may not be able to control.

Remember, the greater the number of people actively accessing the network, the faster this will work.

How to perform MAC spoofing

To carry out MAC spoofing, you will have to bypass the MAC filtering that the target network is using. MAC filtering is commonly used to lockout MAC addresses that have not been authorized to connect to a wireless network. This is usually an effective way to prevent people who may somehow acquire the password from connecting to the network. However, MAC filtering is not an effective security measure when it comes to locking out hackers.

The steps below will show you exactly how to go about spoofing the MAC address of a client who is authorized to connect to the network. The Wi-Fi adapter should be in monitoring mode. Airodump-ng on Kali Linux will be used to recover the MAC address. After this, the Macchanger program will be used to do the spoofing, bypass the filter and connect to the network.

Instructions:

1. Make sure your Wi-Fi adapter is in monitoring mode. To find the wireless network that is being

targeted as well as any clients connected to it, enter this command:

Airodump-ng—c [channel]-bssid [target router MAC Addres]-l wlan0mon

A window will open up, displaying a list of clients who are connected to the network. Their whitelisted MAC addresses will also be shown. These are the addresses you need to spoof to enter the network.

2. Pick one of the whitelisted MAC addresses from the list to use to spoof your own address. Before you can perform the spoofing, you must take down the monitoring interface. Enter the command:

Airmon-ng stop wlan0mon

3. The next step is to take down the wireless interface of the MAC address you intend to spoof. Enter the command:

Ifconfig wlan0 down

4. Then you use the Mcchanger software to change the address. Enter the command:

Macchanger —m [New MAC Address] wlan0

5. Remember, you had taken down the wireless interface in step 3. Now it is time to bring it back up. Use the command:

Ifconfig wlan0 up

Now that the MAC address of your wireless adapter has been changed to that of an authorized user, test and see if the network will authenticate your login. You should be able to connect to the wireless network.

Transmissions

Hacking of wireless networks poses three main threats: Disruption, Alteration and Interception. To prevent malicious hackers from eavesdropping on wireless transmission, you can use:

Signal-hiding methods — Before a malicious hacker can intercept wireless transmissions, they first have to locate the wireless access point. An organization can make this more difficult by switching off the SSID (service set identifier) being broadcast by the access point, assigning a cryptic name to the SSID, lowering signal strength to provide just enough requisite coverage or stationing access points away from exterior walls and windows. There are also more effective but expensive techniques, such as employing directional antennas to restrict the signal within a specific area or using TEMPEST (a technique to block the emission of wireless signals).

Stronger encryption of all wireless traffic — This is very important, especially for organizations that must protect the confidentiality of their information being broadcast wirelessly. This measure reduces the risks of a man-in-the-middle attack.

Stronger authentication procedures — This should apply to users as well as their devices. This minimizes man-in-the-middle attacks.

Countermeasures against Denial of Service Attacks

Malicious hackers may, at times, attempt to bring down the servers of an organization, but in some cases, a DOS attack may be unintentional. There are certain steps that can be taken to minimize the risks of this form of attack:

- Performing site surveys carefully to determine the location of signals emanating from other devices. This should be used as a guide in deciding where the access points should be located.

- Conducting regular audits of network performance and activity to determine areas with problems. If there are any offending devices, they should be removed. Measures should also be taken to enhance signal coverage and strength in problem areas.

Access Points

Wireless access points that are poorly configured are a major vulnerability and may allow malicious hackers unauthorized access to confidential information. To secure wireless access points, the following countermeasures must be taken:

- Eliminate all rogue access points — The best way to do this is to use 802. Ix to prevent any rogue devices from plugging into and connecting to the wireless network.

- Ensure all authentic access points are properly configured — Make sure that all default settings are changed since they are publicly available and hackers can easily exploit them.

- Authenticate every device using 802. Ix protocol — a strong authentication system will prevent unauthorized devices from setting up backdoors. This protocol ensures stringent authentication before assigning any device to an IP address.

Devices

There are two perspectives when it comes to assessing security threats against wireless devices: Theft/Loss and Compromise. Laptops and PDAs usually contain a lot of confidential and sensitive information and therefore must be protected from theft or loss. Wireless client devices can also be compromised when a malicious hacker gains access to stored data in the device. Hackers can also use the device to launch attacks on other systems and networks.

Networks

- Encryption — This is the best way to secure a wireless network. Most base stations, access points and wireless routers come with inbuilt encryption mechanisms that enable scrambling of network communications. Always make sure that the router you buy comes with an encryption feature. Most manufacturers turn this feature off, so ensure that you manually turn it on before you start using your router.

- Anti-spyware, anti-virus and firewalls — Make sure that your wireless network is protected in the same way as a wired connection. Keep all your software updated and always check whether your firewall is switched on.

- Switch off your router's identifier broadcasting - This is the mechanism that a wireless router uses for broadcasting its presence in an area. However, there is no need to announce the presence of a network if the users know that it is already there. Malicious hackers tend to search for the identifier broadcast to zero in on potential targets.

- Change default identifier — Every router has a default ID given to it by its manufacturer. You may have switched off the identifier broadcaster, but hackers can still attack the network if they find out the default ID, which is publicly accessible. Change the identifier and do not forget to configure the new ID into your computer.

- Change the default password — Every router is assigned a default password by the manufacturer. This is for purposes of configuring the device initially. These default passwords are easy to find, so make sure that you change your router password to something that will be very difficult to crack. Also, try to make your password as long as possible.

- Specify the devices authorized to connect to the network — Configure your router to only allow specific Mac addresses to connect to the network. However, do not rely on this technique alone, as Mac spoofing is still possible.

- Shut the network down when unused — Whenever a wireless network is not being used, make sure that it is switched off. This will limit the window of opportunity that hackers can use to penetrate the network.

- Be vigilant in W-Fi hotspots — Most people love to use the free Wi-Fi at airports, cafes, hotels and other public places. These wireless networks are rarely secured, so do not assume that they are.

The Users

There is no greater way to secure a wireless network than educating and training all users. Users are not just people who connect to the network but IT personnel and administrators as well. It is very important to teach people how to behave in a way that will maintain the security of the wireless network. This user training and education must be a periodic endeavor.

Let us face it. It is not possible to completely eliminate every risk that a wireless network comes with. Eventually, a hacker will get through. However, there are actions that can be taken to maintain a reasonable level of general security. This is possible using systematic risk evaluation and management techniques. Every component of a wireless network must be considered when establishing countermeasures against malicious hackers.

Chapter 5: Uses and Applications of Kali Linux

The uses of Kali Linux are wide-ranging. Below, I have outlined and discussed some of them. Feel free to download the documentation from the links provided in chapter 2. Now let us get down to the serious stuff.

Penetration testing

This is a mechanism that is utilized by organizations to ascertain the robustness of their security infrastructure. Here, security professionals will play the role of the attackers, whereby they will attempt to discover flaws and vulnerabilities in a system before the malicious fellows do. One key objective is the identification and reporting of vulnerabilities to companies and organizations. As organizations become increasingly security conscious and the cost of security breaches rises exponentially, many large organizations are beginning to contract out security services. One of these critical security services is penetration testing. A
penetration test is essentially a legal, commissioned hack to demonstrate the vulnerability of a firm's

network and systems. Generally, organizations conduct a vulnerability assessment first to find potential weaknesses in their network, operating systems and services. I emphasize potential, as this vulnerability scan includes a significant number of false positives (things identified as vulnerabilities that are, in reality, not vulnerabilities). It is the role of the penetration tester to attempt to hack, or penetrate, these vulnerabilities. Only then can the organization know whether the weakness is real and decide to invest time and money to close the vulnerability.

Espionage and military

Cyber espionage can be said to be the practice of accessing information and secrets without the knowledge and permission of the entities being targeted. They can be ordinary individuals, rivals, competitors, groups, governments or even enemies. The objectives here are broad. They can be political, economic, personal or even military-related. The techniques used, too, are diverse. Hackers can use malicious software, cracking techniques, proxy servers, among others, to attain their stated objectives. Espionage can be carried out online by professionals from their computer desks or it can be done by infiltration using trained moles and conventional spies. In some circumstances, it can be carried by amateurish hackers with malicious intent and software programmers. It is common knowledge that every nation on earth carries out some form of cyber espionage or even cyber warfare, albeit covertly. Gathering intelligence on military activities of other countries has been made more cost-effective by hacking. Thus, a hacker has their place cut out in the defense systems of any nation.

Forensics:

For years, the popularity of Forensic Linux Live Boot environments has become well known. There are so many forensic tools that are Linux based on this distribution. Using Kali, forensic experts can do all that pertains to their tradecraft starting from the initial triage, data imaging all the way to case management and full analysis.

Reverse Engineering:

Recently, reverse engineering has become an indispensable skill in various sectors, including law enforcement. Reverse Engineering is a primary method that is used in the identification of vulnerabilities and the development of exploits. That is on the offensive side of it. Defensively speaking, reverse engineering can be utilized in the analysis of malware that has been used to target a given system. Here, the objective will be to establish the capabilities of a given piece of tradecraft.

Wireless Attacks:

Kali supports a wide range of wireless hacking tools. What makes wireless networks a commonly attacked vector is their pervasive nature. Kali Linux also supports multiple wireless cards and is a hacker's favorite choice for conducting attacks against different types of wireless networks.

Password Attacks:

Kali Linux can be used for conducting password attacks where a user encounters an authentication system. The OS comes with numerous useful tools and utilities for this purpose. We have both offline and online password attack tools that a Kali Linux user can use to deal with hashing and encryption systems.

Database Assessment:

Kali Linux is capable of database attacks such as SQL injection and attacking credentials. All this is made possible by the tools present in Kali's vast repositories that can be used for testing attack vectors ranging from data extraction and analysis to SQL injection.

Sniffing and Spoofing:

Again, Kali Linux has plenty of tools an aspiring hacker or a professional one can use to get access to data as it is being transmitted over the network. You can use spoofing tools to impersonate a networks' legitimate user and then use the sniffing tools if you wish to capture and analyze data you have just captured. These tools are a lethal combination when used together.

Stress Testing

To check whether your system is stable, you carry out a stress test on it. In this scenario, you will use the numerous tools provided by Kali Linux to generate more than normal traffic. This way you will be able to know the limits of your system. The tools for stress testing can either be proprietary or open-source. As an expert, it is essential that you know all the tools that are used for testing a system's availability.

Hardware Hacking

Another application of Kali Linux is in hardware hacking. Kali Linux comes with the following tools that can be used to accomplish this task.

- **android-sdk** - The Android SDK provides you the API libraries and developer tools necessary to build, test and debug apps for Android.

- **apktool** - It is a tool for reverse engineering 3rd party, closed, binary Android apps. It can decode resources to the nearly original form and rebuild them after making some modifications; it makes possible to debug smali code step by step. Also, it makes working with the app easier because of project-like files structure and automation of some repetitive tasks like building apk, etc.

- **Arduino** - This is an electronics prototyping platform that is open-source. It is based on easy-to-use, flexible software and hardware.

- **Sakis3G** - Sakis3G is a tweaked shell script that is supposed to work out-of-the-box for establishing a 3G connection with any combination of modem or operator. It automatically setups your USB or Bluetooth™ modem and may even detect operator settings. You should try it when anything else fails.

- **Smali** - smali/baksmali is an assembler/disassembler for the dex format used by dalvik, Android's Java VM implementation. The syntax is loosely based on Jasmin's/dedexer's syntax and supports the full functionality of the dex format (annotations, debug info, line info, etc.)

Chapter 6: Introduction to Cybersecurity

Introduction

We define cybersecurity as being the protection of computer systems, computer networks, and their associated programs from attacks that are of a digital form. Typically, cyberattacks are carried out with the intent of gaining access, modification or even destruction of information that is sensitive. They also attempt to extorting money from victims and are meant to interrupt the normal processes of a business.

Confidentiality, Integrity and Availability

The three are famously referred to as the CIA triad. We can describe it as a model whose purpose is to guide information security policies within any given organization. To prevent confusing the triad with the American Central Intelligence Agency, we sometimes refer to it as the AIC triad. The three elements are the most critical components of security. In our case, we can say that availability is defined as a guarantee of access that is reliable to information by people with authorization, confidentiality is said to be a set of protocols that are used to limiting access to information and integrity is the undertaking given to show that the information at hand is both accurate and trustworthy.

Confidentiality:

This is a rough equivalent of privacy. While ensuring that the right people can have access to crucial information, it is also prudent that vigorous measures are undertaken to make sure that there is confidentiality. There should be restricted access to the data in question by those who are authorized to view it. Out there, it is not uncommon to categorized data based on the type and amount of damage that can result from it falling into unauthorized persons. Stringent measures can more or less be implemented depending on these categories. Guarding the confidentiality of data sometimes requires specialized training for authorized to view/use persons. It would generally involve security risks that could harm that information. It can, without a doubt, help people with the proper authorization to get to know the various risk factors and equip them with countermeasures. Additional aspects of the training may comprise best practices in password-related issues alongside social engineering mechanisms.

This will help them avoid breaching rules governing data-handling with potentially disastrous results in as much as they may have intentions we can describe as being noble. For example, using a routing number or an account number is an effective measure that can be used to ensure confidentiality. We can also employ the use of data encryption to make sure that there is confidentiality. Passwords and user IDs are part of a standard procedure that is becoming a common phenomenon, two-factor authentication. There are different options. They include security tokens (soft tokens or key fobs) and biometric verification.

Furthermore, it is incumbent upon the users to take precautions in ensuring that locations where their information appears and the number of times required to send it to complete a transaction is at a minimal. In cases where we have critical data, extra measures may be necessary. Such actions can involve storing the information on disconnected storage devices on air-gapped computers or it can even be stored in the form of hard copies only.

Integrity:

This component of the triad comprises ensuring the trustworthiness, consistency, and accuracy of data throughout its complete life cycle. It is of immense importance that data that is in transit is not altered. Solid steps need to be taken to make sure that no modification on the data by unauthorized people happens. For instance, in cases where we have a confidentiality breach. Here, the countermeasures can involve user access controls and file permissions. To prevent accidental deletion or erroneous changes by authorized users, we can employ the use of version control. In place, there also need to exist mechanisms to help in the detection of data changes, which may result from non-human events, including a server crash or an electromagnetic pulse. We can include checksums and cryptographic checksums to help with the integrity verification of data. Lastly, it may be necessary to have some form of redundancies and backups that will help in the restoration back to its former state.

Availability:

The rigorous maintenance of all the hardware ensures that there will always be availability fo the services rendered by this hardware. Failing equipment should be promptly and adequately repaired to keep in order a properly functioning operating system environment that is devoid of any software conflicts. One aspect of maintenance that should also be carried out is updating all the necessary system components. It will also be to provide ample bandwidth for communications and to ensure a minimal occurrence of bottlenecks. Mitigation of hardware failures and their repercussions can be done using high-availability clusters, redundancy, RAID and even failovers.

For the worst-case scenarios that occur, disaster recovery that is both adaptive and fast is essential. For this to be possible, the disaster recovery plan laid down has to be comprehensive. Prevention of data loss or connection interruptions needs to also account for unpredictable events. Examples include fire and natural disasters. Copies of back up data can be securely stored at a location that is geographically-isolated to prevent loss of data resulting from such occurrences. Such sites also need to be water and fire-resistant. To guard against issues such as downtime and inaccessibility of data due to denial-of-service attacks and network intrusions, we can employ the use of extra security equipment, for instance, proxy servers, firewalls and software.

Issues arising from the CIA:

The CIA paradigm faces immense challenges where big data is involved. This is primarily because of the sheer volume needing to be kept safe, the variety of formats of the data, and, finally, the multiplicity of the originating sources. Disaster recovery plans and duplicate sets of data all make the already high cost even higher. Additionally, oversight is often lacking since the main objective of big data is for analytics purposes, i.e., gathering data and using it to make some kind of useful interpretation. We all know this fellow, Edward Snowden, who brought this issue to light. Security agencies carry out the collection of enormous volumes of peoples' private data throughout the world. To safeguard individual information from exposure in the IoT environment, we have special considerations known as the Internet of Things privacy. This means that almost any logical or physical entity can be assigned a unique identifier to enable autonomous communications over a network, including the Internet.

The transmitted data from a particular endpoint may not, on its own, necessarily result in any privacy issues. The catch is, however, when the fragmented data from multiple endpoints is accessed, gathered and analyzed, sensitive information can be obtained. Securing the Internet of Things is itself a formidable challenge since it comprises numerous Internet-enabled devices besides computers. Such devices are, in most cases, often set up with default passwords that are weak or in some cases, the devices are unpatched. Unless IoT is protected adequately, there is a likelihood that it may be used as a separate vector of attack or be made a part of a thingbot. Recently, it has been demonstrated by researchers that it is possible to compromise a network just by using a Wi-Fi-enabled light bulb. It is essential for us that we consider the security of the numerous network-capable products that are under development.

Encryption

We define encryption as a mechanism through which plaintext or other data type are changed from their currently readable form to an encoded way. It is only an entity having access to a decryption key that can decode the data. This is an important measure that usually is used to provide end-to-end data security across networks. Encryption, as a proactive security measure, is commonly used all over the internet for purposes of protecting crucial information belonging to users, which is being exchanged between servers and browsers. That can include private information such as payment information, passwords and other personal information. Individuals, together with organizations, may also opt to use encryption to ensure the safety of sensitive data that is stored on mobile devices, servers and computers.

How encryption works

Plaintext data, also known as unencrypted data, is encrypted through the use of an encryption algorithm plus an encryption key. The result of this is a ciphertext that can be seen only in its original form if decrypted with the correct key. On the other hand, decryption is the reverse of encryption. The steps used in encryption are followed in a reverse fashion. In the modern age, we have two commonly used encryption algorithms. They are symmetric and asymmetric encryptions.

When it comes to the symmetric encryption mechanism, a single key is utilized for encryption. The Advanced Encryption Standard (AES) is one of the most used symmetric-key ciphers. It was designed primarily to protect classified information for governments. This mechanism is faster in comparison to asymmetric encryption. The sender must, however, share the encryption key with the recipient. The keys need to be managed in a secure fashion. This uses an asymmetric algorithm in most cases.

On the other hand, we have asymmetric cryptography. We can also refer to it as public-key cryptography. Here, two different keys are used. They are, however, mathematically linked. The keys are as follows; one key is public and the other one private. The public key many times can be shared with anyone. The private key has to be kept secret. In asymmetric cryptography, the commonly used encryption algorithm is the RSA. The reason is to some extent that the two keys can encrypt a message, which is to imply the key that is opposite to the one used for the encryption is used to decrypt it. This feature offers a way of ensuring that we not only have confidentiality but also authenticity, non-reputability and integrity of electronic communications and data.

Benefits of Encryption

Confidentiality of digital data, which is stored on computer systems or that which is sent through the internet or any other computer network, is protected by using encryption. Organizations such as Payment Card Industry Data Security Standard (PCI DSS) require that sensitive data be encrypted to keep unauthorized entities from accessing the data. We also have some standards requiring or recommending data encryption. Nowadays, modern encryption algorithms serve an integral role in making sure that the security of communications and IT systems possess not only confidentiality but also the under listed key elements of security:

- Authentication: the origin of a given message should be able to be verified.
- Integrity: This has got to do with keeping the message intact. That is, the contents of

messages have not been altered or deleted from the time it was sent.

- Nonrepudiation: Here, non-repudiation means that a particular sender cannot dispute that they send the message.

Backup and Redundancy

Usually, we use backup where copies of data are created in anticipation of a catastrophic loss. On the other hand, redundancy is a lot more than just data storage. Redundancy aims to provide a continuity of service regardless of what will happen. Data redundancy ensures that the storage of data is done at multiple and heterogeneous locations. We also have what we call network redundancy whereby a given network is configured in such a way that it has numerous alternative systems. The alternative systems serve to ensure continuity of service regardless of what happens.

Data Redundancy

For any organization, it is essential first that regular services are restored as soon as possible after there has been a security breach. Data should be able to be reconstructed as quickly as possible. To this end, businesses have come up with various ways to make sure there is data redundancy. It is common knowledge that these methods come with their own merits in terms of cost-effectiveness, speed and management. The most common way is using off-site tape backups. In this method, magnetic tapes are used to store a complete bit-for-bit copy of a storage volume. The tapes can be transferred to an off-site storage facility where they can be easily retrieved whenever there is a catastrophic failure. Besides, we can use Cloud Backup to safeguard data against losses.

Network Redundancy

Most of the infrastructure we use for our networks are unbelievably fragile. For instance, when a router burns out due to one reason or another, the result is that there will be a prolonged period of network downtime. To mitigate against this, businesses make sure that networks they use have an adequate redundancy so that they can survive and provide services in cases of an emergency. Fundamentally, network redundancy means that no matter what type of failure occurs, a network will still be up and running.

To be able to do this, we can have multiple network devices such as hubs, routers and switches configured to stand in for one of them that fails. We also have ISP redundancy, where a gateway in the network is joined to more than one separate ISP. Just like with the devices, one ISP will take over whenever there is a failure. In cases where a network is functioning correctly, we can use the ISPs to share the traffic resulting in reduced congestion of the network. This here is called load sharing.

Preventing a SPOFF

SPOFF is full for a single point of failure. We do not desire that one critical part of a system failure can render the entire system unusable. Any planning needs to mitigate this phenomenon. A single point of failure can be reduced or eliminated by way of redundancy. This will make sure that there is not a single component that can prevent the proper working of a system.

Chapter 7: Network Scanning and Management

Introduction

The ability to scan for and connect to other network devices from your system is crucial to becoming a successful hacker, and with wireless technologies like WiFi

and Bluetooth becoming the standard, finding and controlling WiFi and Bluetooth connections is vital. If someone can hack a wireless connection, they can gain entry to a device and access to confidential information. The first step, of course, is to learn how to find these devices. In this chapter, we are going to examine two of the most common wireless technologies in Linux: WiFi and Bluetooth.

Network Scanning

We say that it is the utilization of a computer network for purposes of collecting information about IT systems. We carry out scanning of networks primarily to help us do system maintenance or a security assessment. Hackers can also conduct a network scanning exercise before launching their attacks. The following are some of the reasons we scan networks:

- Identification of the present TCP and UDP network services, which may be actively being executed on the targets.
- To get to understand the systems for filtering that are in between the targeted hosts and the user.
- Discover the operating systems that are being used through the assessment of their IP responses.
- Analyze a particular host that is being targeted for its number predictability of the TCP sequence. This is to enable the TCP spoofing and attack sequence prediction.

Network scanning comprises of two key aspects: vulnerability scanning and network port scanning. The latter denotes a way of sending data packets through a network over to a systems' specific port numbers. The goal is to discover network services that are present in that particular system. It is an excellent way for troubleshooting issues that a given system has. That way, the problems can be dealt with so that the system is secure. For us to discover known vulnerabilities present in network systems, a method known as vulnerability scanning is used. Through it, we can identify weak spots both in the operating system and the application software. It is these weak points that are usually used to compromise computing systems.

Both vulnerability scanning and network port scanning can be said to be techniques that are used in information gathering. On the flip side, they can be a prelude to an attack when they are put to use by anonymous entities. Such entities usually have malicious intentions. The inverse mapping is another technique for network scanning. It is useful when it comes to collecting IP addresses that are not mapped to live hosts. By doing so, it will be aiding in the focussing attention on addresses that are worth focussing on, that is, those that are feasible. There are three stages in which information gathering can be accomplished.

i.   The footprinting stage
ii. The scanning stage
iii. The enumeration stage

This, therefore, implies that network scanning is among the crucial steps an attacker needs to be able to gather information.

Network scanning with ifconfig

The ifconfig command is one of the essential tools that can be used for examining and interacting with active network interfaces. You can use it to query your active network connections by simply entering ifconfig in the terminal.

Scanning Wireless Networks with iwconfig

If you have a wireless adapter, you can use the iwconfig command to gather crucial information for wireless hacking, such as the adapter's IP address, its MAC address, what mode it's in and more. The information you can glean from this command is particularly important when you're using wireless hacking tools like aircrackng.

Changing your network information

Being able to change your IP address and other network information is a useful skill because it will help you access other networks while appearing as a trusted device on those networks. For example, in a denial of service (DoS) attack, you can spoof your IP so that that the attack appears to come from another source, thus helping you evade IP capture during forensic analysis. This is a relatively simple task in Linux and it's done with the ifconfig command.

Changing Your IP Address

To change your IP address, enter ifconfig, followed by the interface you want to reassign and the new IP address you want to be assigned to that interface. For example, to assign the IP address 192.168.181.115 to interface eth0, you would enter the following:

Kali >ifconfig eth0 192.168.181.115
kali >

When you do this correctly, Linux will go back to the command prompt and say nothing. This is a good thing! Then, when you again check your network connections with ifconfig, you should see that your IP address has changed to the new IP address you just assigned.

Changing Your Network Mask and Broadcast Address

You can also change your network mask (netmask) and broadcast address with the ifconfig command. For instance, if you want to assign that same eth0 interface with a netmask of 255.255.0.0 and a broadcast address of 192.168.1.255, you would enter the following:

Kali >ifconfig eth0 192.168.181.115 netmask 255.255.0.0 broadcast
192.168.1.255
kali >

Once again, if you've done everything correctly, Linux responds with a new command prompt. Now enter ifconfig again to verify that each of the parameters has been changed accordingly.

Spoofing Your MAC Address

You can also use ifconfig to change your MAC address. The MAC address is globally unique and is often used as a security measure to keep hackers out of networks —or to trace them. Changing your MAC address to spoof a different MAC address is almost trivial and neutralizes those security measures. Thus, it's an instrumental technique for bypassing network access controls. To spoof your MAC address, use the ifconfig command's down option to take down the interface (eth0 in this case). Then enter the ifconfig command followed by the interface name (hw for hardware, ether for Ethernet) and the new spoofed MAC address. Finally, bring the interface back up with the up option for the change to take place.

IP Addresses assignment

Linux has a Dynamic Host Configuration Protocol (DHCP) server that runs a daemon, a process that runs in the background, called dhcpd or the dhcp daemon. The DHCP server will carry out the assignment of IP addresses to all of the systems that are located on the subnet. It also keeps a log of which IP address is allocated to which machine at any one time. This makes it an excellent resource for forensic analysts to trace hackers after an attack. For that reason, it's useful to understand how the DHCP server works. Usually, to connect to the internet from a LAN, you must have a DHCP-assigned IP.

Therefore, after setting a static IP address, you must return and get a new DHCP-assigned IP address. To do this, you can always reboot your system, but I will show you how to retrieve a new DHCP without having to shut your system down and restart it. To request an IP address from DHCP, all that is required is to call the DHCP server using dhclient, followed by an interface that you wish to assign the address. The different Linux distros use different DHCP clients. Kali, for instance, is based on Debian that uses dhclient.

Manipulating the Domain Name System (DNS)

Hackers can find a treasure trove of information on a target in its Domain Name
System. This is a key element of the internet and although it's designed to translate domain names to IP addresses, a hacker can use it to garner information on the target.

- **Examining DNS with dig**

DNS is the service that translates a domain name like google.com to the appropriate IP address. This way, your system knows how to get to it. Without DNS, it would mean that we would be required to remember the thousands of IP addresses that belong to the websites we visit frequently. Dig is one of the commands any aspiring hacker needs to know. It offers a way to gather DNS information about a target domain. The stored DNS information can be a crucial piece of early reconnaissance to obtain before attacking. This information could include the IP address of the target's nameserver (the server that translates the target's name to an IP address), the target's email server and potentially any subdomains and IP addresses. You can also use the dig command to get information on email servers connected to a domain by adding the mx option (mx is short for mail exchange server). This information is critical for attacks on email systems.

- **Changing Your DNS Server**

In some cases, you may want to use another DNS server. To do so, you will edit a plaintext file named /etc/resolv.conf on the system. Open that file in a text editor. Then, on your command line, enter the precise name of your editor, followed by the location of the file and the filename.

Wi-Fi Networks

Firstly, let us look at WiFi. Before doing so, here is a small introduction to the various WiFi security protocols that usually are frequently used. The original, Wired Equivalent Privacy (WEP), was severely flawed and easily cracked. Its replacement, WiFi Protected Access (WPA), was a bit more secure. Finally, WPA2PSK, which is much more secure and uses a preshared key (PSK) that all users share, is now used by nearly all WiFi AP's (except enterprise WiFi).

Basic Wireless Commands

ifconfig

To perform a network interface configuration in Unix-based operating systems, one needs ifconfig. It is an administration utility that is found in the system. Ifconfig has utilities that are utilized in the configuration, querying and controlling of the parameters of the TCP/IP interface. As an interactive tool, ifconfig can be used to show settings of the network interface and analyze them.

In summary, ifconfig does the following:

- The command enables the viewing of settings of a network;
- Carrying out enabling of a network Interface and also disabling it;
- Network Interface IP address assigning ;
- Assigning network interfaces a netmask ;
- Allocating a Broadcast to Network Interface;
- Assigning an IP, Netmask and Broadcast to Network Interface;
- Changing MTU for a Network Interface;
- Enabling and disabling Promiscuous Mode;
- Addition and removal of New Alias to Network Interface;
- Changing the MAC address of Network Interface.

iwevent

This command displays Wireless Events received through the RTNetlink socket. Each line shows the specific Wireless Event, which describes what has happened on the specified wireless interface. This command doesn't take any arguments.

iwlist

This command can be used for scanning wireless networks available and also for displaying any other information about the wireless networks which are not displayed when the iwconfig command is used. Iwlist is utilized in the generation of wireless access points that are nearby together with their SSIDs and their MAC addresses.

iwspy

This command is used for monitoring nodes in a network. It can also be used for recording the link quality of the nodes.

ifrename

This command is used for renaming wireless network interfaces depending on multiple criteria that are static to allocate names consistently to each interface. The interface names usually are dynamic by default. This command helps users decide the name of the network interface.

iwgetid

This is used in the reporting of the NWID, ESSID or address of the access point of the wireless network presently being used. By default, iwgetid will display the devices' ESSID. Suppose that it is unavailable, it will output its NWID instead. The information reported is the same as the one shown by iwconfig. In comparison, it is easier to do integration in various scripts.

Detecting and Connecting to Bluetooth

In recent times, nearly all gadgets, systems and devices have inbuilt Bluetooth. The devices can be computers, iPods, smartphones, speakers, game controllers, keyboards, tablets, among others. The ability to break into Bluetooth networks can result in the compromising of the information on the device, assuming a devices' control and acquisition of a platform to transmit privileges information from and to the device, among other things. We, therefore, need to understand how Bluetooth works if we are to exploit this technology. From this book, you will be able to acquire some basic knowledge that will come in handy during the scanning and connecting to Bluetooth devices in preparation for hacking them.

How Bluetooth Works

First, we can define Bluetooth as a wireless communication technology that enables devices to transmit voice or data wirelessly. This happens over a relatively short distance. This technology was meant to replace the ubiquitous cables that were being used to connect devices while still securing the communications across them. The process of joining two Bluetooth devices is known as pairing. Pretty much any two devices can pair if they are set to a discoverable mode. In the discoverable mode, a Bluetooth device will broadcast the following information about themselves:

- Technical information
- Name
- List of services
- Class

Upon pairing, two Bluetooth devices will exchange a link key. The devices will store the key to be used in the identification of the other device in future pairings. Every device has a unique identifier and usually a manufacturer-assigned name. These will be useful pieces of data when we want to identify and access a device.

Bluetooth Scanning and Reconnaissance

Linux has an implementation of the Bluetooth protocol stack called BlueZ that we are going to use to scan for Bluetooth signals. Most Linux distributions, including Kali Linux, have it as an inbuilt feature by default. BlueZ possesses utilities that can help us scan and manage Bluetooth capable devices. Examples of the utilities are outlined below:

- hciconfig: this is an equivalent of ifconfig in Linux, but made for Bluetooth capable devices.
- hcitool: this is a tool that we use to perform inquiries. The inquiries can be the device ID, name, class or even its clock information. This helps the devices to work in sync.
- hcidump: sniffing of Bluetooth communications is carried out by this tool, it, therefore, gives us a chance to capture data that is being sent over the Bluetooth signal.

The first scanning and reconnaissance step with Bluetooth is to check whether the Bluetooth adapter on the system that we are using is recognized and enabled so we can use it to scan for other devices.

Scanning for Bluetooth Devices with hcitool

Now that we know our adapter is up, we can use another tool in the BlueZ suite called hcitool, which is used to scan for other Bluetooth devices within range. With the simple scan command, we can find out Bluetooth devices that are transmitting using their discover beacons. That is, the devices set to their discovery mode. Most of the tools for Bluetooth hacking you are likely to encounter will be using these commands in a script. You should be able to create your tools from these commands using Python script or even bash script.

Using the sdptool to scanning for services

The service discovery protocol, SDP, as it is commonly known, is a protocol of Bluetooth that is used in the searching of Bluetooth services (Bluetooth is a suite of services), and, helpfully, BlueZ provides the sdptool tool for browsing a device for the services it offers. It is also important to note that the device does not have to be in discovery mode to be scanned. The syntax is as follows:

sdptool browse MACaddress

Seeing Whether the Devices Are Reachable with l2ping

Once we have gathered the MAC addresses of all nearby devices, we can send out pings to these devices, whether they are in discovery mode or not, to see whether they are in reach. This lets us know whether they are active and within range. To send out a ping, we use the l2ping command with the following syntax:

l2ping MACaddress

Summary

Wireless devices represent the future of connectivity and hacking. Linux has developed specialized commands for scanning and connecting to Wi-Fi APs in the first step toward hacking those systems. The aircrack-ng suite of wireless hacking tools includes both airmon-ng and airodump-ng, which enable us to scan and gather vital information from in-range wireless devices. The BlueZ suite includes hciconfig, hcitool and other tools capable of scanning and information gathering, which are necessary for hacking the Bluetooth devices within range. It also includes many other tools worth exploring.

Chapter 8: Web Security

Web Security

Just like physical stores, homes, government locations, web applications alongside websites are also susceptible to their security arrangements and protocols being circumvented. What is needed to counter cyber-crimes and the compromising of web applications is robust and reliable security measures.

Web security does this exactly. A functional definition of web security for us can be that it is a set of protocols and protection measures employed in the safeguarding of your website together with your web applications against hacking and against unsanctioned access by personnel who are unauthorized. The integral division of Information Security can protect web services, websites and web applications. This provides crucial security for anything that is carried out on the Internet.

Normally, there exist multiple considerations that are involved when we are dealing with web protection and/or web security. For an application on the web or a website to be said to be secure, it must be backed up by a variety of techniques and checkpoints to guarantee its security. We always have standards of security that need to be adhered to. OWASP is responsible for the highlighting and implementation of these standards. Web developers who have plenty of experienced normally adhere to OWASP standards and keenly study the Web Hacking Incident Database to be able to know vulnerabilities that lead to websites being hacked and how they are hacked.

Common website security threats

Websites can be attacked in more than one way. Before proceeding, we need to understand some common threats to website security. These are what we shall be looking to avoid and be prepared for during the planning of security measures. Some of these include Spam, Viruses and malware, WHOIS domain registration, and DDoS attacks, among many others.

How to safeguard your website

After getting to know common security threats, let us now focus on how we can prevent them. The assumption that your website is secure is not correct. As long as you have not instituted any safeguard mechanisms, there is a high chance that it can be attacked. Here are a few steps you are required to effect to better the security of your website:

- **Restrict file uploads**

It is risky to let visitors on your website upload files. The uploads may contain a script meant to exploit vulnerabilities present on your website. All uploads need to be treated as a threat to the security of the website.

- **Use HTTPS protocol**

This tells the visitors of a given website that essentially, they are dealing with a proper server. This translates to "no one can intercept the interactions they are having or the content they are viewing."

- **Secure your personal computer**

Security starts with you! It is important that you take care of the security of your devices. Hackers can use your PC as a gateway to your website. Ensure that you have antivirus software that is updated with the latest definitions. This will protect you from many malicious attacks including from file downloads. It is also possible to inject malware to the websites through stolen FTP login credentials. It is important that you frequently scan your devices for malware and viruses regularly.

- **Change your default CMS settings**

We have seen that numerous attacks are normally automated these days. Malicious users do program bots to help them locate sites still using their default settings. Make it hard for them. Upon installation of a CMS you own, modify the settings which are still on default mode:

- ✓ Settings required for comments
- ✓ Controls that users require
- ✓ Information visibility
- ✓ Permissions for files

Above are settings you can change right away.

- **Software updates**

All the software must stay up to date. This includes the CMS, plugins, Word Press software, among many others. The updates bring improved functionality, security patches to cover vulnerabilities, fixes for bugs and software glitches, and so on.

- **Select a web hosting plan that is safe**

Web hosting plans that are shared have higher chances of getting compromised. In as much as they are appealing to users due to the potential cost savings, the levels of protection are reduced. As such, they are not a secure option. Remember, cheap is expensive!

- **Limit access to users**

Errors caused by human beings account for a majority of cybersecurity attacks. Reducing or limiting humans can contribute greatly to error reduction. It is not necessary for every employee to access your website. Guests, web designers and consultants likewise, do not deserve automatic access. The least privilege principle needs to be implemented to secure your website.

- **Do a password change**

Password changing is a significant shot in the arm for web security. So, change your password. Changing the password alone is even not enough; make it a habit to change it often.

- **Monitor your security**

You can get utilities that can help you monitor your websites' security online. Such utilities can help you with conducting security audits, which can help to expose potential vulnerabilities. In so doing, you can launch countermeasures before an attack happens.

- **Make a backup for your website**

It is said that when you have been forewarned, you should forearm yourself. It is good to always be prepared for the worse. In this case, the worst that can happen is your website getting compromised. A backup ensures you are at peace since there will be no data that is lost in the event of a compromise.

Conclusion

May I take this opportunity to thank you for being able to make it to the end of this informative book, *Kali Linux*. I want to believe that it has been edifying, and through it, you are now able to hit the ground running in matters revolving around hacking. Also, I hope that you have gained the relevant expertise to enable you to begin your hacking career or better your skills if you are already one. I sincerely hope that you have enjoyed turning pages right from the first topic which was Introduction to Kali Linux, all through The Basics of Kali Linux, The Hacking Process, Wireless Network Hacking, Uses and Applications of Kali Linux, Introduction to Cybersecurity, Network Scanning and Management and Web Security. I trust that by studying this book, you have gotten to learn plenty of practical concepts that you need to become a hacking expert.

By now, you must have been able to get access to a vast body of theoretical knowledge regarding the various types of attacks that can be launched on your systems, the reason for launching them and how you are able to safeguard your infrastructure against such attacks. These are your first steps towards becoming a professional hacker. The book covers topical issues like wireless network attacks, cyber-attacks and penetration testing, among others. It, therefore, means that you are now in a good position to discern network attack mechanisms that occur in the real world and prescribe appropriate remedies.

I have also given you a few security measures you can implement to keep your networks safe. The formatting is such that the language is a user-friendly language that you can understand the importance of securing your networks. Going forward, the next step is to put the concepts you have acquired from this book into practice. They say practice makes perfect and it is by practicing that one can become an expert in the field of hacking, more so using Kali Linux. Let the knowledge you have acquired from the book work for you.

Finally, if you found this book useful in any way, a review on Amazon is always welcome!

Lightning Source UK Ltd.
Milton Keynes UK
UKHW020229041220
374592UK00003B/461